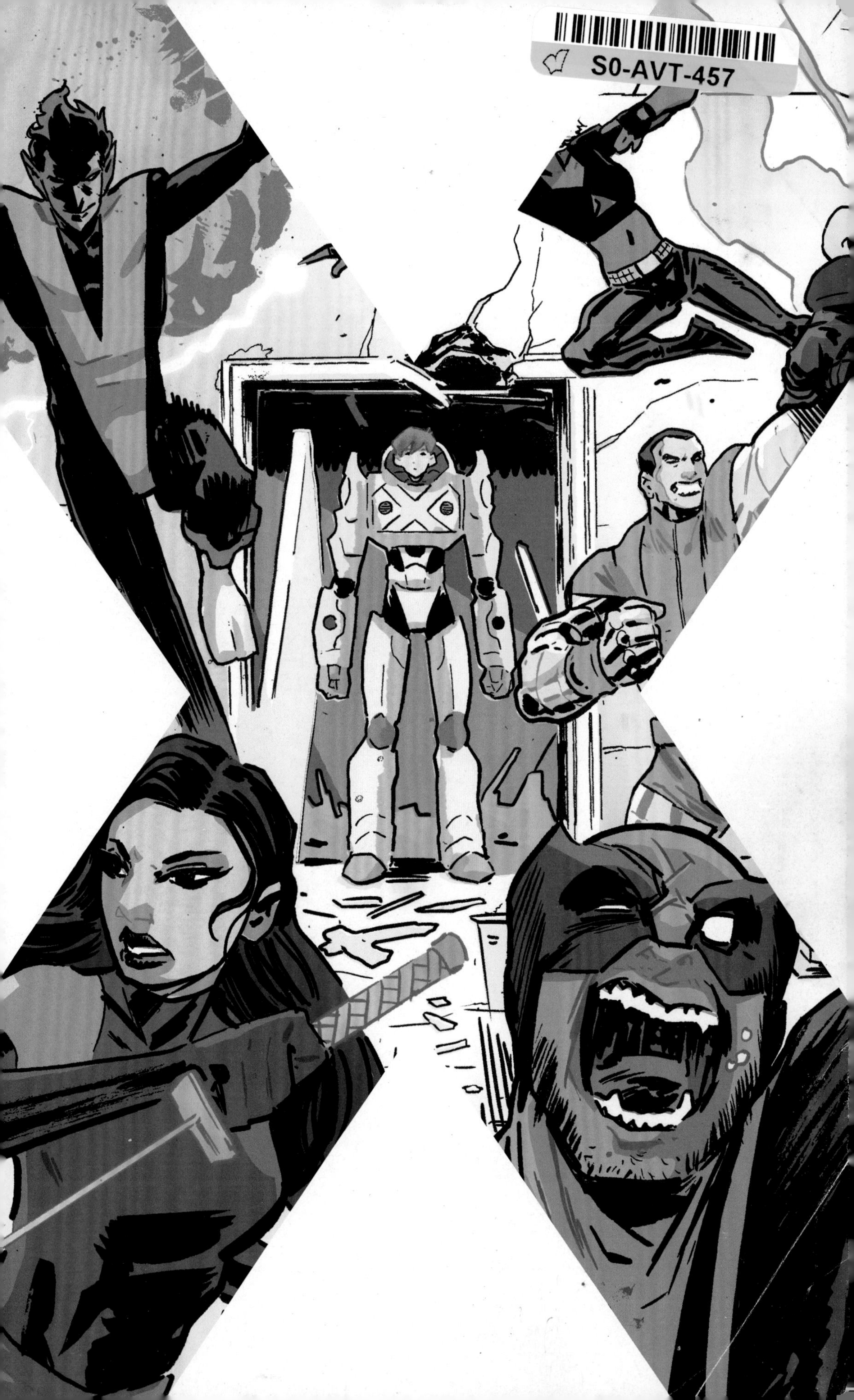

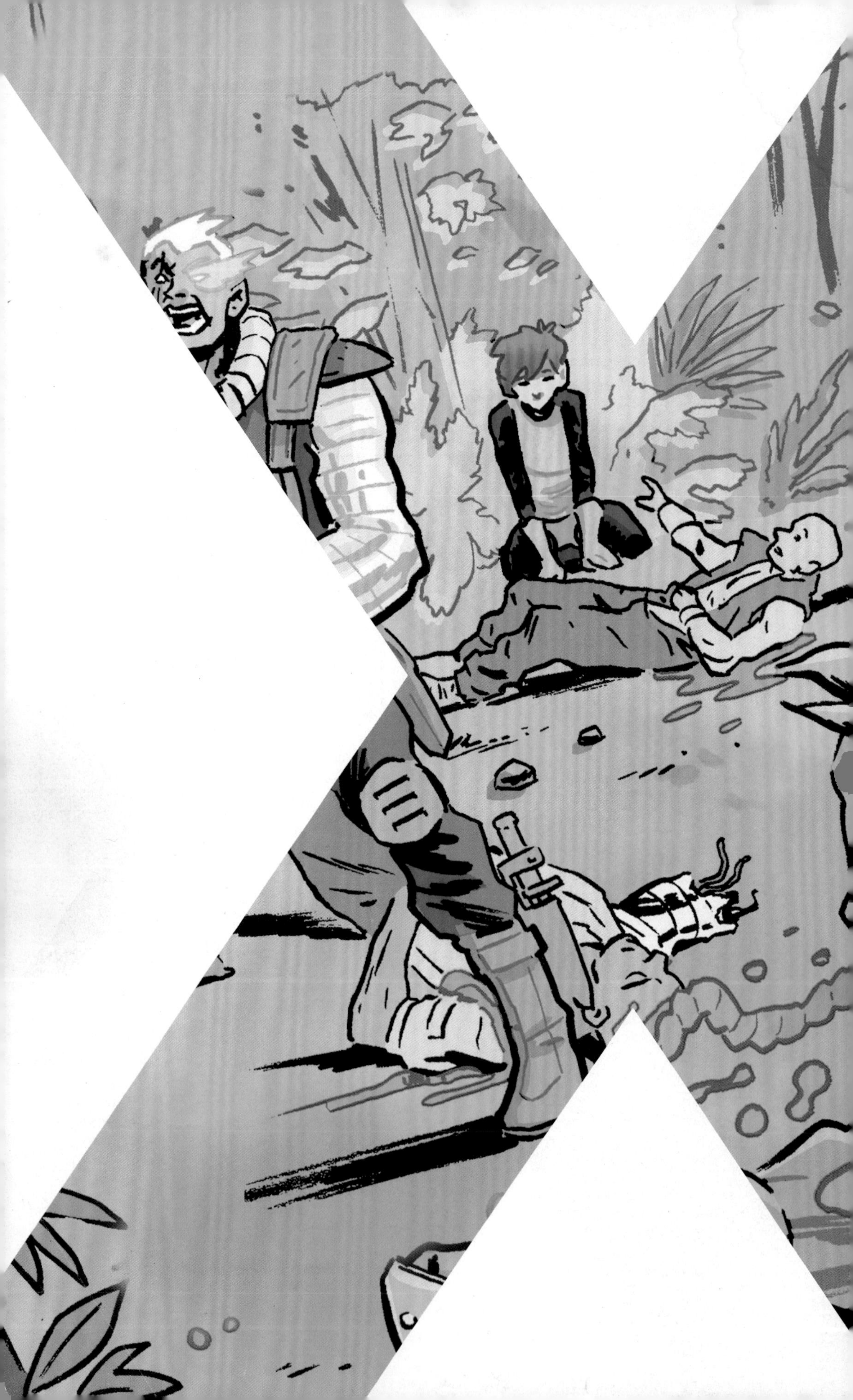

MAX **BEMIS**
WRITER

MICHAEL **WALSH**
ARTIST

RUTH **REDMOND**
COLORIST

VC's CLAYTON **COWLES**
LETTERER

MICHAEL **WALSH**
COVER ART

HEATHER **ANTOS**
ASSISTANT EDITOR

JORDAN **WHITE**
EDITOR

MEN
WORST X-MAN EVER

AXEL **ALONSO**
EDITOR IN CHIEF

JOE **QUESADA**
CHIEF CREATIVE OFFICER

DAN **BUCKLEY**
PUBLISHER

X-MEN CREATED BY
STAN **LEE** AND JACK **KIRBY**

COLLECTION EDITOR **SARAH BRUNSTAD**
ASSOCIATE MANAGING EDITOR **ALEX STARBUCK**
SENIOR EDITOR, SPECIAL PROJECTS **JENNIFER GRÜNWALD**
EDITOR, SPECIAL PROJECTS **MARK D. BEAZLEY**
VP, PRODUCTION & SPECIAL PROJECTS **JEFF YOUNGQUIST**
SVP PRINT, SALES & MARKETING **DAVID GABRIEL**
BOOK DESIGNER **ADAM DEL RE**

X-MEN: WORST X-MAN EVER. Contains material originally published in magazine form as X-MEN: WORST X-MAN EVER #1-5. First printing 2016. ISBN# 978-0-7851-9354-8. Published by MARVEL WORLDWIDE, INC., a subsidiary of MARVEL ENTERTAINMENT, LLC. OFFICE OF PUBLICATION: 135 West 50th Street, New York, NY 10020. Copyright © 2016 MARVEL No similarity between any of the names, characters, persons, and/or institutions in this magazine with those of any living or dead person or institution is intended, and any such similarity which may exist is purely coincidental. **Printed in Canada.** ALAN FINE, President, Marvel Entertainment; DAN BUCKLEY, President, TV, Publishing & Brand Management; JOE QUESADA, Chief Creative Officer; TOM BREVOORT, SVP of Publishing; DAVID BOGART, SVP of Business Affairs & Operations, Publishing & Partnership; C.B. CEBULSKI, VP of Brand Management & Development, Asia; DAVID GABRIEL, SVP of Sales & Marketing, Publishing; JEFF YOUNGQUIST, VP of Production & Special Projects; DAN CARR, Executive Director of Publishing Technology; ALEX MORALES, Director of Publishing Operations; SUSAN CRESPI, Production Manager; STAN LEE, Chairman Emeritus. For information regarding advertising in Marvel Comics or on Marvel.com, please contact Vit DeBellis, Integrated Sales Manager, at vdebellis@marvel.com. For Marvel subscription inquiries, please call 888-511-5480. **Manufactured between 7/1/2016 and 8/8/2016 by SOLISCO PRINTERS, SCOTT, QC, CANADA.**

10 9 8 7 6 5 4 3 2 1

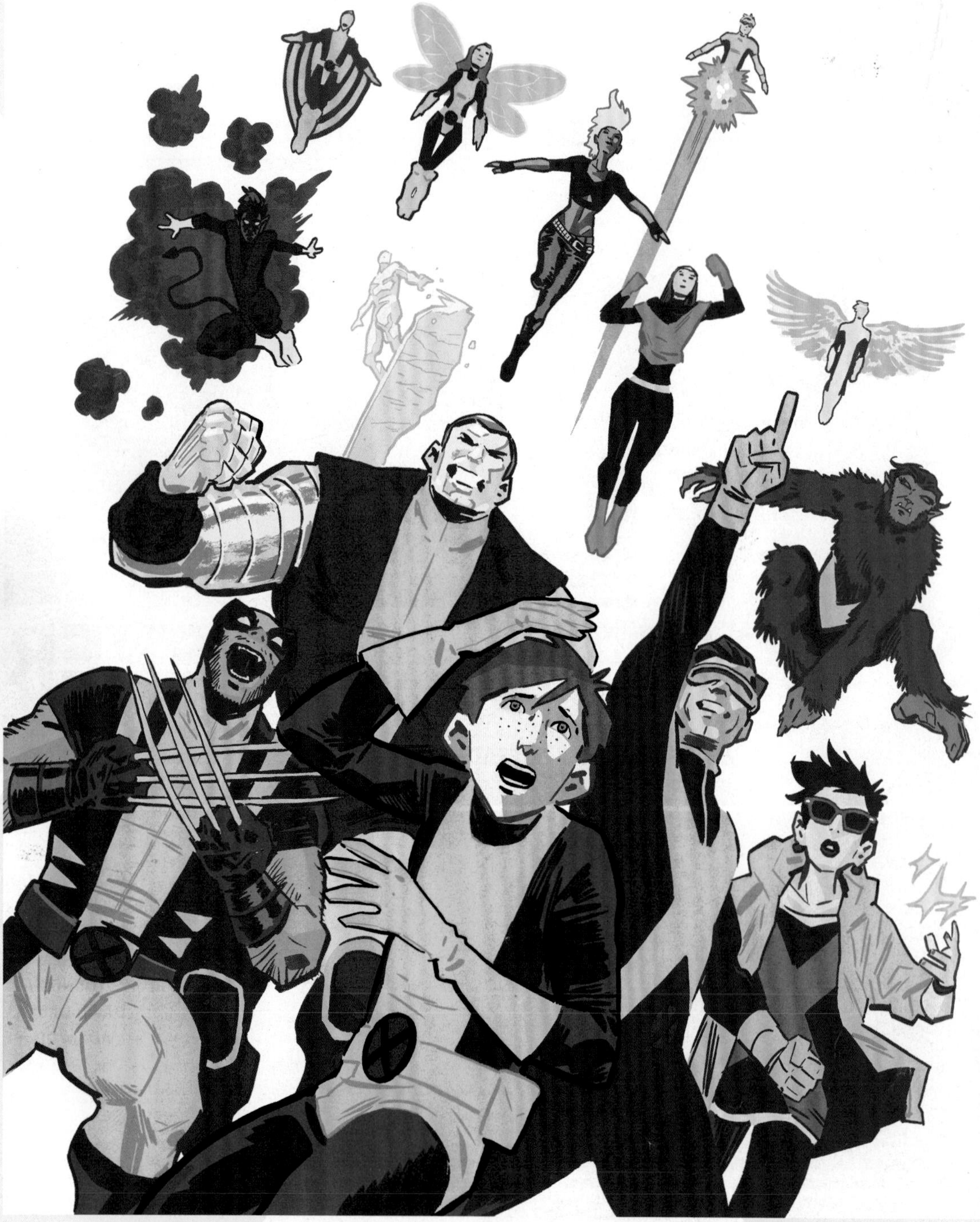

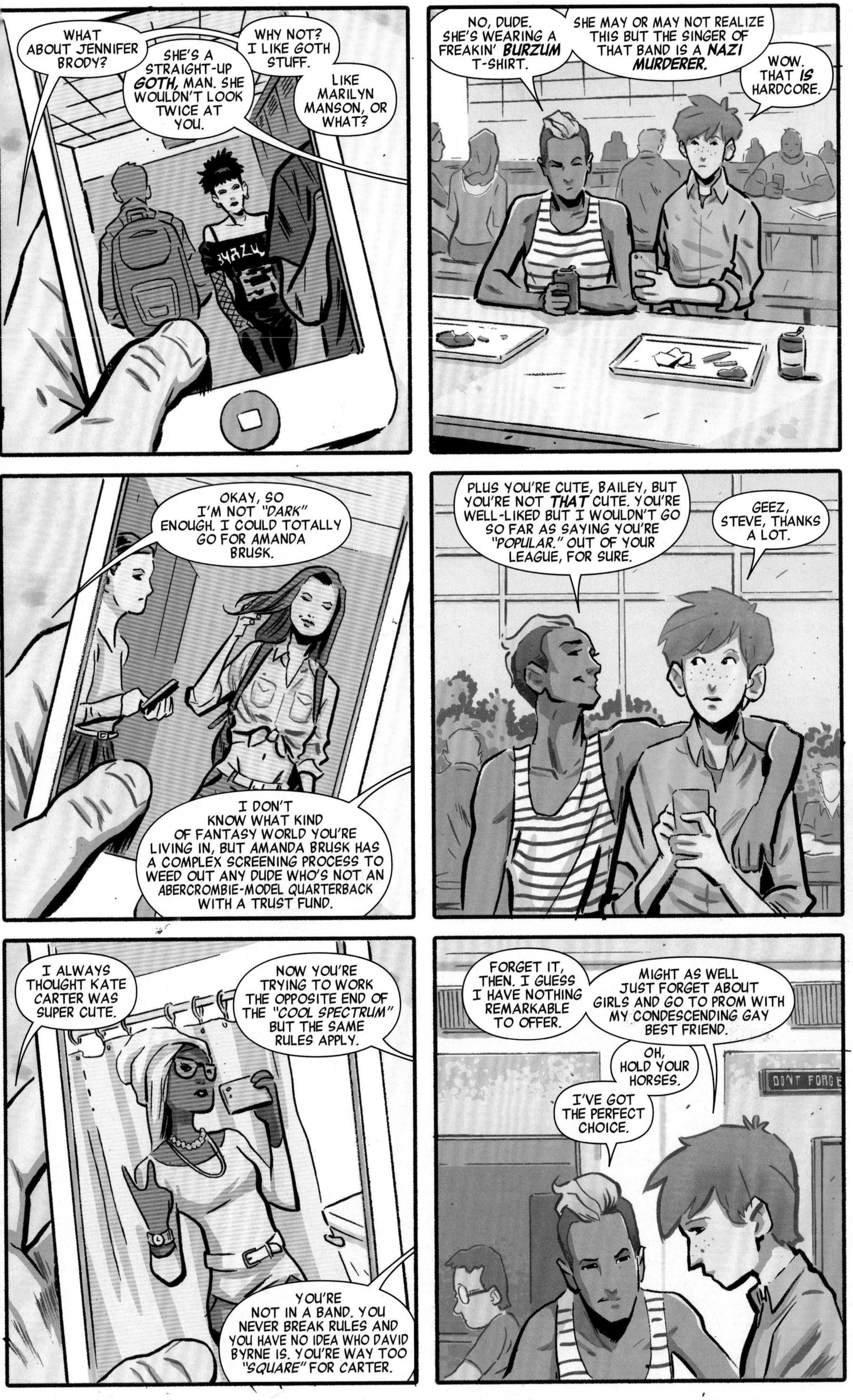
WHAT ABOUT JENNIFER BRODY?
WHY NOT? I LIKE GOTH STUFF.
SHE'S A STRAIGHT-UP GOTH, MAN. SHE WOULDN'T LOOK TWICE AT YOU.
LIKE MARILYN MANSON, OR WHAT?
NO, DUDE. SHE'S WEARING A FREAKIN' BURZUM T-SHIRT.
SHE MAY OR MAY NOT REALIZE THIS BUT THE SINGER OF THAT BAND IS A NAZI MURDERER.
WOW. THAT IS HARDCORE.
OKAY, SO I'M NOT "DARK" ENOUGH. I COULD TOTALLY GO FOR AMANDA BRUSK.
I DON'T KNOW WHAT KIND OF FANTASY WORLD YOU'RE LIVING IN, BUT AMANDA BRUSK HAS A COMPLEX SCREENING PROCESS TO WEED OUT ANY DUDE WHO'S NOT AN ABERCROMBIE-MODEL QUARTERBACK WITH A TRUST FUND.
PLUS YOU'RE CUTE, BAILEY, BUT YOU'RE NOT THAT CUTE. YOU'RE WELL-LIKED BUT I WOULDN'T GO SO FAR AS SAYING YOU'RE "POPULAR." OUT OF YOUR LEAGUE, FOR SURE.
GEEZ, STEVE, THANKS A LOT.
I ALWAYS THOUGHT KATE CARTER WAS SUPER CUTE.
NOW YOU'RE TRYING TO WORK THE OPPOSITE END OF THE "COOL SPECTRUM" BUT THE SAME RULES APPLY.
YOU'RE NOT IN A BAND. YOU NEVER BREAK RULES AND YOU HAVE NO IDEA WHO DAVID BYRNE IS. YOU'RE WAY TOO "SQUARE" FOR CARTER.
FORGET IT, THEN. I GUESS I HAVE NOTHING REMARKABLE TO OFFER.
MIGHT AS WELL JUST FORGET ABOUT GIRLS AND GO TO PROM WITH MY CONDESCENDING GAY BEST FRIEND.
OH, HOLD YOUR HORSES.
I'VE GOT THE PERFECT CHOICE.

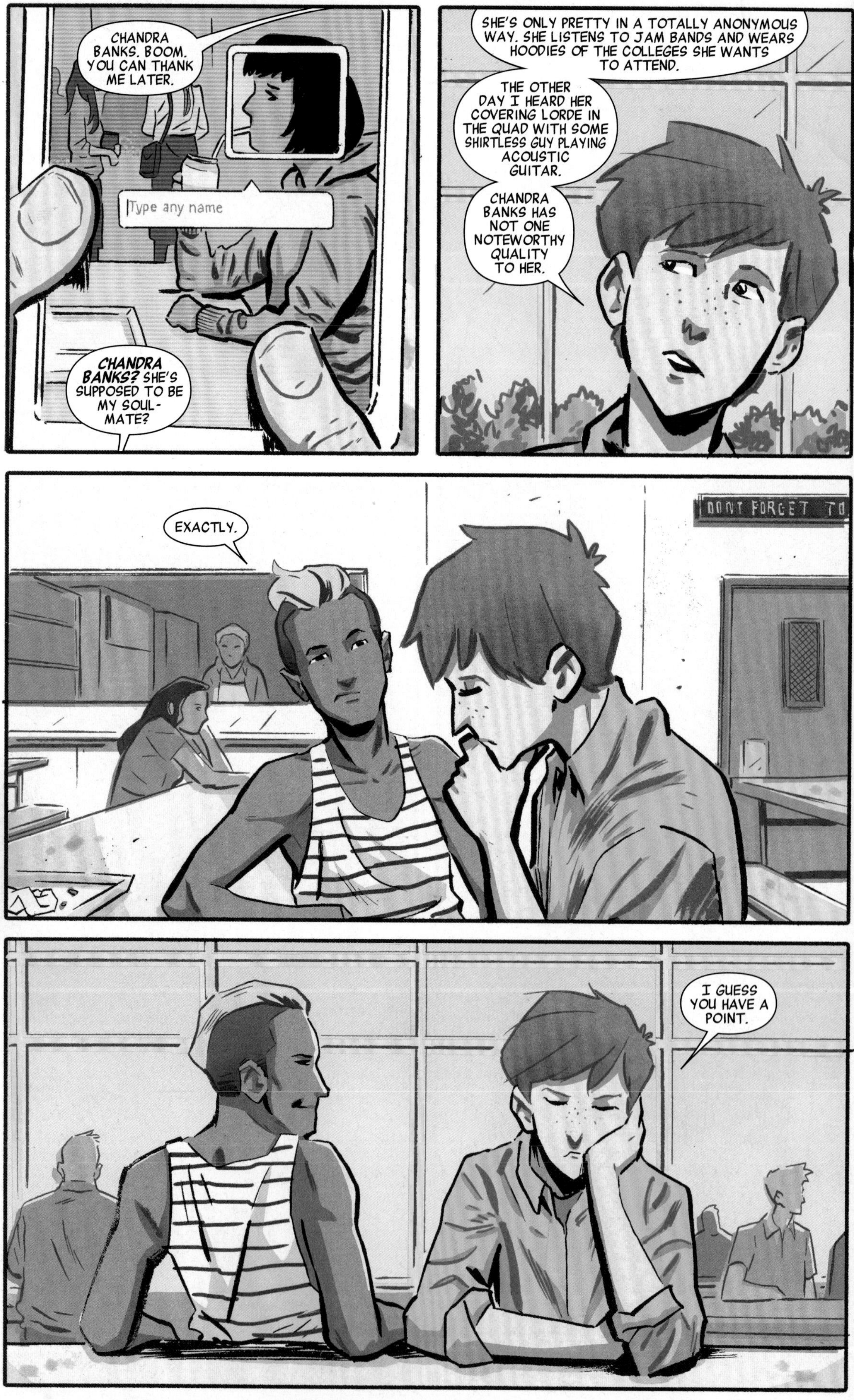
CHANDRA BANKS. BOOM. YOU CAN THANK ME LATER.
Type any name
CHANDRA BANKS? SHE'S SUPPOSED TO BE MY SOUL-MATE?
SHE'S ONLY PRETTY IN A TOTALLY ANONYMOUS WAY. SHE LISTENS TO JAM BANDS AND WEARS HOODIES OF THE COLLEGES SHE WANTS TO ATTEND.
THE OTHER DAY I HEARD HER COVERING LORDE IN THE QUAD WITH SOME SHIRTLESS GUY PLAYING ACOUSTIC GUITAR.
CHANDRA BANKS HAS NOT ONE NOTEWORTHY QUALITY TO HER.
DON'T FORGET TO
EXACTLY.
I GUESS YOU HAVE A POINT.

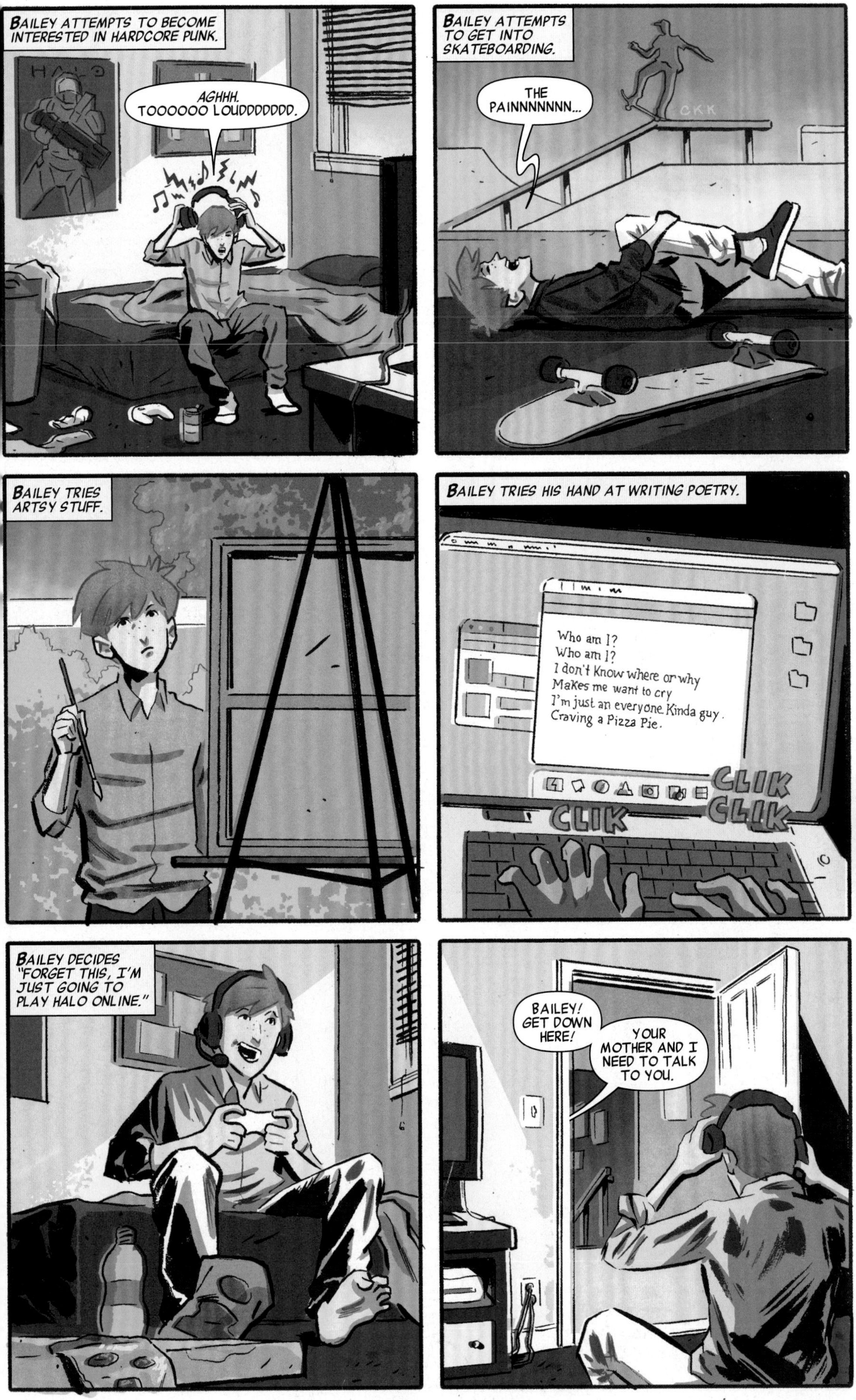
BAILEY ATTEMPTS TO BECOME INTERESTED IN HARDCORE PUNK.
AGHHH. TOOOOOO LOUDDDDDDD.
BAILEY ATTEMPTS TO GET INTO SKATEBOARDING.
THE PAINNNNNNN...
BAILEY TRIES ARTSY STUFF.
BAILEY TRIES HIS HAND AT WRITING POETRY.
Who am I?
Who am I?
I don't Know where or why
Makes me want to cry
I'm just an everyone Kinda guy.
Craving a Pizza Pie.
CLIK
CLIK
CLIK
BAILEY DECIDES "FORGET THIS, I'M JUST GOING TO PLAY HALO ONLINE."
BAILEY! GET DOWN HERE!
YOUR MOTHER AND I NEED TO TALK TO YOU.

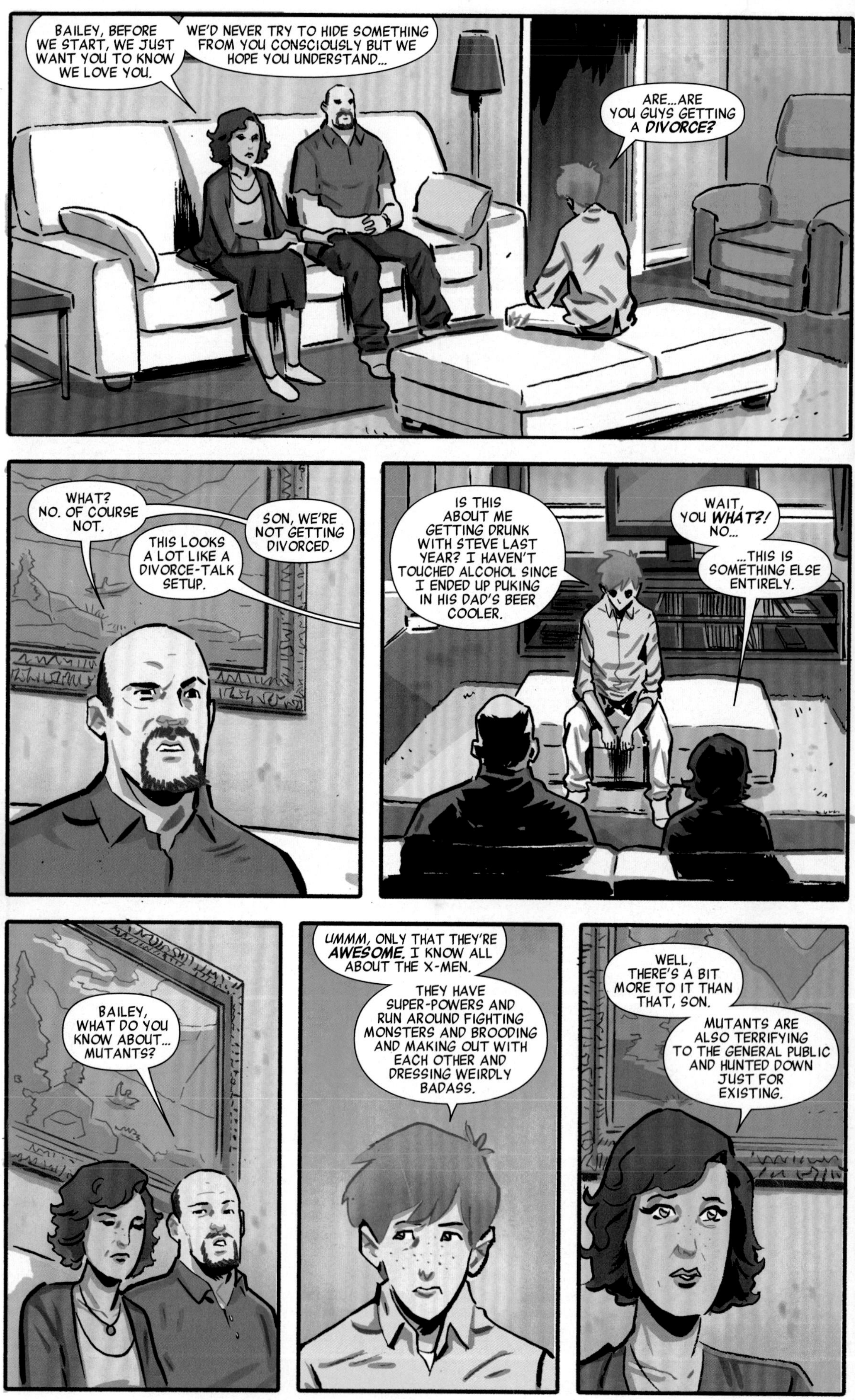
BAILEY, BEFORE WE START, WE JUST WANT YOU TO KNOW WE LOVE YOU.
WE'D NEVER TRY TO HIDE SOMETHING FROM YOU CONSCIOUSLY BUT WE HOPE YOU UNDERSTAND...
ARE...ARE YOU GUYS GETTING A DIVORCE?
WHAT? NO. OF COURSE NOT.
SON, WE'RE NOT GETTING DIVORCED.
THIS LOOKS A LOT LIKE A DIVORCE-TALK SETUP.
IS THIS ABOUT ME GETTING DRUNK WITH STEVE LAST YEAR? I HAVEN'T TOUCHED ALCOHOL SINCE I ENDED UP PUKING IN HIS DAD'S BEER COOLER.
WAIT, YOU WHAT?! NO...
...THIS IS SOMETHING ELSE ENTIRELY.
BAILEY, WHAT DO YOU KNOW ABOUT... MUTANTS?
UMMM, ONLY THAT THEY'RE AWESOME. I KNOW ALL ABOUT THE X-MEN.
THEY HAVE SUPER-POWERS AND RUN AROUND FIGHTING MONSTERS AND BROODING AND MAKING OUT WITH EACH OTHER AND DRESSING WEIRDLY BADASS.
WELL, THERE'S A BIT MORE TO IT THAN THAT, SON.
MUTANTS ARE ALSO TERRIFYING TO THE GENERAL PUBLIC AND HUNTED DOWN JUST FOR EXISTING.

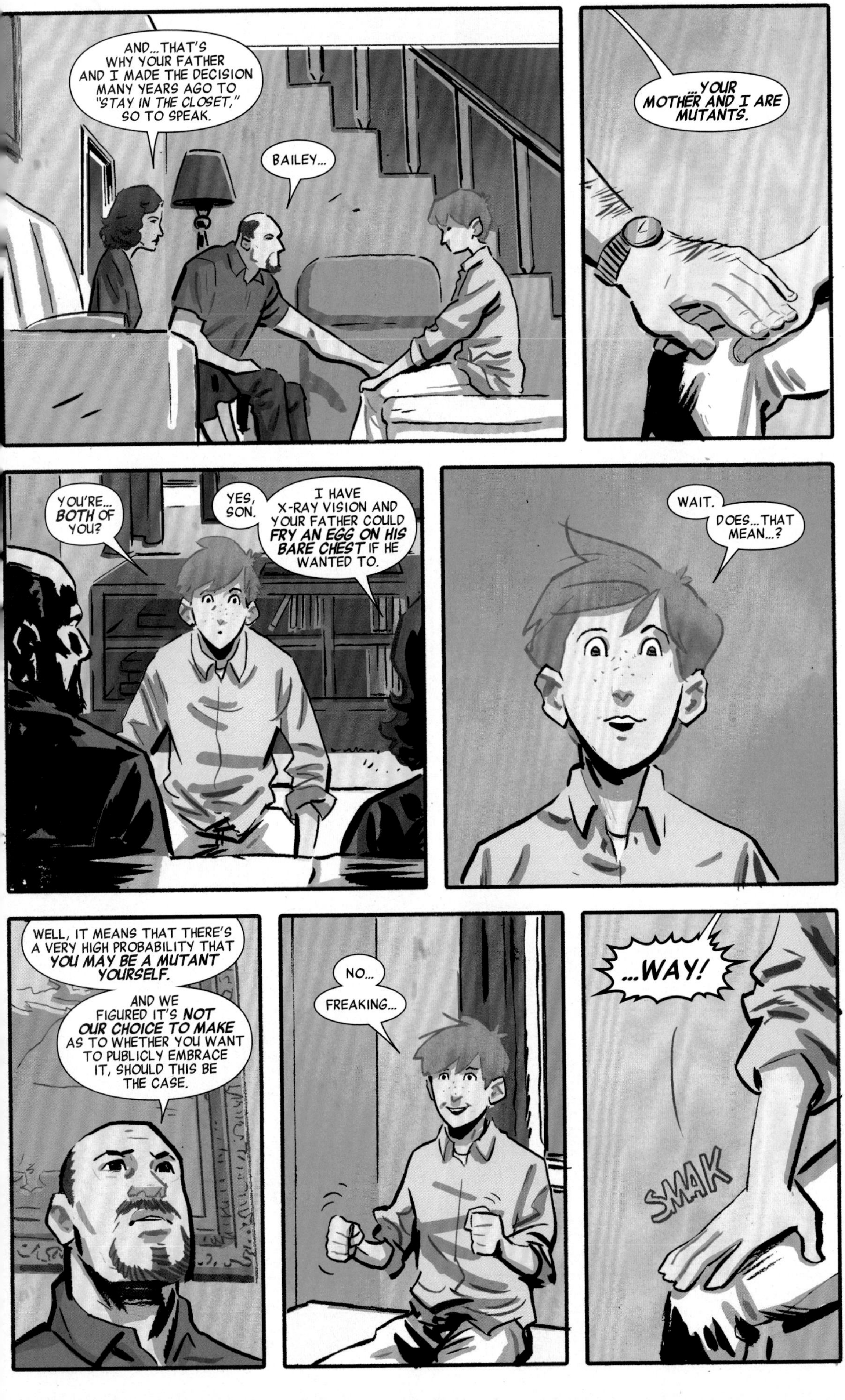
AND...THAT'S WHY YOUR FATHER AND I MADE THE DECISION MANY YEARS AGO TO "STAY IN THE CLOSET," SO TO SPEAK.
BAILEY...
...YOUR MOTHER AND I ARE MUTANTS.
YOU'RE... BOTH OF YOU?
YES, SON.
I HAVE X-RAY VISION AND YOUR FATHER COULD FRY AN EGG ON HIS BARE CHEST IF HE WANTED TO.
WAIT.
DOES...THAT MEAN...?
WELL, IT MEANS THAT THERE'S A VERY HIGH PROBABILITY THAT YOU MAY BE A MUTANT YOURSELF.
AND WE FIGURED IT'S NOT OUR CHOICE TO MAKE AS TO WHETHER YOU WANT TO PUBLICLY EMBRACE IT, SHOULD THIS BE THE CASE.
NO...
FREAKING...
...WAY!
SMAK

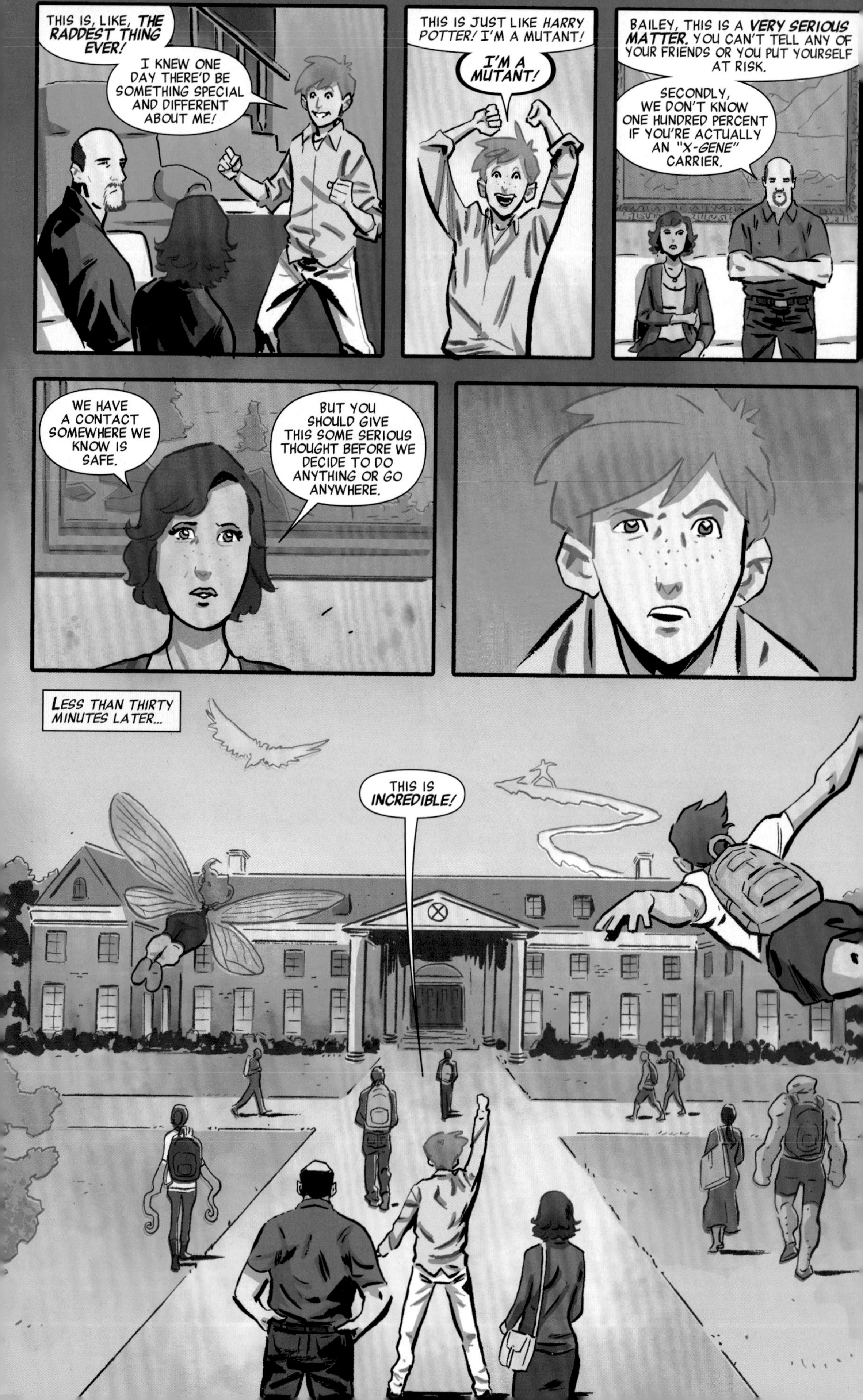
THIS IS, LIKE, THE RADDEST THING EVER!
I KNEW ONE DAY THERE'D BE SOMETHING SPECIAL AND DIFFERENT ABOUT ME!
THIS IS JUST LIKE HARRY POTTER! I'M A MUTANT!
I'M A MUTANT!
BAILEY, THIS IS A VERY SERIOUS MATTER. YOU CAN'T TELL ANY OF YOUR FRIENDS OR YOU PUT YOURSELF AT RISK.
SECONDLY, WE DON'T KNOW ONE HUNDRED PERCENT IF YOU'RE ACTUALLY AN "X-GENE" CARRIER.
WE HAVE A CONTACT SOMEWHERE WE KNOW IS SAFE.
BUT YOU SHOULD GIVE THIS SOME SERIOUS THOUGHT BEFORE WE DECIDE TO DO ANYTHING OR GO ANYWHERE.
LESS THAN THIRTY MINUTES LATER...
THIS IS INCREDIBLE!

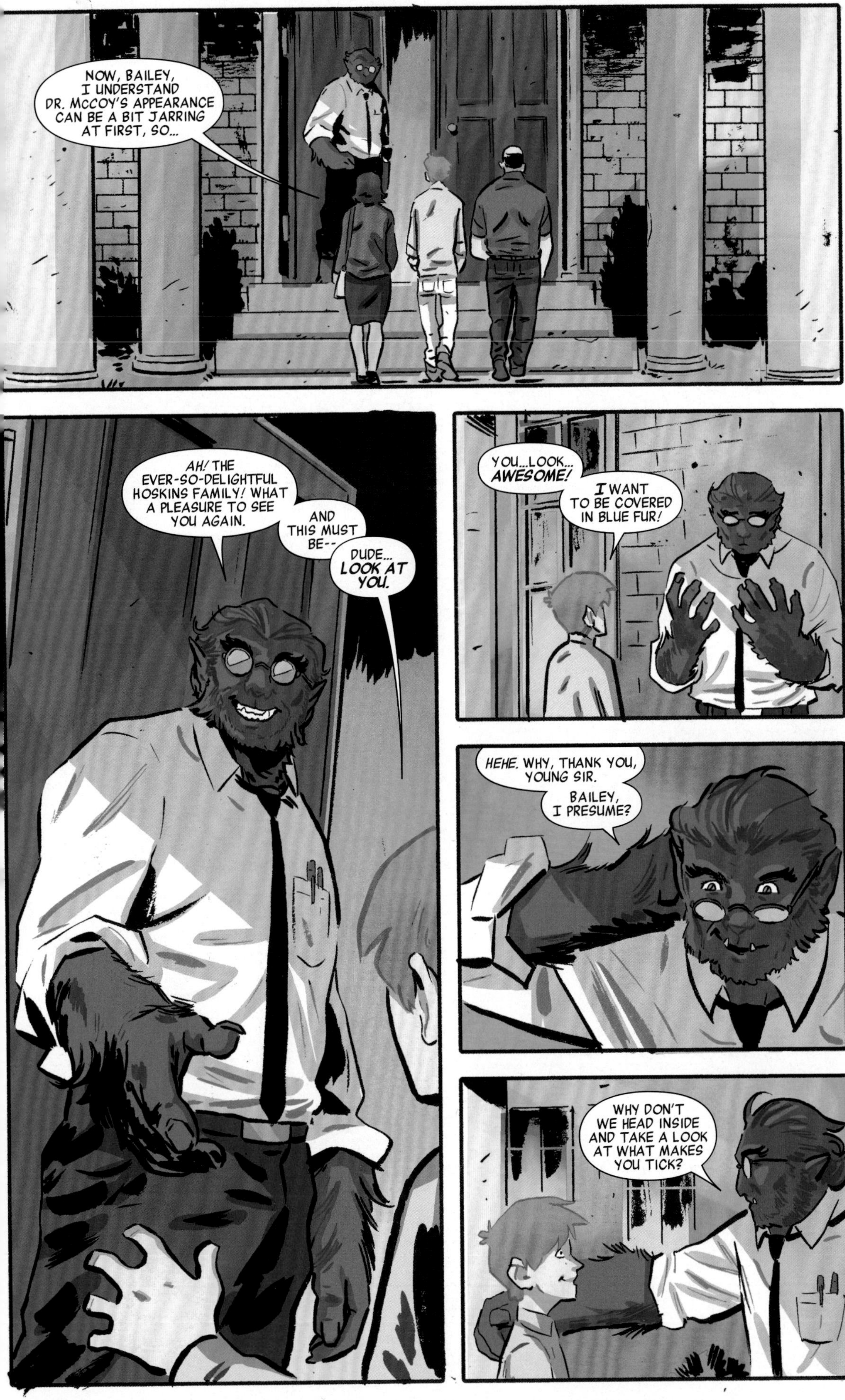
NOW, BAILEY, I UNDERSTAND DR. McCOY'S APPEARANCE CAN BE A BIT JARRING AT FIRST, SO...
AH! THE EVER-SO-DELIGHTFUL HOSKINS FAMILY! WHAT A PLEASURE TO SEE YOU AGAIN.
AND THIS MUST BE--
DUDE... LOOK AT YOU.
YOU...LOOK... AWESOME!
I WANT TO BE COVERED IN BLUE FUR!
HEHE. WHY, THANK YOU, YOUNG SIR.
BAILEY, I PRESUME?
WHY DON'T WE HEAD INSIDE AND TAKE A LOOK AT WHAT MAKES YOU TICK?

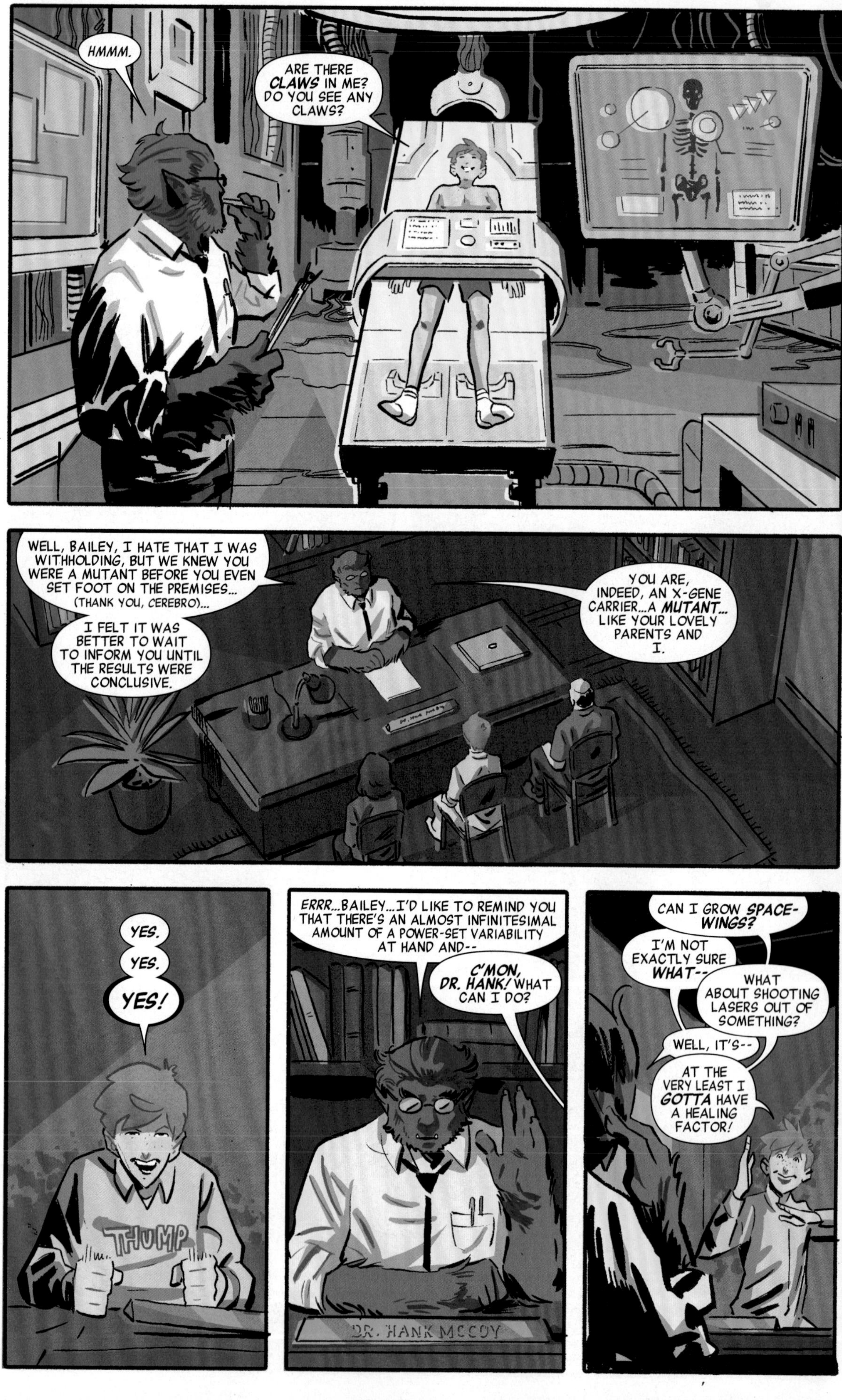
HMMM.
ARE THERE CLAWS IN ME? DO YOU SEE ANY CLAWS?
WELL, BAILEY, I HATE THAT I WAS WITHHOLDING, BUT WE KNEW YOU WERE A MUTANT BEFORE YOU EVEN SET FOOT ON THE PREMISES... (THANK YOU, CEREBRO)...
I FELT IT WAS BETTER TO WAIT TO INFORM YOU UNTIL THE RESULTS WERE CONCLUSIVE.
YOU ARE, INDEED, AN X-GENE CARRIER...A MUTANT... LIKE YOUR LOVELY PARENTS AND I.
YES.
YES.
YES!
THUMP
ERRR...BAILEY...I'D LIKE TO REMIND YOU THAT THERE'S AN ALMOST INFINITESIMAL AMOUNT OF A POWER-SET VARIABILITY AT HAND AND--
C'MON, DR. HANK! WHAT CAN I DO?
DR. HANK MCCOY
CAN I GROW SPACE-WINGS?
I'M NOT EXACTLY SURE WHAT--
WHAT ABOUT SHOOTING LASERS OUT OF SOMETHING?
WELL, IT'S--
AT THE VERY LEAST I GOTTA HAVE A HEALING FACTOR!

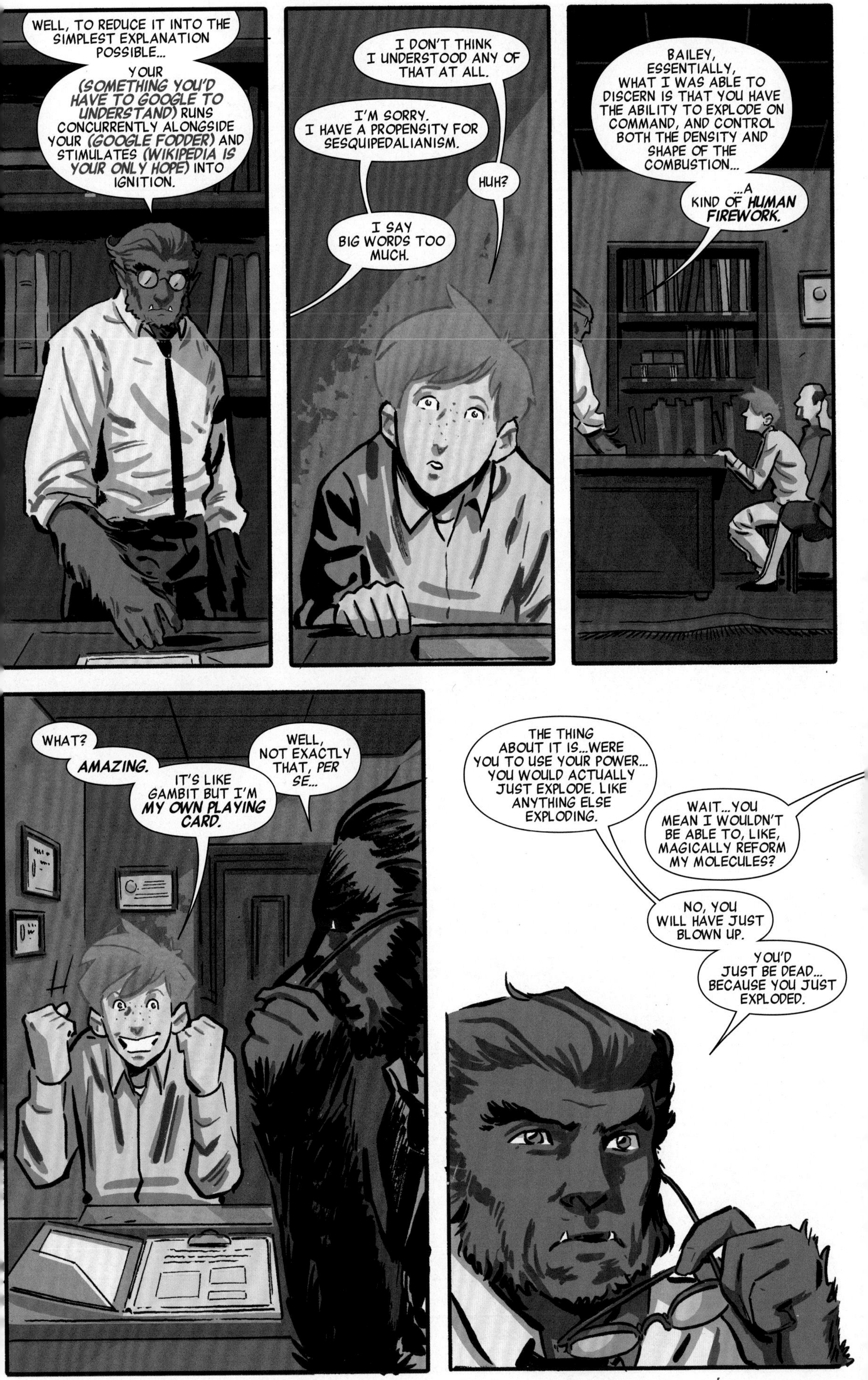
WELL, TO REDUCE IT INTO THE SIMPLEST EXPLANATION POSSIBLE...
YOUR (SOMETHING YOU'D HAVE TO GOOGLE TO UNDERSTAND) RUNS CONCURRENTLY ALONGSIDE YOUR (GOOGLE FODDER) AND STIMULATES (WIKIPEDIA IS YOUR ONLY HOPE) INTO IGNITION.
I DON'T THINK I UNDERSTOOD ANY OF THAT AT ALL.
I'M SORRY. I HAVE A PROPENSITY FOR SESQUIPEDALIANISM.
HUH?
I SAY BIG WORDS TOO MUCH.
BAILEY, ESSENTIALLY, WHAT I WAS ABLE TO DISCERN IS THAT YOU HAVE THE ABILITY TO EXPLODE ON COMMAND, AND CONTROL BOTH THE DENSITY AND SHAPE OF THE COMBUSTION...
...A KIND OF HUMAN FIREWORK.
WHAT?
AMAZING.
IT'S LIKE GAMBIT BUT I'M MY OWN PLAYING CARD.
WELL, NOT EXACTLY THAT, PER SE...
THE THING ABOUT IT IS...WERE YOU TO USE YOUR POWER... YOU WOULD ACTUALLY JUST EXPLODE. LIKE ANYTHING ELSE EXPLODING.
WAIT...YOU MEAN I WOULDN'T BE ABLE TO, LIKE, MAGICALLY REFORM MY MOLECULES?
NO, YOU WILL HAVE JUST BLOWN UP.
YOU'D JUST BE DEAD... BECAUSE YOU JUST EXPLODED.

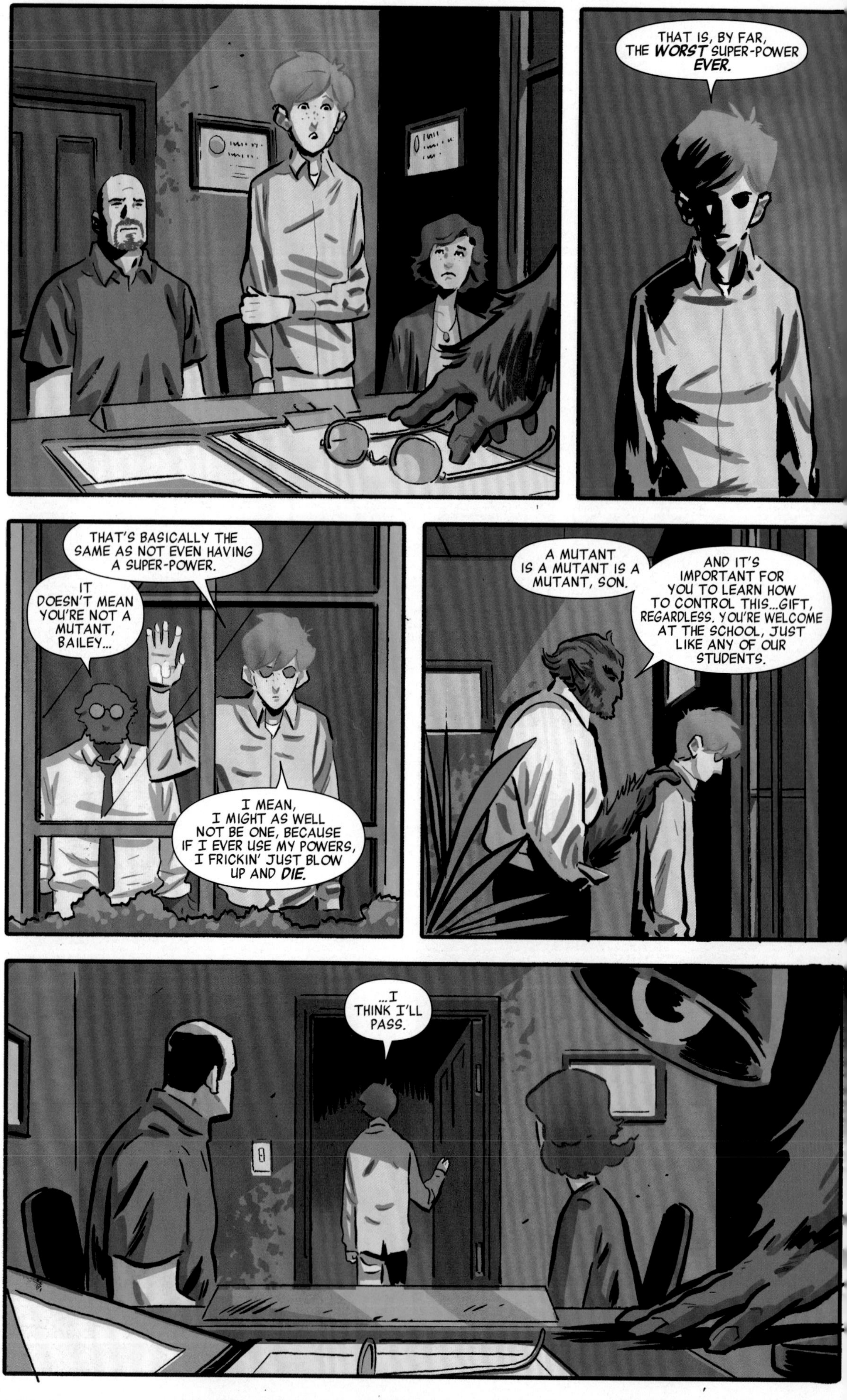
THAT IS, BY FAR, THE WORST SUPER-POWER EVER.
THAT'S BASICALLY THE SAME AS NOT EVEN HAVING A SUPER-POWER.
IT DOESN'T MEAN YOU'RE NOT A MUTANT, BAILEY...
I MEAN, I MIGHT AS WELL NOT BE ONE, BECAUSE IF I EVER USE MY POWERS, I FRICKIN' JUST BLOW UP AND DIE.
A MUTANT IS A MUTANT IS A MUTANT, SON.
AND IT'S IMPORTANT FOR YOU TO LEARN HOW TO CONTROL THIS...GIFT, REGARDLESS. YOU'RE WELCOME AT THE SCHOOL, JUST LIKE ANY OF OUR STUDENTS.
...I THINK I'LL PASS.

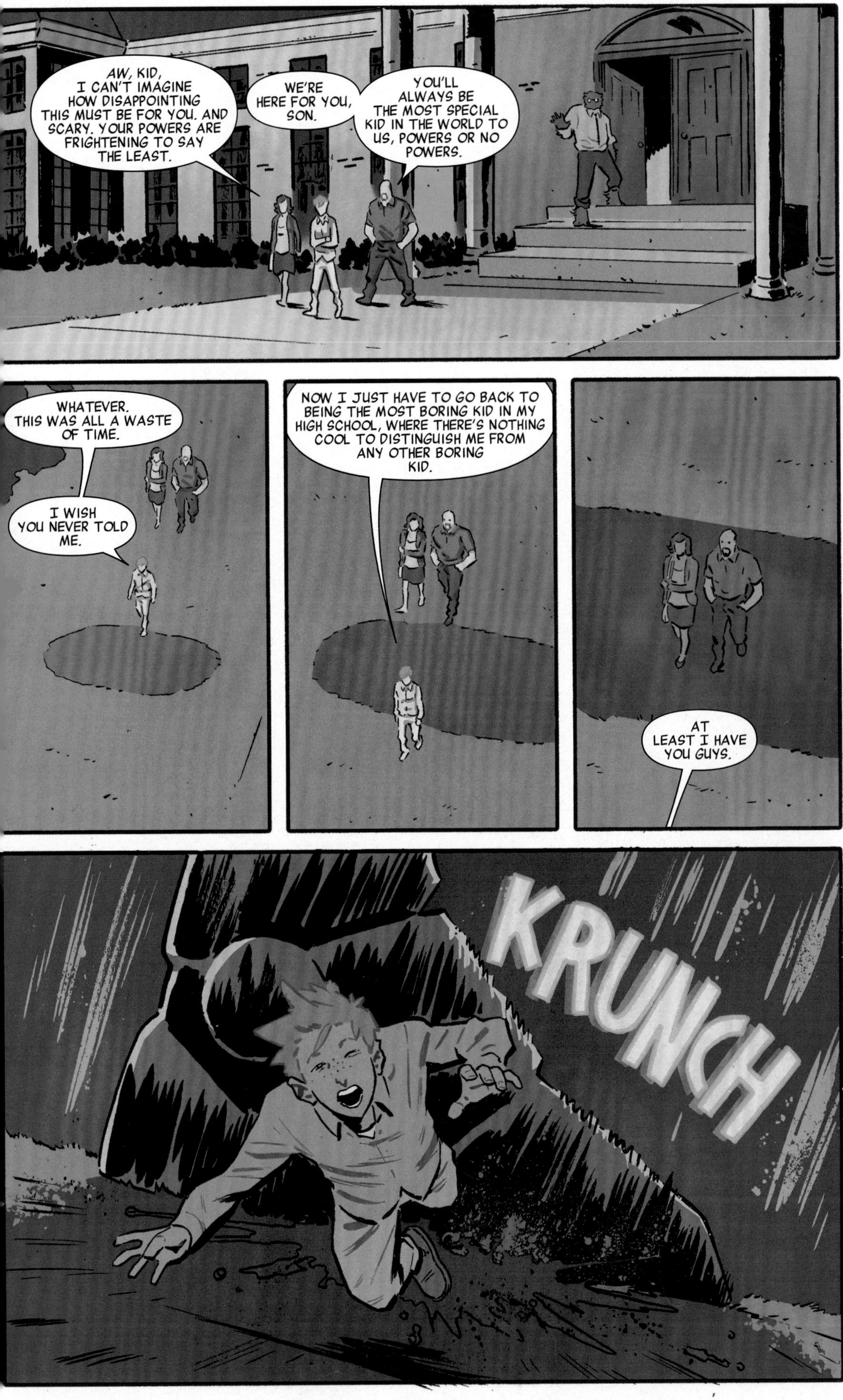
AW, KID, I CAN'T IMAGINE HOW DISAPPOINTING THIS MUST BE FOR YOU. AND SCARY. YOUR POWERS ARE FRIGHTENING TO SAY THE LEAST.
WE'RE HERE FOR YOU, SON.
YOU'LL ALWAYS BE THE MOST SPECIAL KID IN THE WORLD TO US, POWERS OR NO POWERS.
WHATEVER. THIS WAS ALL A WASTE OF TIME.
I WISH YOU NEVER TOLD ME.
NOW I JUST HAVE TO GO BACK TO BEING THE MOST BORING KID IN MY HIGH SCHOOL, WHERE THERE'S NOTHING COOL TO DISTINGUISH ME FROM ANY OTHER BORING KID.
AT LEAST I HAVE YOU GUYS.
KRUNCH

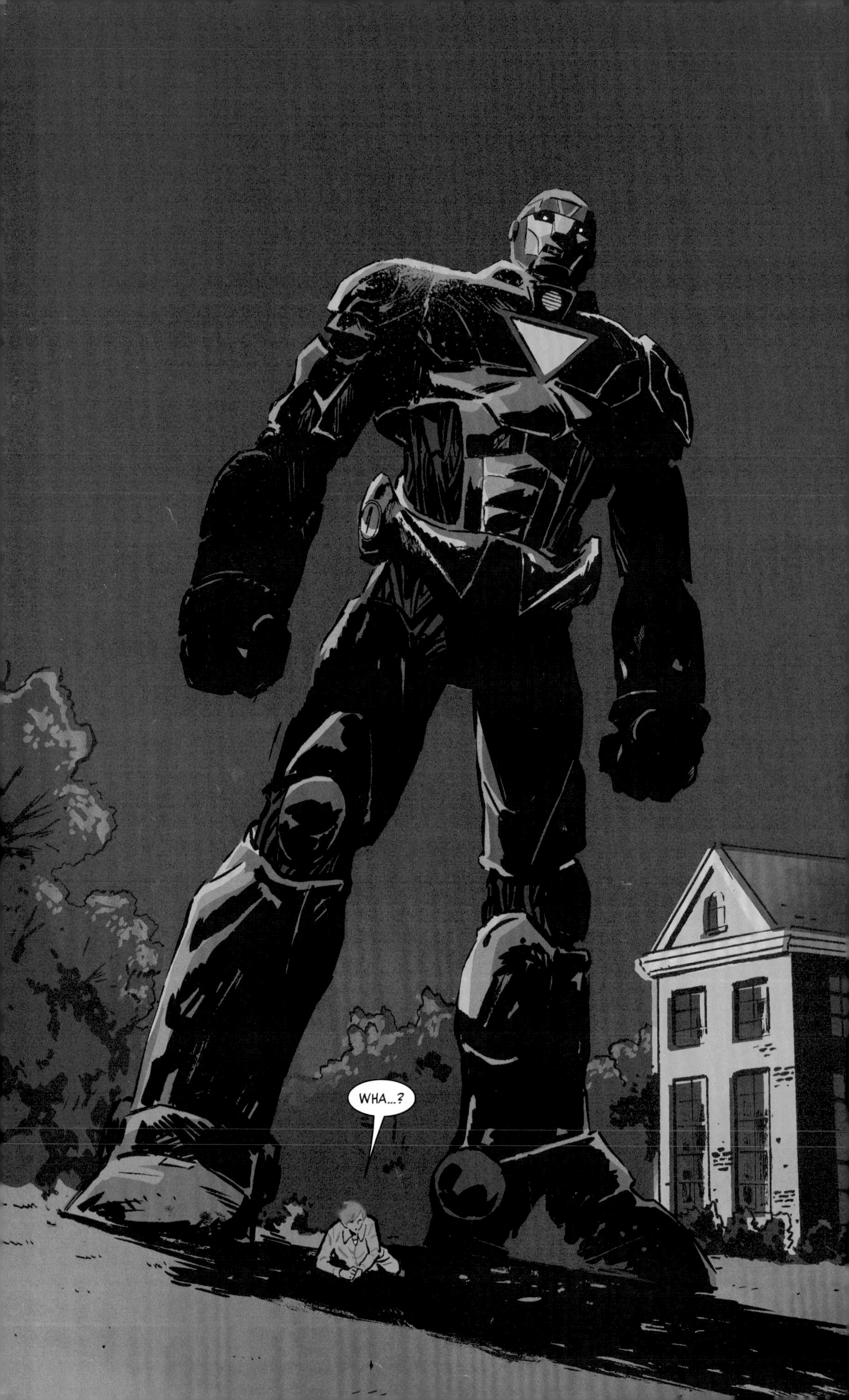
WHA...?

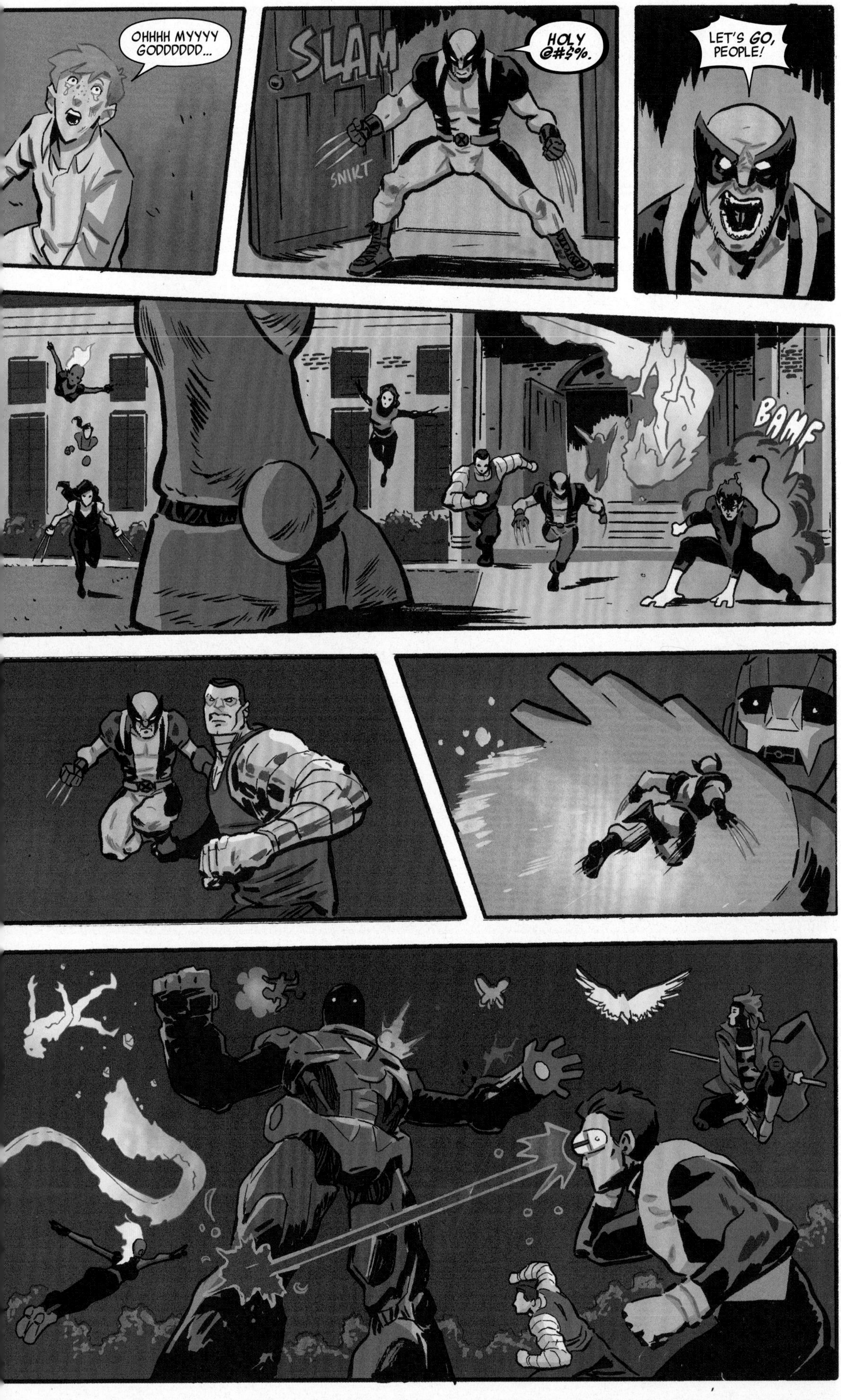
OHHHH MYYYY GODDDDDD...
SLAM
SNIKT
HOLY @#$%.
LET'S GO, PEOPLE!
BAMF

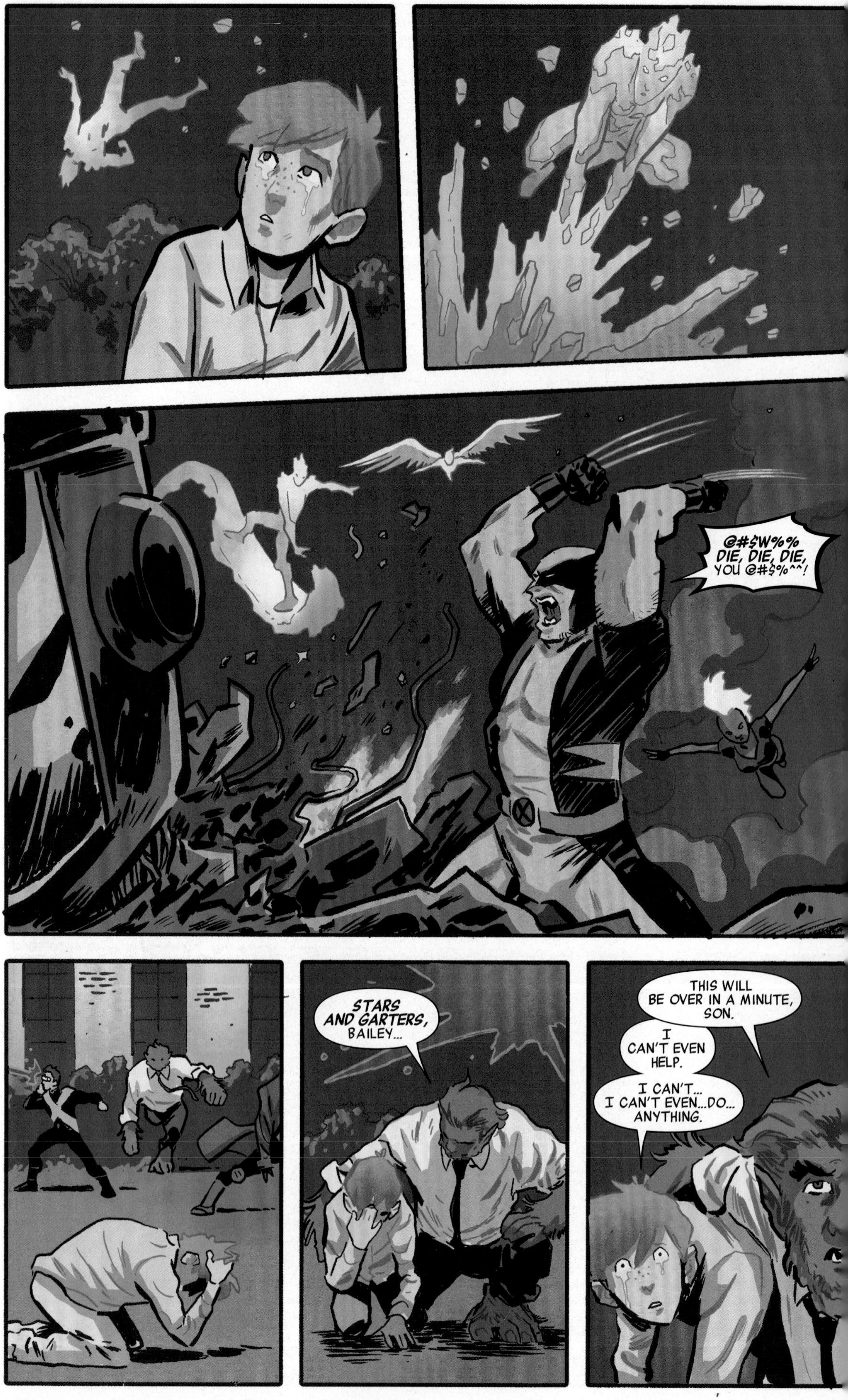
@#$W%%
DIE, DIE, DIE,
YOU @#$%^^!
STARS AND GARTERS, BAILEY...
THIS WILL BE OVER IN A MINUTE, SON.
I CAN'T EVEN HELP.
I CAN'T... I CAN'T EVEN...DO... ANYTHING.

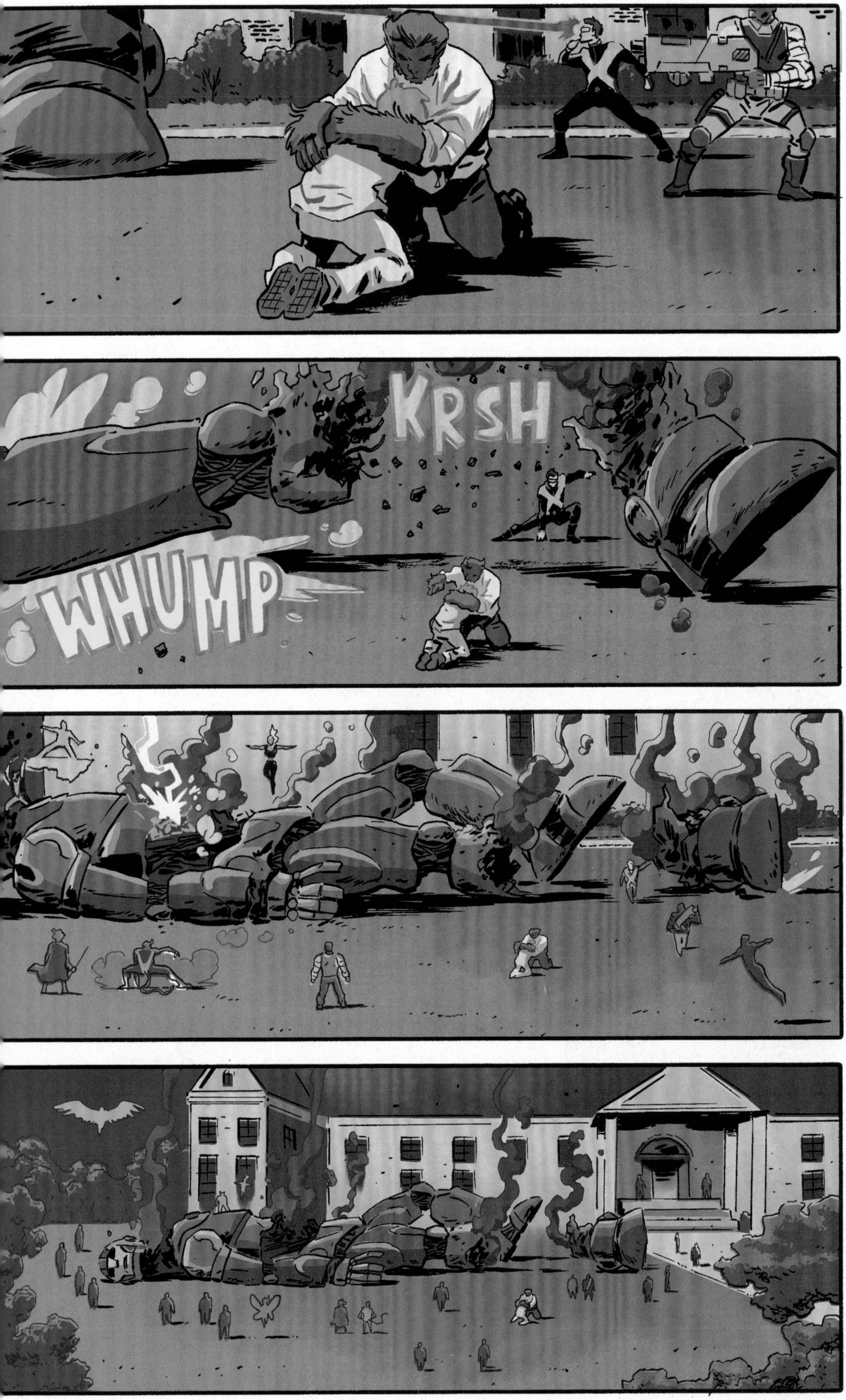

KRSH
WHUMP

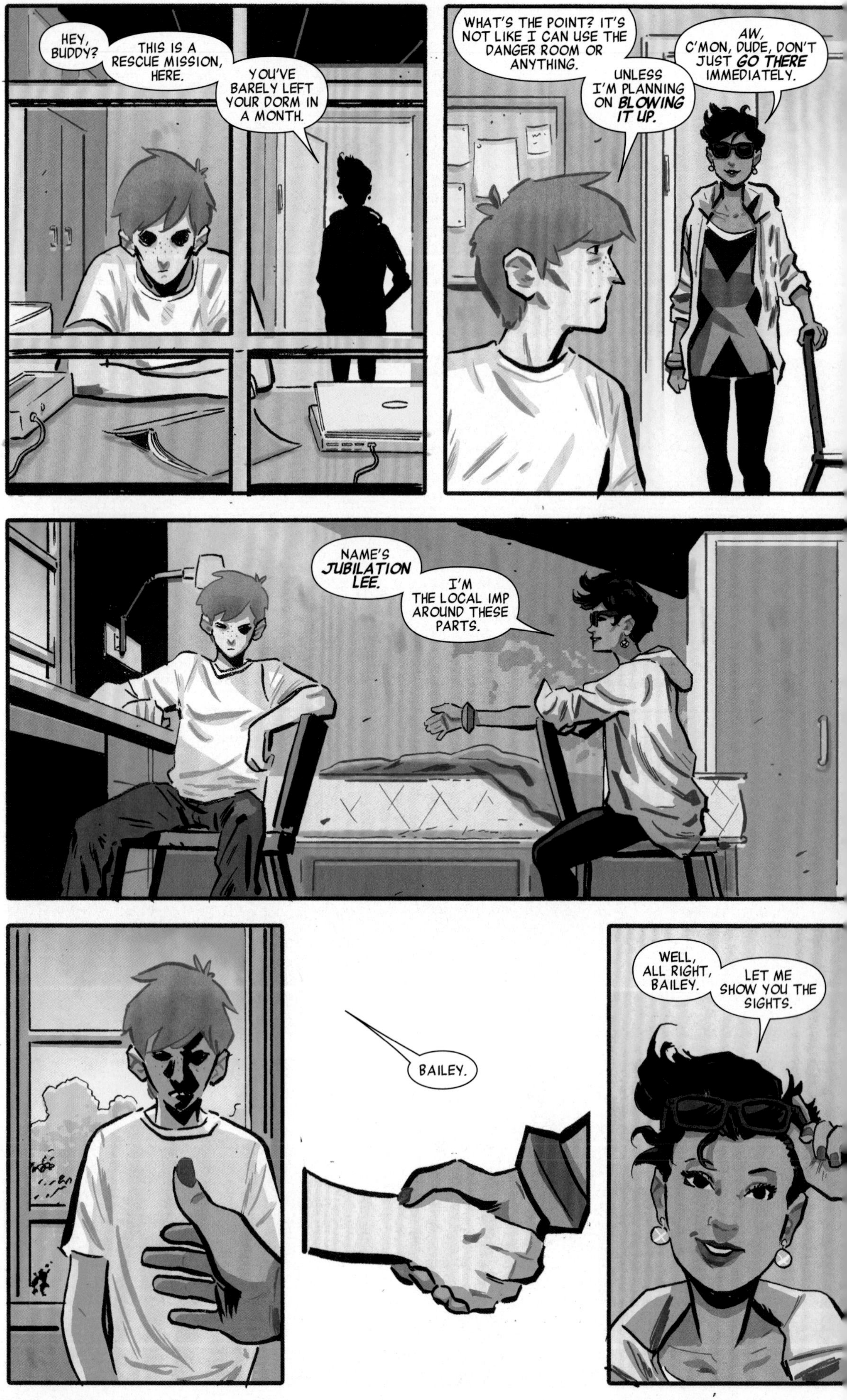
HEY, BUDDY?
THIS IS A RESCUE MISSION, HERE.
YOU'VE BARELY LEFT YOUR DORM IN A MONTH.
WHAT'S THE POINT? IT'S NOT LIKE I CAN USE THE DANGER ROOM OR ANYTHING.
UNLESS I'M PLANNING ON *BLOWING IT UP.*
AW, C'MON, DUDE, DON'T JUST *GO THERE* IMMEDIATELY.
NAME'S *JUBILATION LEE.*
I'M THE LOCAL IMP AROUND THESE PARTS.
BAILEY.
WELL, ALL RIGHT, BAILEY.
LET ME SHOW YOU THE SIGHTS.

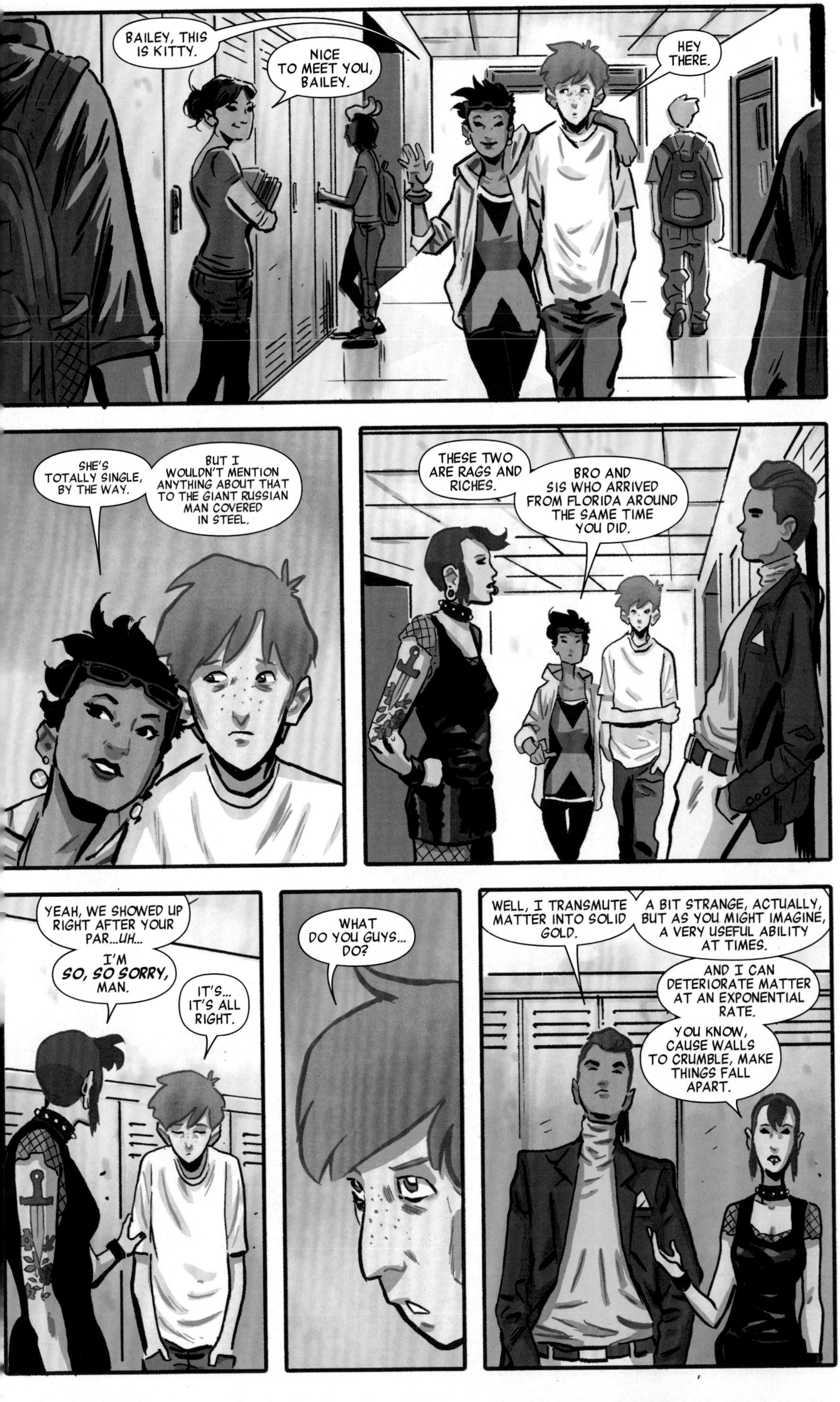
BAILEY, THIS IS KITTY.
NICE TO MEET YOU, BAILEY.
HEY THERE.
SHE'S TOTALLY SINGLE, BY THE WAY.
BUT I WOULDN'T MENTION ANYTHING ABOUT THAT TO THE GIANT RUSSIAN MAN COVERED IN STEEL.
THESE TWO ARE RAGS AND RICHES.
BRO AND SIS WHO ARRIVED FROM FLORIDA AROUND THE SAME TIME YOU DID.
YEAH, WE SHOWED UP RIGHT AFTER YOUR PAR...UH...
I'M ***SO, SO SORRY,*** MAN.
IT'S... IT'S ALL RIGHT.
WHAT DO YOU GUYS... DO?
WELL, I TRANSMUTE MATTER INTO SOLID GOLD.
A BIT STRANGE, ACTUALLY, BUT AS YOU MIGHT IMAGINE, A VERY USEFUL ABILITY AT TIMES.
AND I CAN DETERIORATE MATTER AT AN EXPONENTIAL RATE.
YOU KNOW, CAUSE WALLS TO CRUMBLE, MAKE THINGS FALL APART.

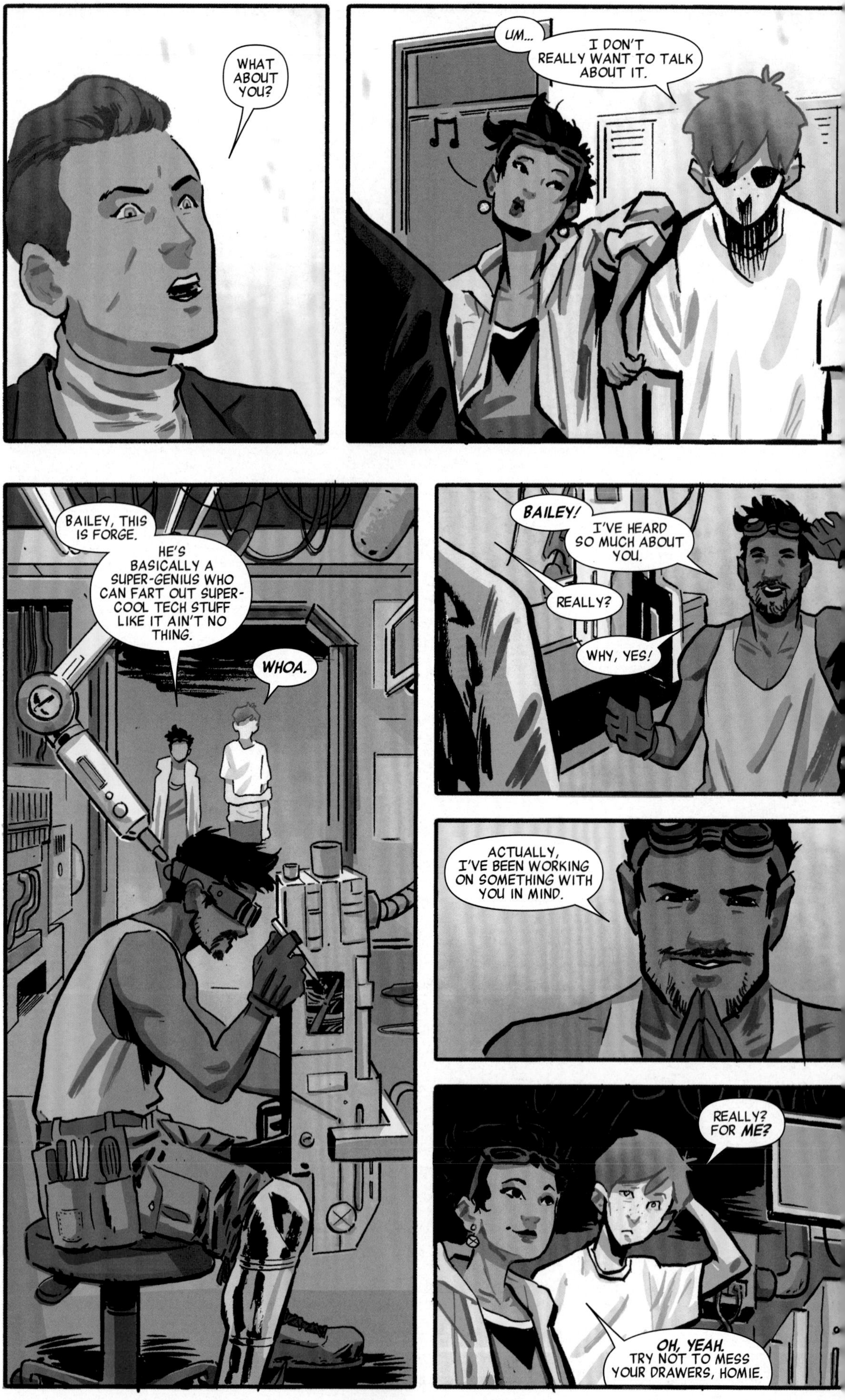
WHAT ABOUT YOU?
UM...
I DON'T REALLY WANT TO TALK ABOUT IT.
BAILEY, THIS IS FORGE.
HE'S BASICALLY A SUPER-GENIUS WHO CAN FART OUT SUPER-COOL TECH STUFF LIKE IT AIN'T NO THING.
WHOA.
BAILEY!
I'VE HEARD SO MUCH ABOUT YOU.
REALLY?
WHY, YES!
ACTUALLY, I'VE BEEN WORKING ON SOMETHING WITH YOU IN MIND.
REALLY? FOR ME?
OH, YEAH. TRY NOT TO MESS YOUR DRAWERS, HOMIE.

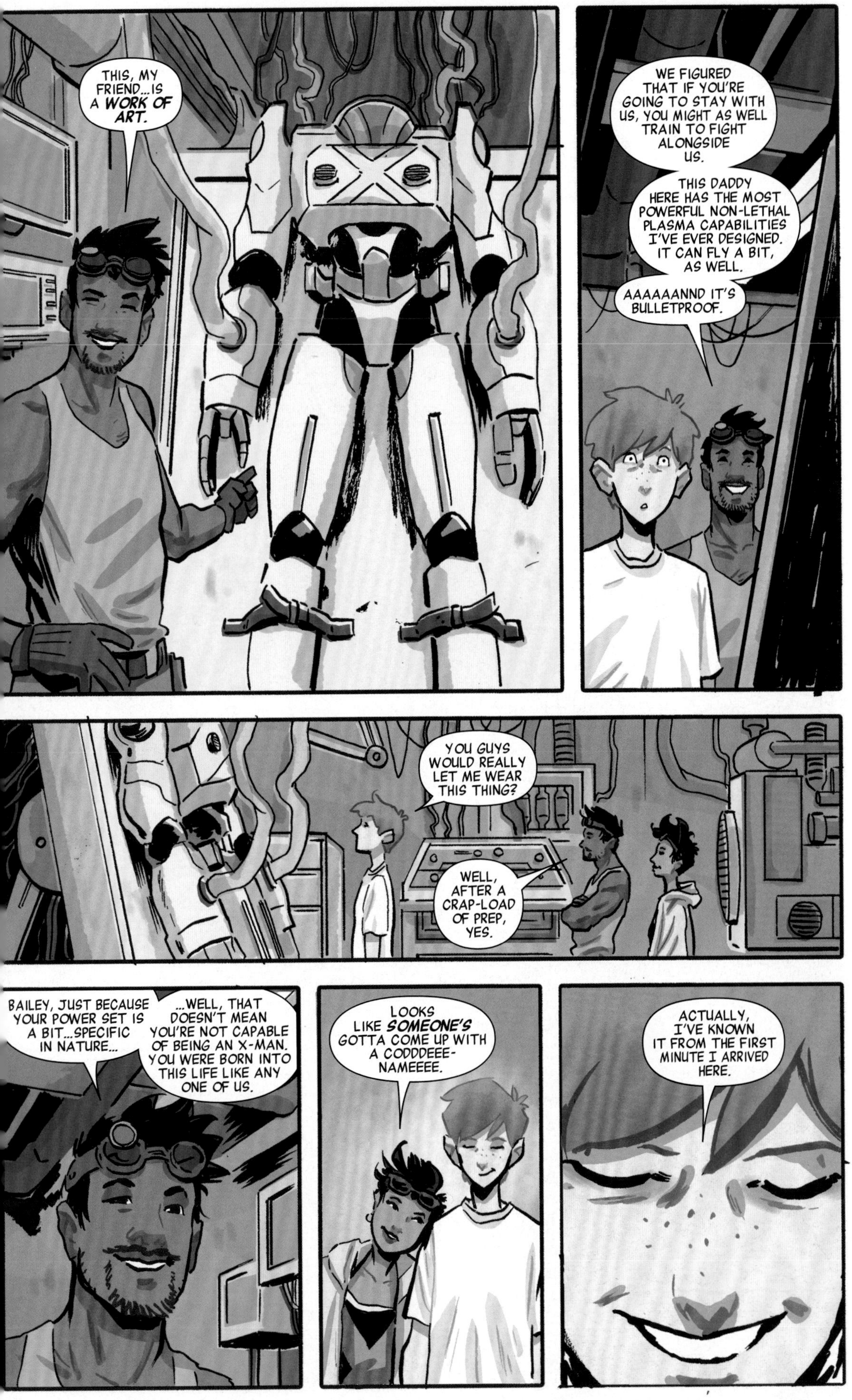
THIS, MY FRIEND...IS A WORK OF ART.
WE FIGURED THAT IF YOU'RE GOING TO STAY WITH US, YOU MIGHT AS WELL TRAIN TO FIGHT ALONGSIDE US.
THIS DADDY HERE HAS THE MOST POWERFUL NON-LETHAL PLASMA CAPABILITIES I'VE EVER DESIGNED. IT CAN FLY A BIT, AS WELL.
AAAAAANND IT'S BULLETPROOF.
YOU GUYS WOULD REALLY LET ME WEAR THIS THING?
WELL, AFTER A CRAP-LOAD OF PREP, YES.
BAILEY, JUST BECAUSE YOUR POWER SET IS A BIT...SPECIFIC IN NATURE...
...WELL, THAT DOESN'T MEAN YOU'RE NOT CAPABLE OF BEING AN X-MAN. YOU WERE BORN INTO THIS LIFE LIKE ANY ONE OF US.
LOOKS LIKE SOMEONE'S GOTTA COME UP WITH A CODDDEEE-NAMEEEE.
ACTUALLY, I'VE KNOWN IT FROM THE FIRST MINUTE I ARRIVED HERE.

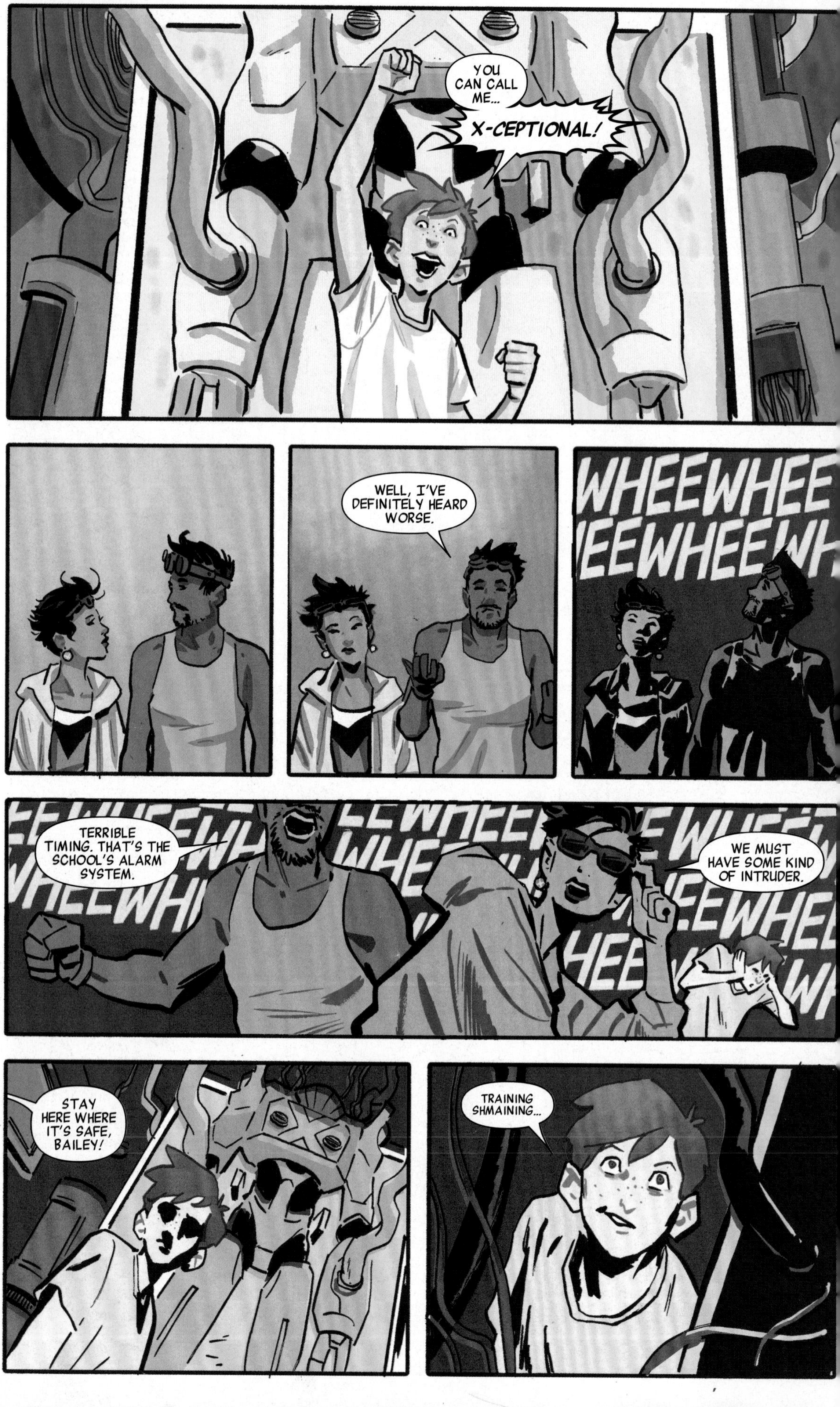
YOU CAN CALL ME...
X-CEPTIONAL!
WELL, I'VE DEFINITELY HEARD WORSE.
WHEEWHEE
TERRIBLE TIMING. THAT'S THE SCHOOL'S ALARM SYSTEM.
WE MUST HAVE SOME KIND OF INTRUDER.
STAY HERE WHERE IT'S SAFE, BAILEY!
TRAINING SHMAINING...

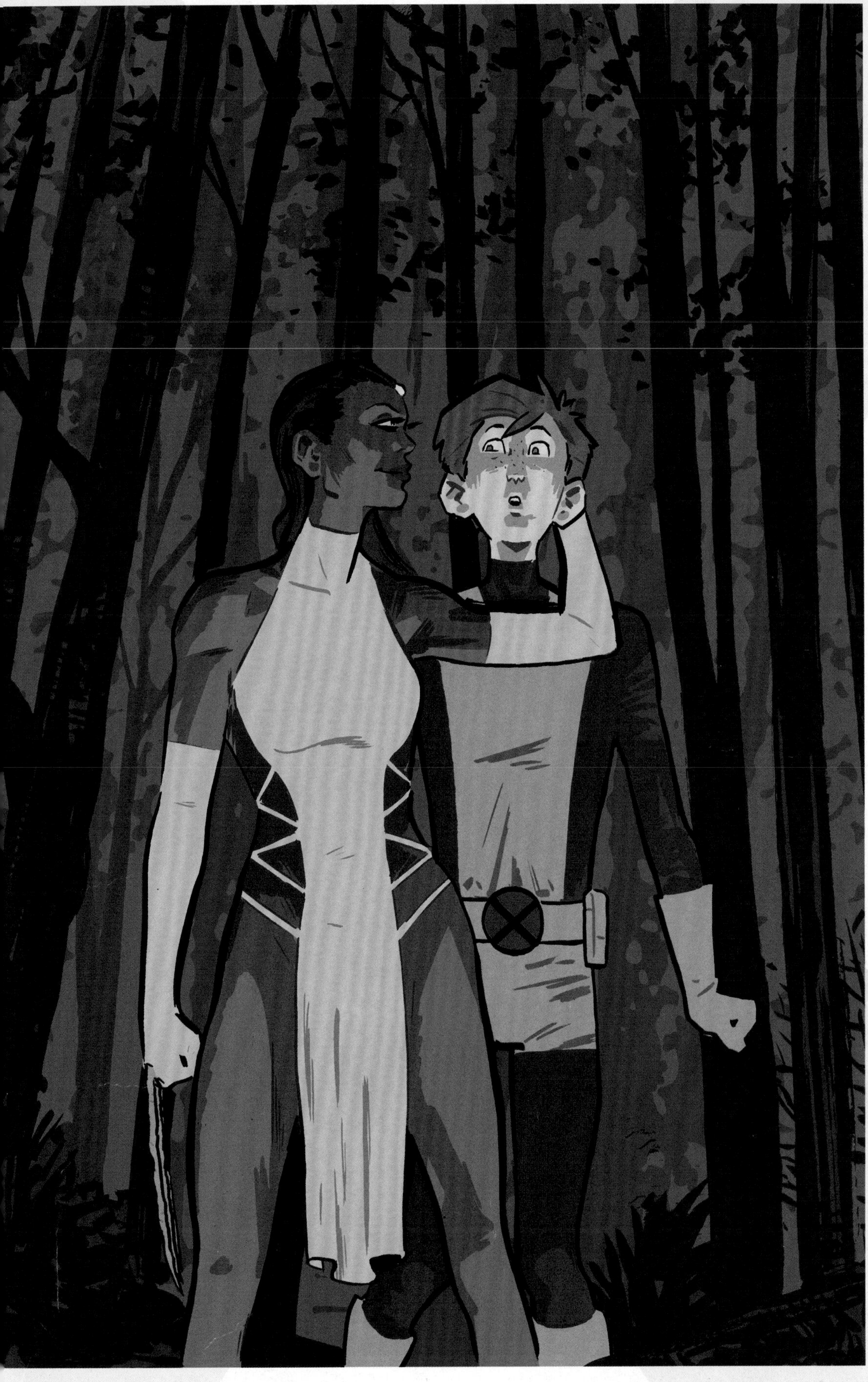

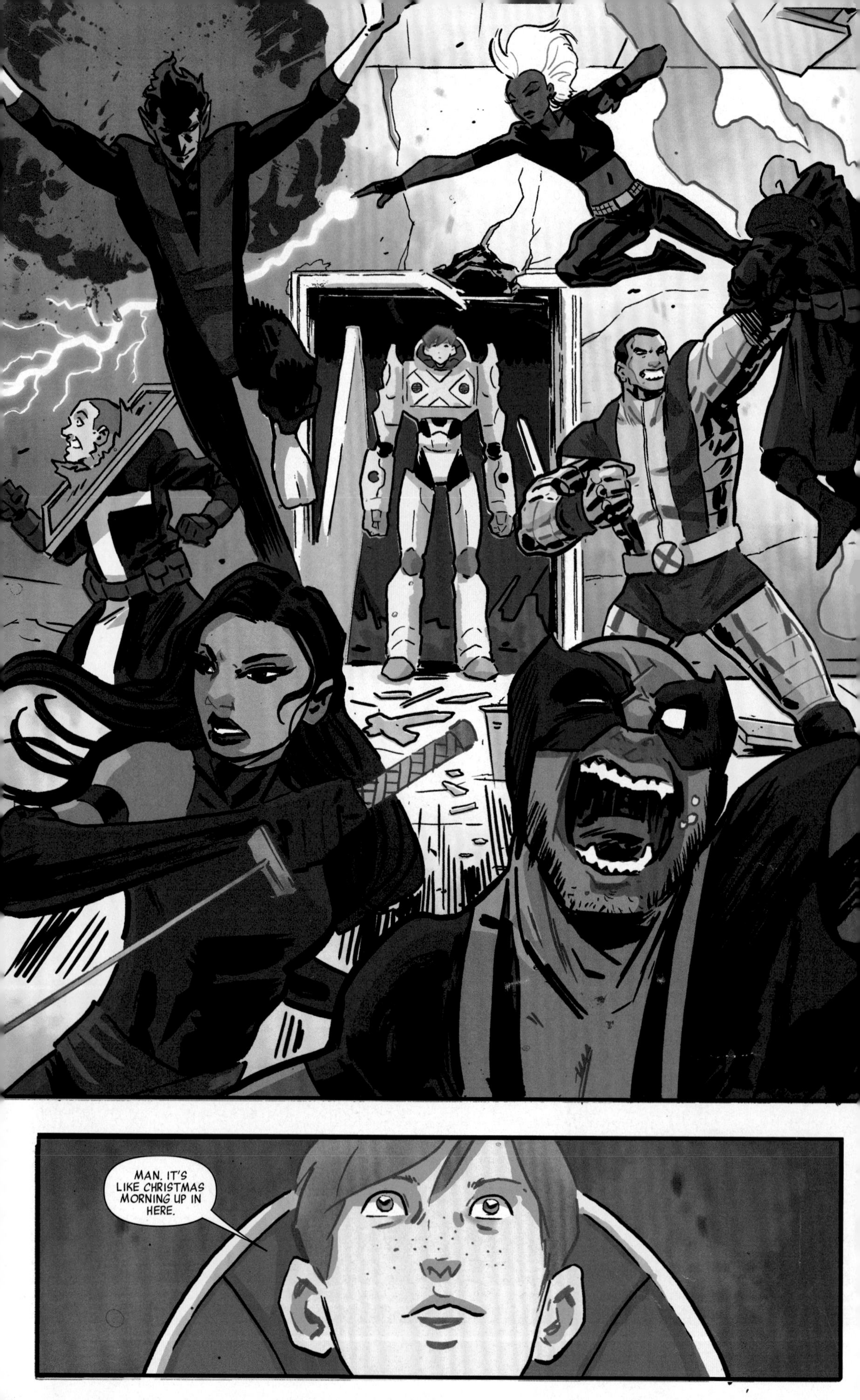
MAN. IT'S LIKE CHRISTMAS MORNING UP IN HERE.

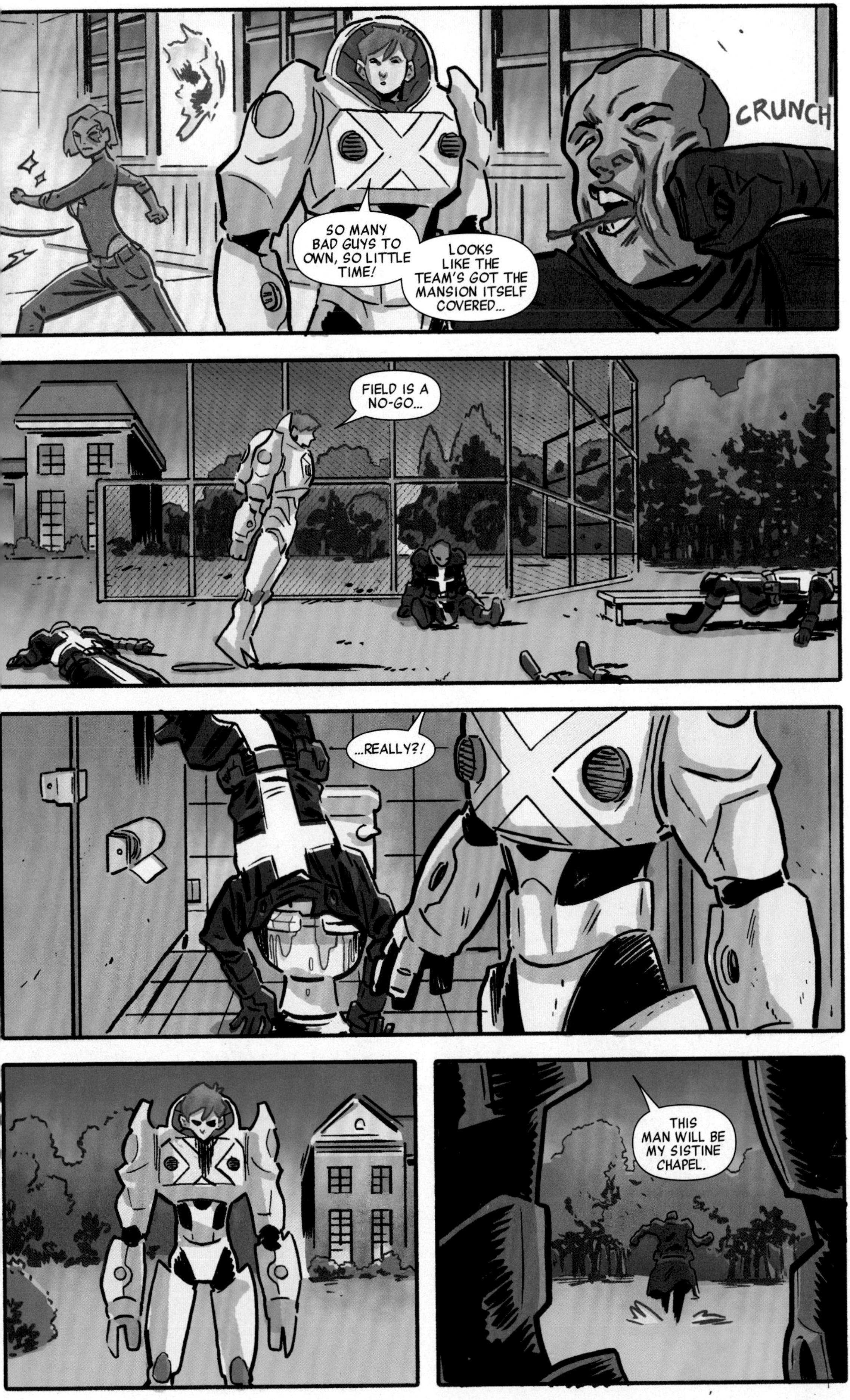
CRUNCH
SO MANY BAD GUYS TO OWN, SO LITTLE TIME!
LOOKS LIKE THE TEAM'S GOT THE MANSION ITSELF COVERED...
FIELD IS A NO-GO...
...REALLY?!
THIS MAN WILL BE MY SISTINE CHAPEL.

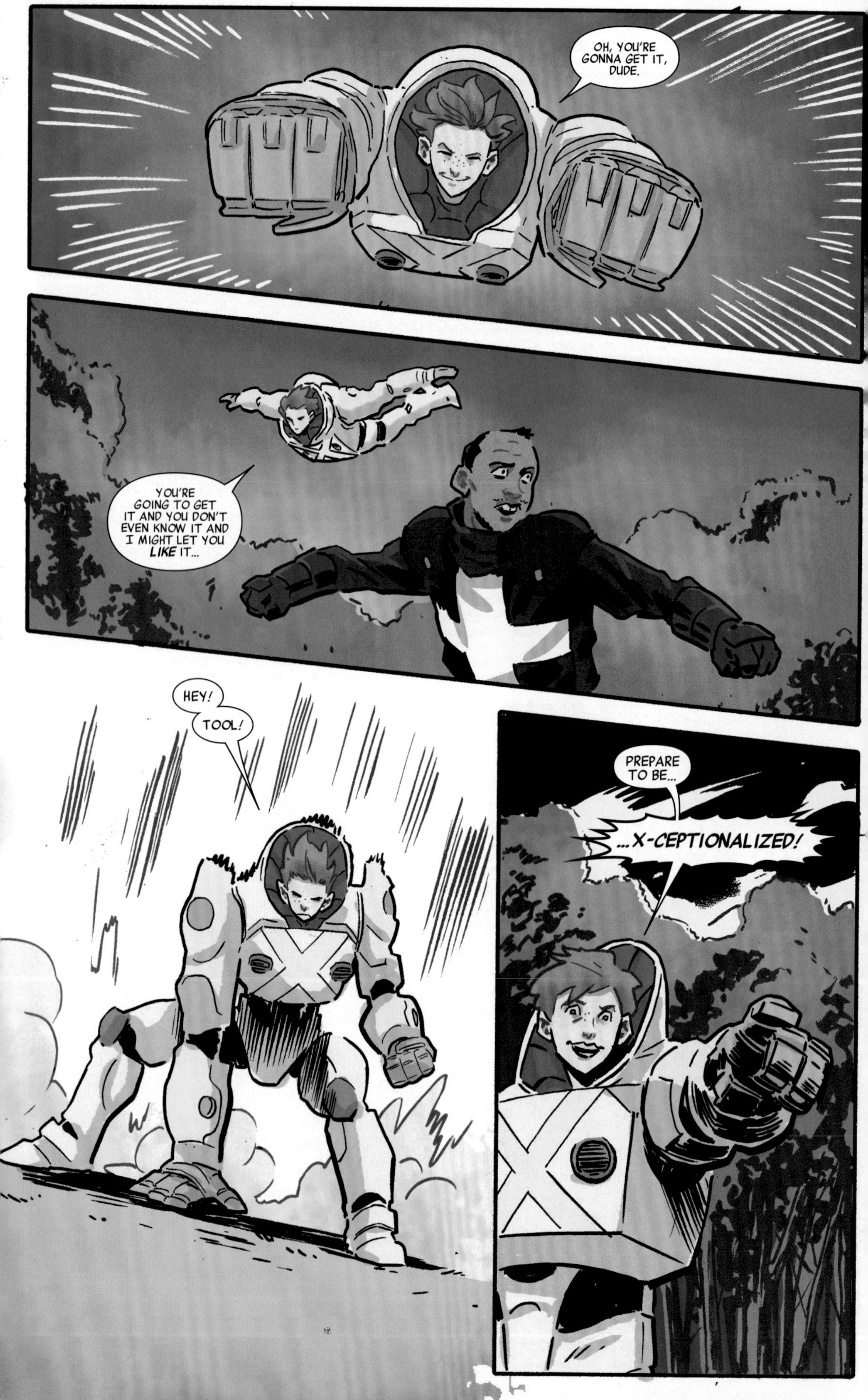
OH, YOU'RE GONNA GET IT, DUDE.
YOU'RE GOING TO GET IT AND YOU DON'T EVEN KNOW IT AND I MIGHT LET YOU LIKE IT...
HEY!
TOOL!
PREPARE TO BE...
...X-CEPTIONALIZED!

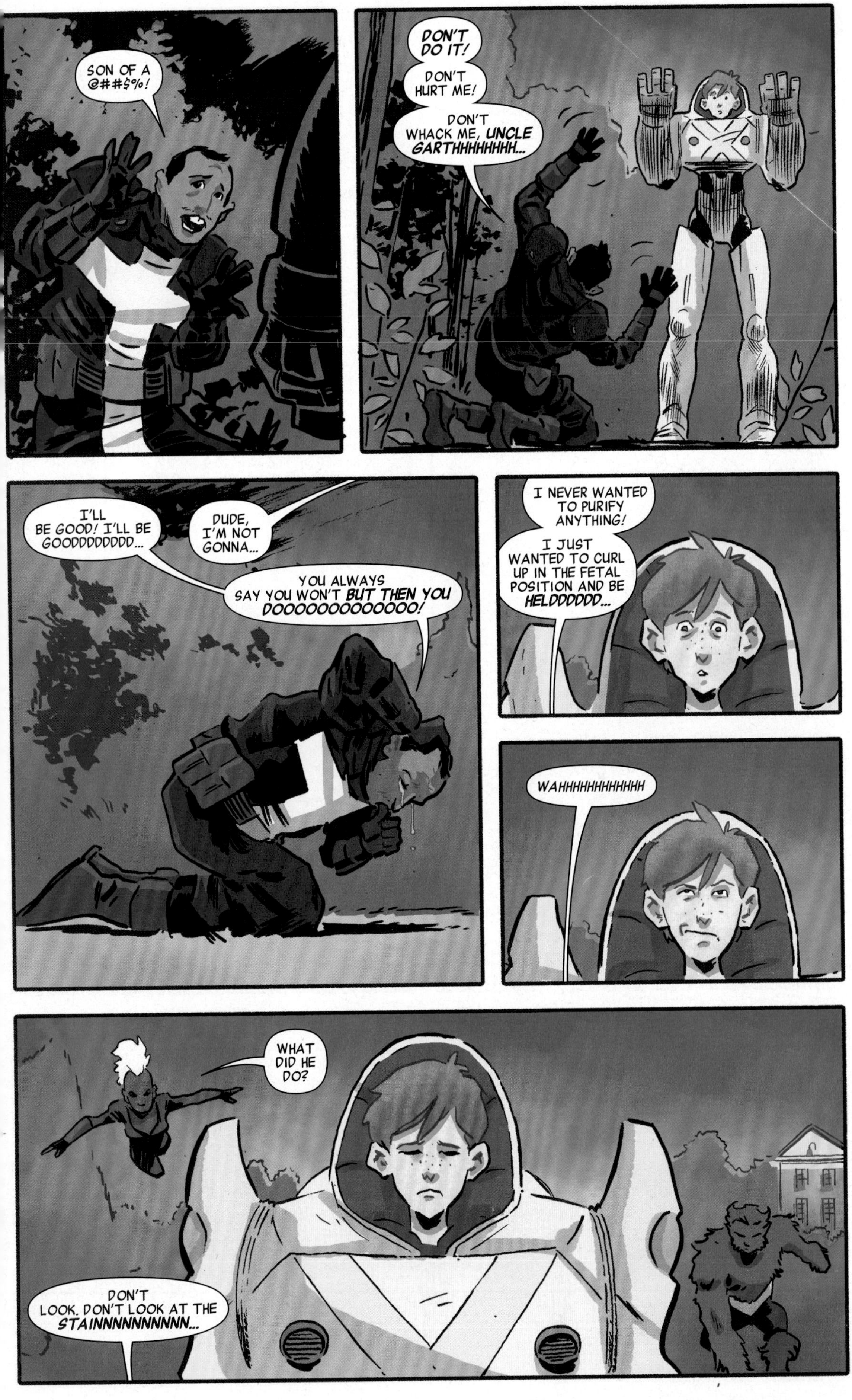

SON OF A @##$%!
DON'T DO IT!
DON'T HURT ME!
DON'T WHACK ME, UNCLE GARTHHHHHHHH...
I'LL BE GOOD! I'LL BE GOODDDDDDDD...
DUDE, I'M NOT GONNA...
YOU ALWAYS SAY YOU WON'T BUT THEN YOU DOOOOOOOOOOOOO!
I NEVER WANTED TO PURIFY ANYTHING!
I JUST WANTED TO CURL UP IN THE FETAL POSITION AND BE HELDDDDDD...
WAHHHHHHHHHHHH
WHAT DID HE DO?
DON'T LOOK. DON'T LOOK AT THE STAINNNNNNNNNN...

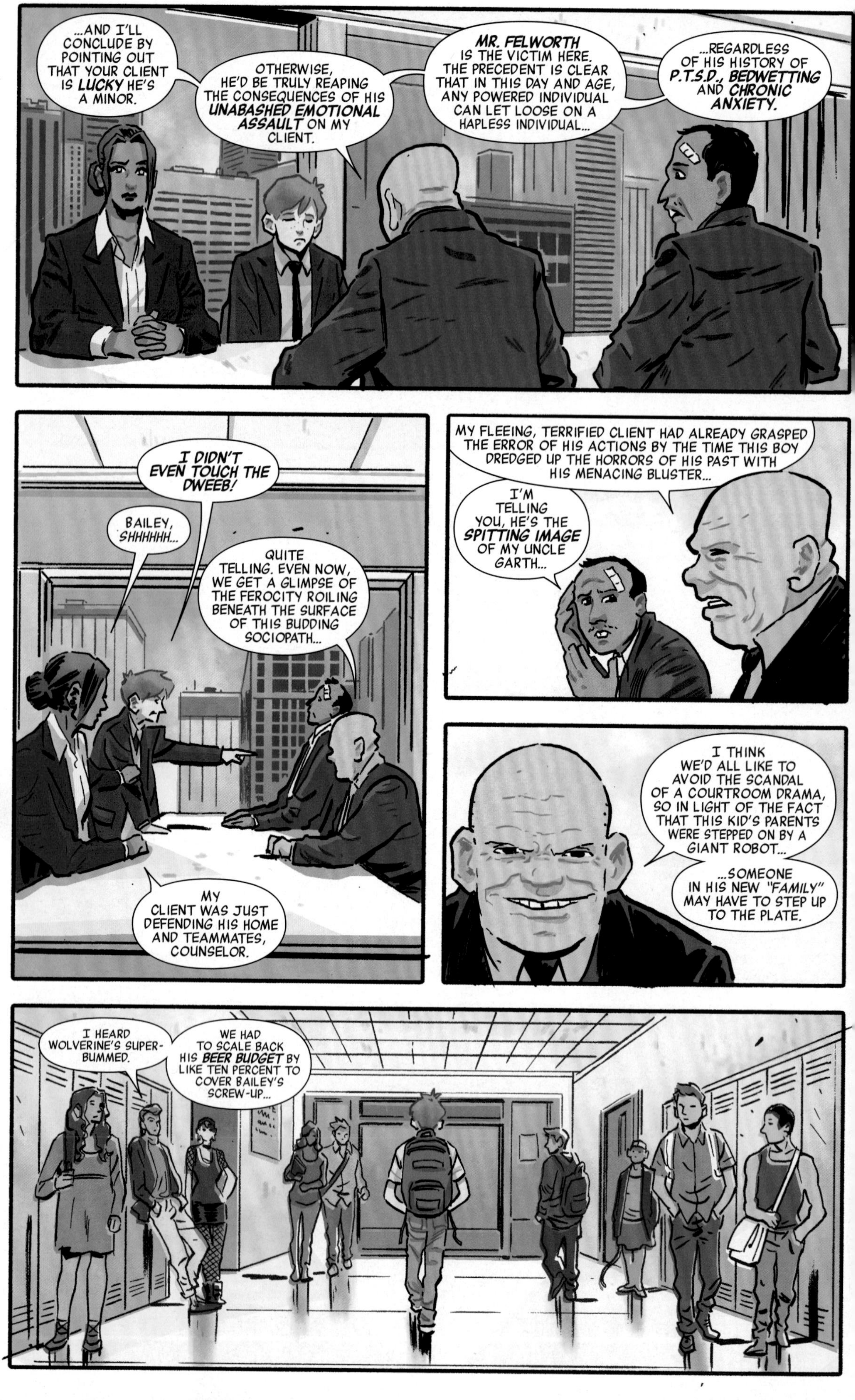
...AND I'LL CONCLUDE BY POINTING OUT THAT YOUR CLIENT IS LUCKY HE'S A MINOR.
OTHERWISE, HE'D BE TRULY REAPING THE CONSEQUENCES OF HIS UNABASHED EMOTIONAL ASSAULT ON MY CLIENT.
MR. FELWORTH IS THE VICTIM HERE. THE PRECEDENT IS CLEAR THAT IN THIS DAY AND AGE, ANY POWERED INDIVIDUAL CAN LET LOOSE ON A HAPLESS INDIVIDUAL...
...REGARDLESS OF HIS HISTORY OF P.T.S.D., BEDWETTING AND CHRONIC ANXIETY.
I DIDN'T EVEN TOUCH THE DWEEB!
BAILEY, SHHHHHH...
QUITE TELLING. EVEN NOW, WE GET A GLIMPSE OF THE FEROCITY ROILING BENEATH THE SURFACE OF THIS BUDDING SOCIOPATH...
MY CLIENT WAS JUST DEFENDING HIS HOME AND TEAMMATES, COUNSELOR.
MY FLEEING, TERRIFIED CLIENT HAD ALREADY GRASPED THE ERROR OF HIS ACTIONS BY THE TIME THIS BOY DREDGED UP THE HORRORS OF HIS PAST WITH HIS MENACING BLUSTER...
I'M TELLING YOU, HE'S THE SPITTING IMAGE OF MY UNCLE GARTH...
I THINK WE'D ALL LIKE TO AVOID THE SCANDAL OF A COURTROOM DRAMA, SO IN LIGHT OF THE FACT THAT THIS KID'S PARENTS WERE STEPPED ON BY A GIANT ROBOT...
...SOMEONE IN HIS NEW "FAMILY" MAY HAVE TO STEP UP TO THE PLATE.
I HEARD WOLVERINE'S SUPER-BUMMED.
WE HAD TO SCALE BACK HIS BEER BUDGET BY LIKE TEN PERCENT TO COVER BAILEY'S SCREW-UP...

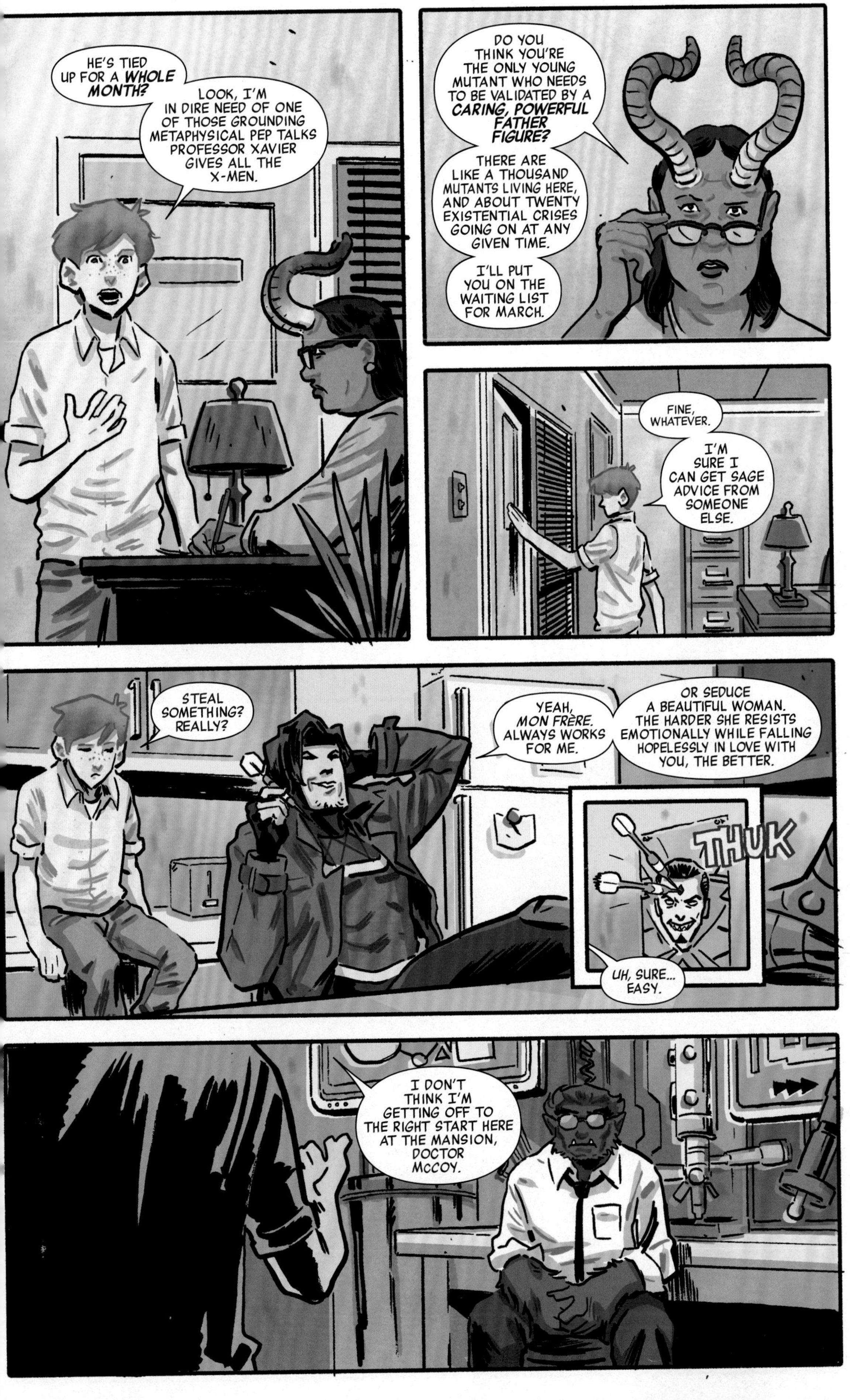

HE'S TIED UP FOR A *WHOLE MONTH?*
LOOK, I'M IN DIRE NEED OF ONE OF THOSE GROUNDING METAPHYSICAL PEP TALKS PROFESSOR XAVIER GIVES ALL THE X-MEN.
DO YOU THINK YOU'RE THE ONLY YOUNG MUTANT WHO NEEDS TO BE VALIDATED BY A *CARING, POWERFUL FATHER FIGURE?*
THERE ARE LIKE A THOUSAND MUTANTS LIVING HERE, AND ABOUT TWENTY EXISTENTIAL CRISES GOING ON AT ANY GIVEN TIME.
I'LL PUT YOU ON THE WAITING LIST FOR MARCH.
FINE, WHATEVER.
I'M SURE I CAN GET SAGE ADVICE FROM SOMEONE ELSE.
STEAL SOMETHING? REALLY?
YEAH, *MON FRÈRE.* ALWAYS WORKS FOR ME.
OR SEDUCE A BEAUTIFUL WOMAN. THE HARDER SHE RESISTS EMOTIONALLY WHILE FALLING HOPELESSLY IN LOVE WITH YOU, THE BETTER.
THUK
UH, SURE... EASY.
I DON'T THINK I'M GETTING OFF TO THE RIGHT START HERE AT THE MANSION, DOCTOR McCOY.

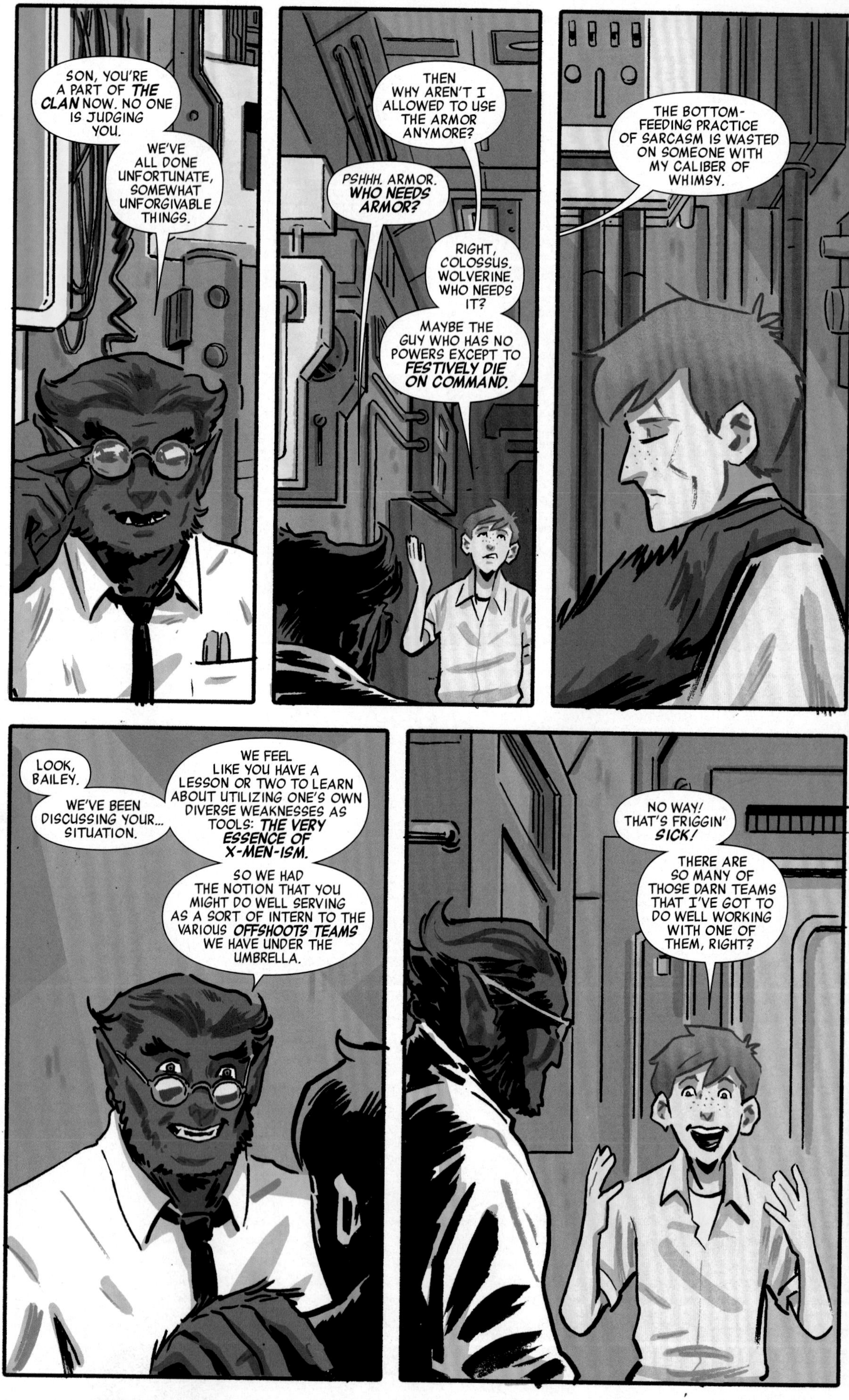
SON, YOU'RE A PART OF THE CLAN NOW. NO ONE IS JUDGING YOU.
WE'VE ALL DONE UNFORTUNATE, SOMEWHAT UNFORGIVABLE THINGS.
THEN WHY AREN'T I ALLOWED TO USE THE ARMOR ANYMORE?
PSHHH. ARMOR. WHO NEEDS ARMOR?
RIGHT, COLOSSUS. WOLVERINE. WHO NEEDS IT?
MAYBE THE GUY WHO HAS NO POWERS EXCEPT TO FESTIVELY DIE ON COMMAND.
THE BOTTOM-FEEDING PRACTICE OF SARCASM IS WASTED ON SOMEONE WITH MY CALIBER OF WHIMSY.
LOOK, BAILEY.
WE'VE BEEN DISCUSSING YOUR... SITUATION.
WE FEEL LIKE YOU HAVE A LESSON OR TWO TO LEARN ABOUT UTILIZING ONE'S OWN DIVERSE WEAKNESSES AS TOOLS: THE VERY ESSENCE OF X-MEN-ISM.
SO WE HAD THE NOTION THAT YOU MIGHT DO WELL SERVING AS A SORT OF INTERN TO THE VARIOUS OFFSHOOTS TEAMS WE HAVE UNDER THE UMBRELLA.
NO WAY! THAT'S FRIGGIN' SICK!
THERE ARE SO MANY OF THOSE DARN TEAMS THAT I'VE GOT TO DO WELL WORKING WITH ONE OF THEM, RIGHT?

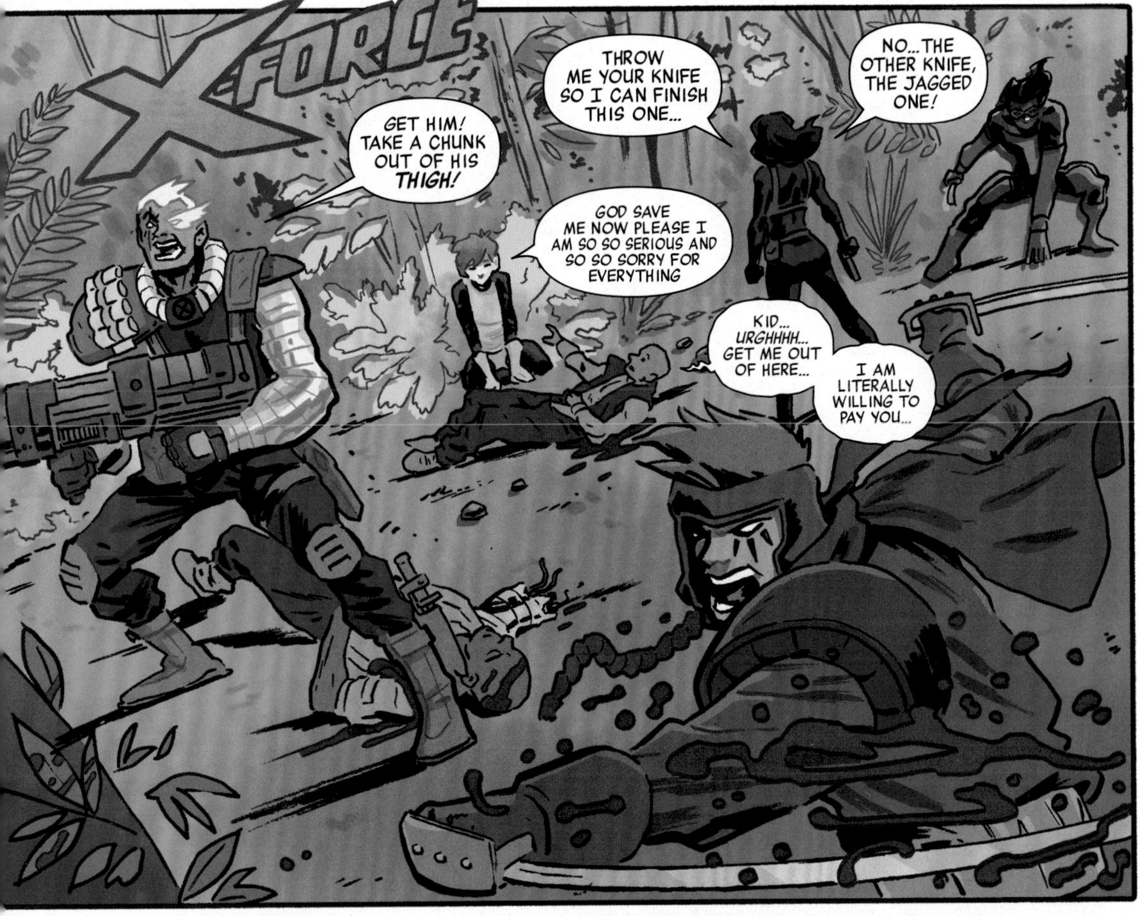
X-FORCE
GET HIM! TAKE A CHUNK OUT OF HIS *THIGH!*
THROW ME YOUR KNIFE SO I CAN FINISH THIS ONE...
NO... THE OTHER KNIFE, THE JAGGED ONE!
GOD SAVE ME NOW PLEASE I AM SO SO SERIOUS AND SO SO SORRY FOR EVERYTHING
KID... *URGHHHH...* GET ME OUT OF HERE...
I AM LITERALLY WILLING TO PAY YOU...

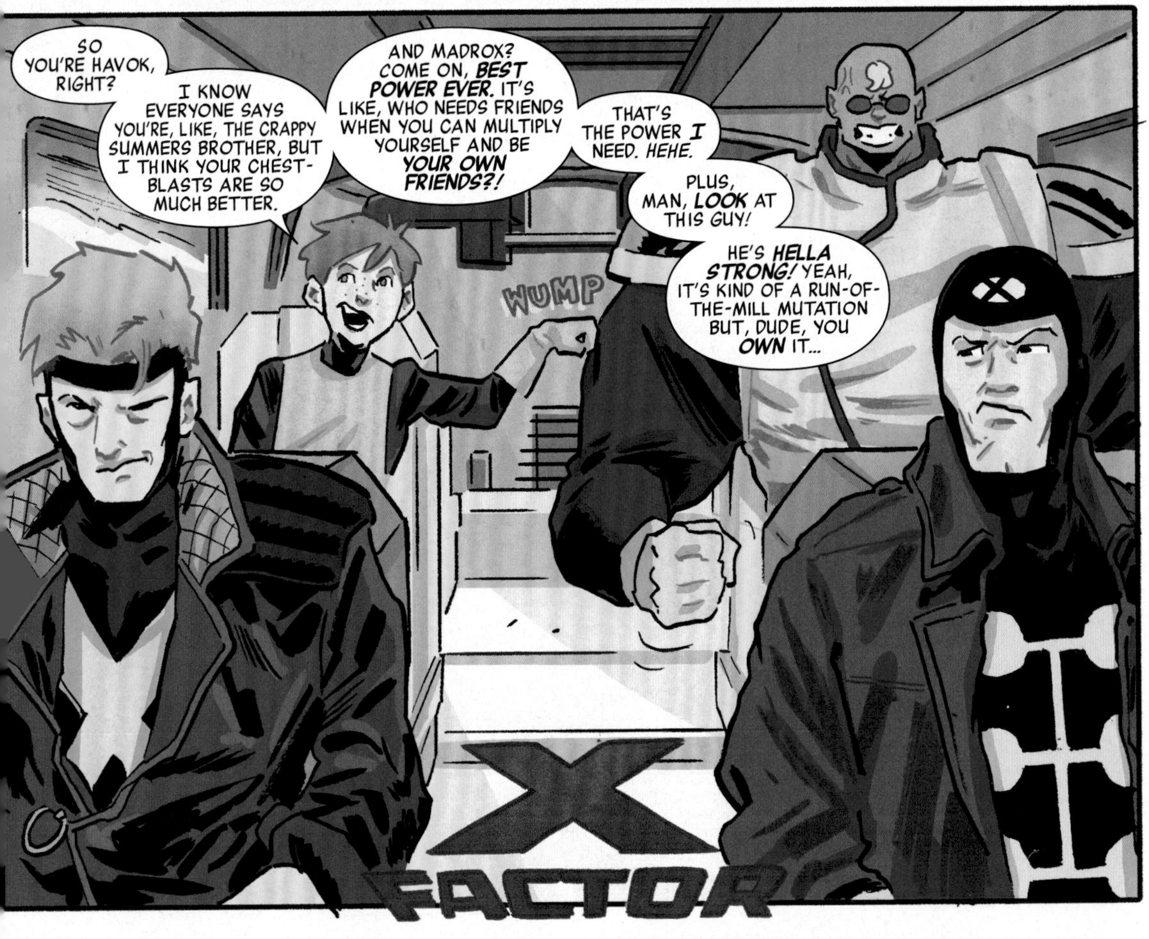
SO YOU'RE HAVOK, RIGHT?
I KNOW EVERYONE SAYS YOU'RE, LIKE, THE CRAPPY SUMMERS BROTHER, BUT I THINK YOUR CHEST-BLASTS ARE SO MUCH BETTER.
AND MADROX? COME ON, ***BEST POWER EVER.*** IT'S LIKE, WHO NEEDS FRIENDS WHEN YOU CAN MULTIPLY YOURSELF AND BE ***YOUR OWN FRIENDS?!***
THAT'S THE POWER ***I*** NEED. *HEHE.*
PLUS, MAN, ***LOOK*** AT THIS GUY!
HE'S ***HELLA STRONG!*** YEAH, IT'S KIND OF A RUN-OF-THE-MILL MUTATION BUT, DUDE, YOU ***OWN*** IT...
WUMP
X FACTOR

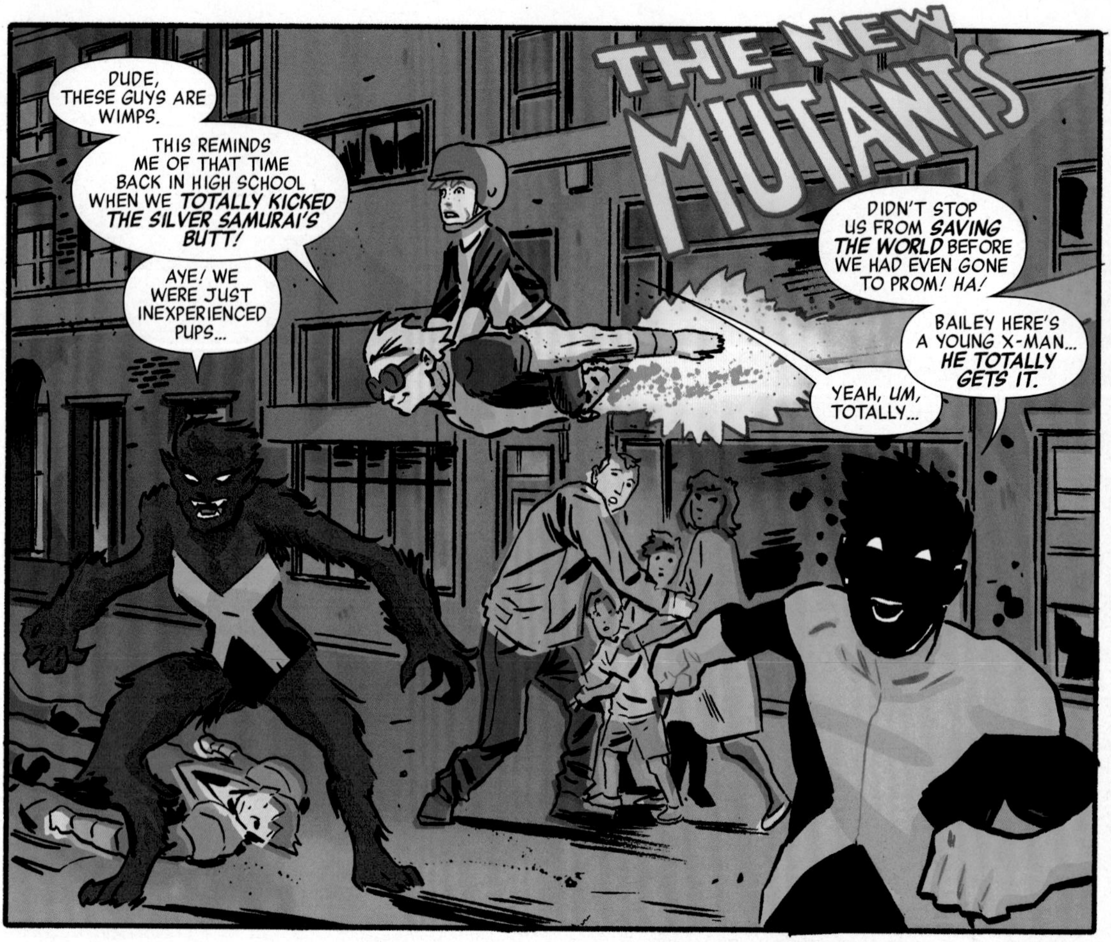
THE NEW MUTANTS
DUDE, THESE GUYS ARE WIMPS.
THIS REMINDS ME OF THAT TIME BACK IN HIGH SCHOOL WHEN WE TOTALLY KICKED THE SILVER SAMURAI'S BUTT!
AYE! WE WERE JUST INEXPERIENCED PUPS...
DIDN'T STOP US FROM SAVING THE WORLD BEFORE WE HAD EVEN GONE TO PROM! HA!
BAILEY HERE'S A YOUNG X-MAN... HE TOTALLY GETS IT.
YEAH, UM, TOTALLY...

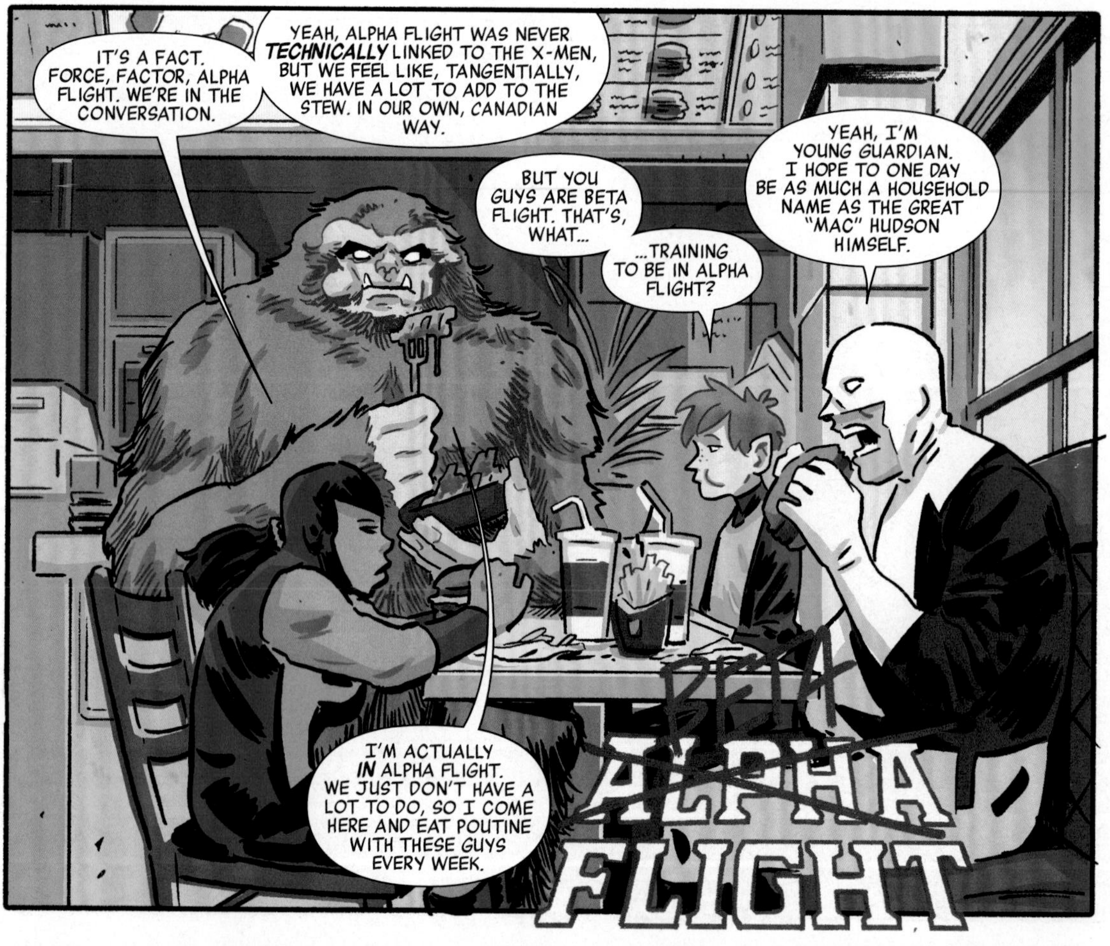
IT'S A FACT. FORCE, FACTOR, ALPHA FLIGHT. WE'RE IN THE CONVERSATION.
YEAH, ALPHA FLIGHT WAS NEVER TECHNICALLY LINKED TO THE X-MEN, BUT WE FEEL LIKE, TANGENTIALLY, WE HAVE A LOT TO ADD TO THE STEW. IN OUR OWN, CANADIAN WAY.
BUT YOU GUYS ARE BETA FLIGHT. THAT'S, WHAT...
...TRAINING TO BE IN ALPHA FLIGHT?
YEAH, I'M YOUNG GUARDIAN. I HOPE TO ONE DAY BE AS MUCH A HOUSEHOLD NAME AS THE GREAT "MAC" HUDSON HIMSELF.
I'M ACTUALLY IN ALPHA FLIGHT. WE JUST DON'T HAVE A LOT TO DO, SO I COME HERE AND EAT POUTINE WITH THESE GUYS EVERY WEEK.
BETA
ALPHA
FLIGHT

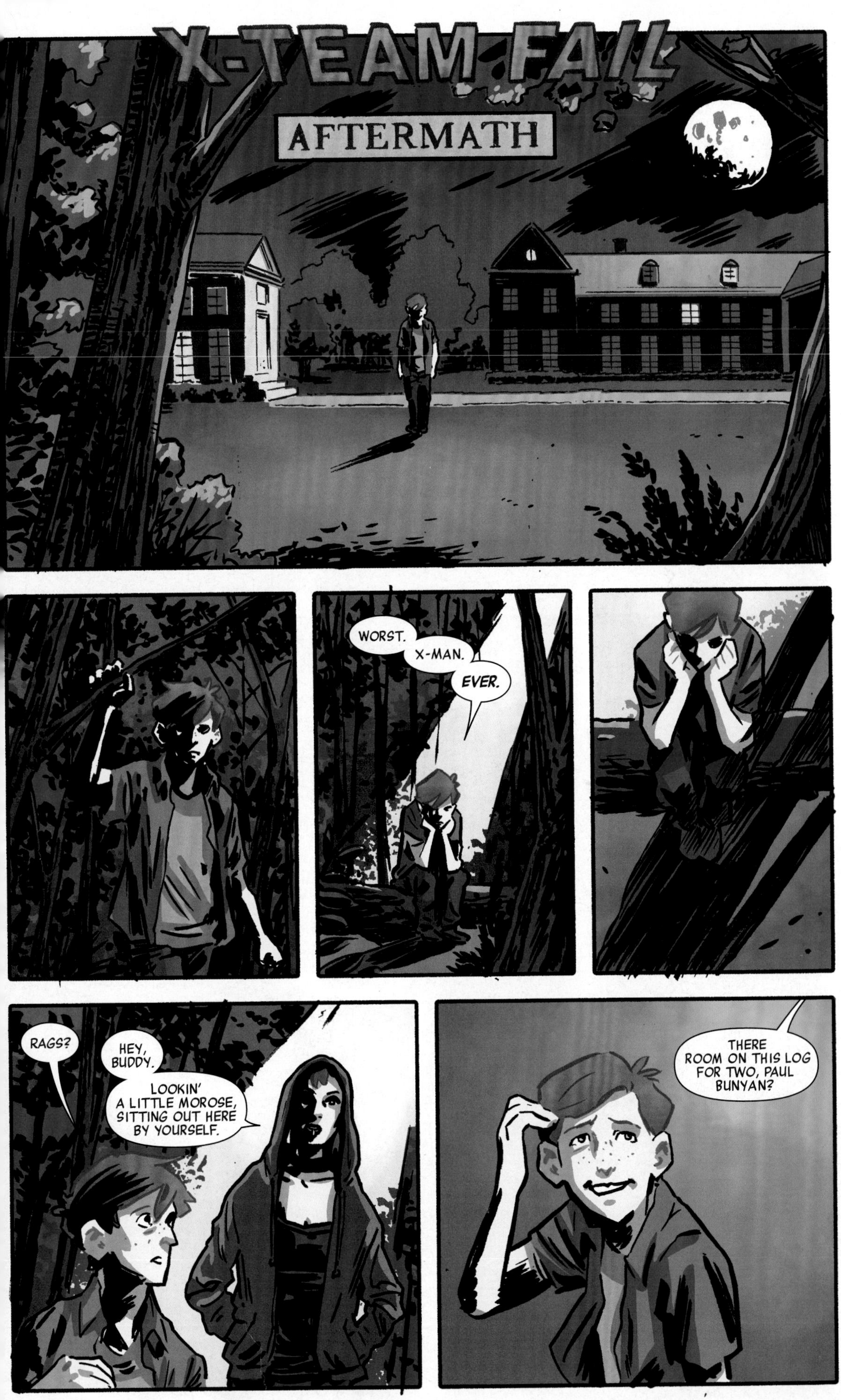
X-TEAM FAIL
AFTERMATH
WORST.
X-MAN.
EVER.
RAGS?
HEY, BUDDY.
LOOKIN' A LITTLE MOROSE, SITTING OUT HERE BY YOURSELF.
THERE ROOM ON THIS LOG FOR TWO, PAUL BUNYAN?

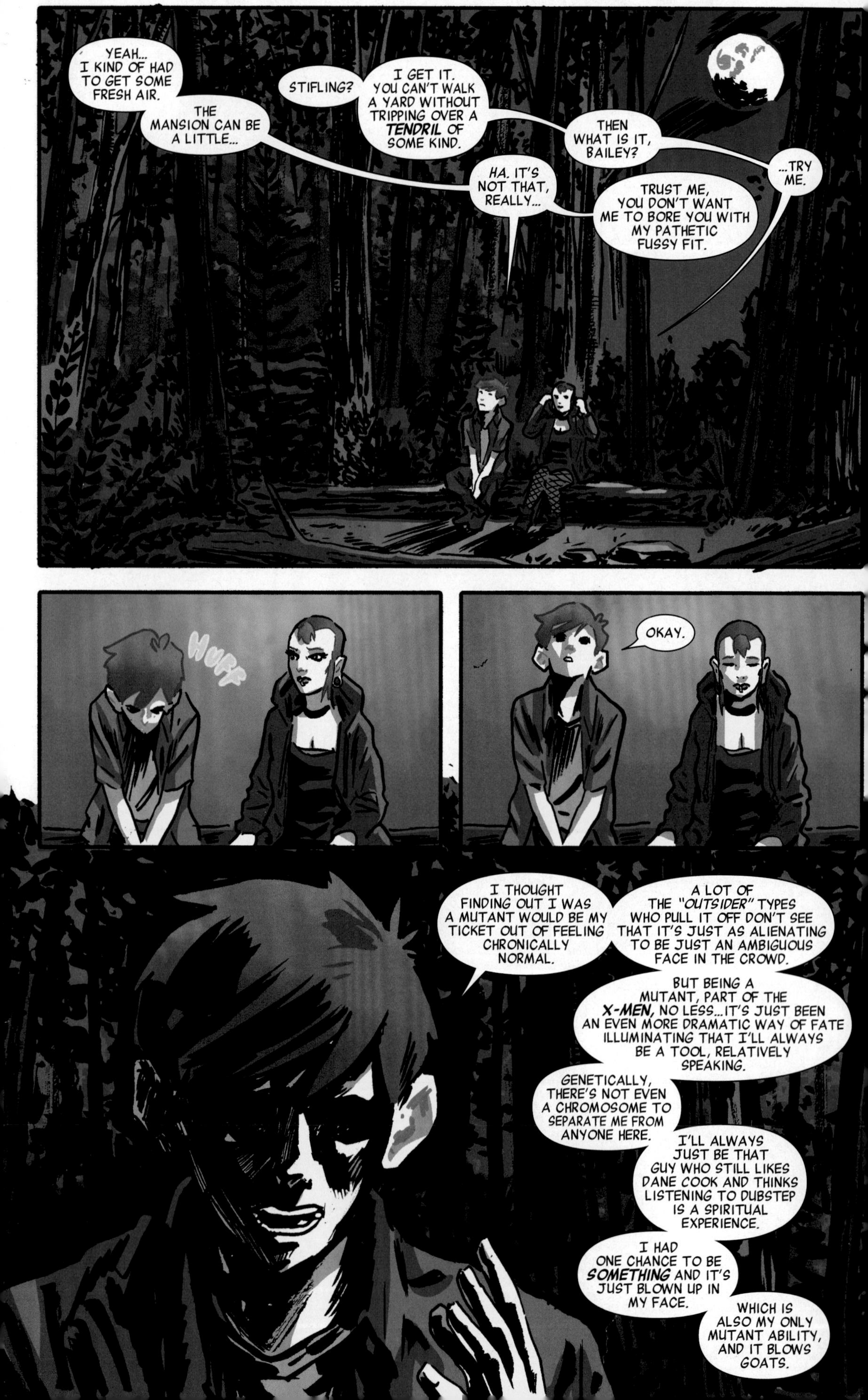
YEAH... I KIND OF HAD TO GET SOME FRESH AIR.
THE MANSION CAN BE A LITTLE...
STIFLING?
I GET IT. YOU CAN'T WALK A YARD WITHOUT TRIPPING OVER A TENDRIL OF SOME KIND.
HA. IT'S NOT THAT, REALLY...
TRUST ME, YOU DON'T WANT ME TO BORE YOU WITH MY PATHETIC FUSSY FIT.
THEN WHAT IS IT, BAILEY?
...TRY ME.
HUFF
OKAY.
I THOUGHT FINDING OUT I WAS A MUTANT WOULD BE MY TICKET OUT OF FEELING CHRONICALLY NORMAL.
A LOT OF THE "OUTSIDER" TYPES WHO PULL IT OFF DON'T SEE THAT IT'S JUST AS ALIENATING TO BE JUST AN AMBIGUOUS FACE IN THE CROWD.
BUT BEING A MUTANT, PART OF THE X-MEN, NO LESS...IT'S JUST BEEN AN EVEN MORE DRAMATIC WAY OF FATE ILLUMINATING THAT I'LL ALWAYS BE A TOOL, RELATIVELY SPEAKING.
GENETICALLY, THERE'S NOT EVEN A CHROMOSOME TO SEPARATE ME FROM ANYONE HERE.
I'LL ALWAYS JUST BE THAT GUY WHO STILL LIKES DANE COOK AND THINKS LISTENING TO DUBSTEP IS A SPIRITUAL EXPERIENCE.
I HAD ONE CHANCE TO BE SOMETHING AND IT'S JUST BLOWN UP IN MY FACE.
WHICH IS ALSO MY ONLY MUTANT ABILITY, AND IT BLOWS GOATS.

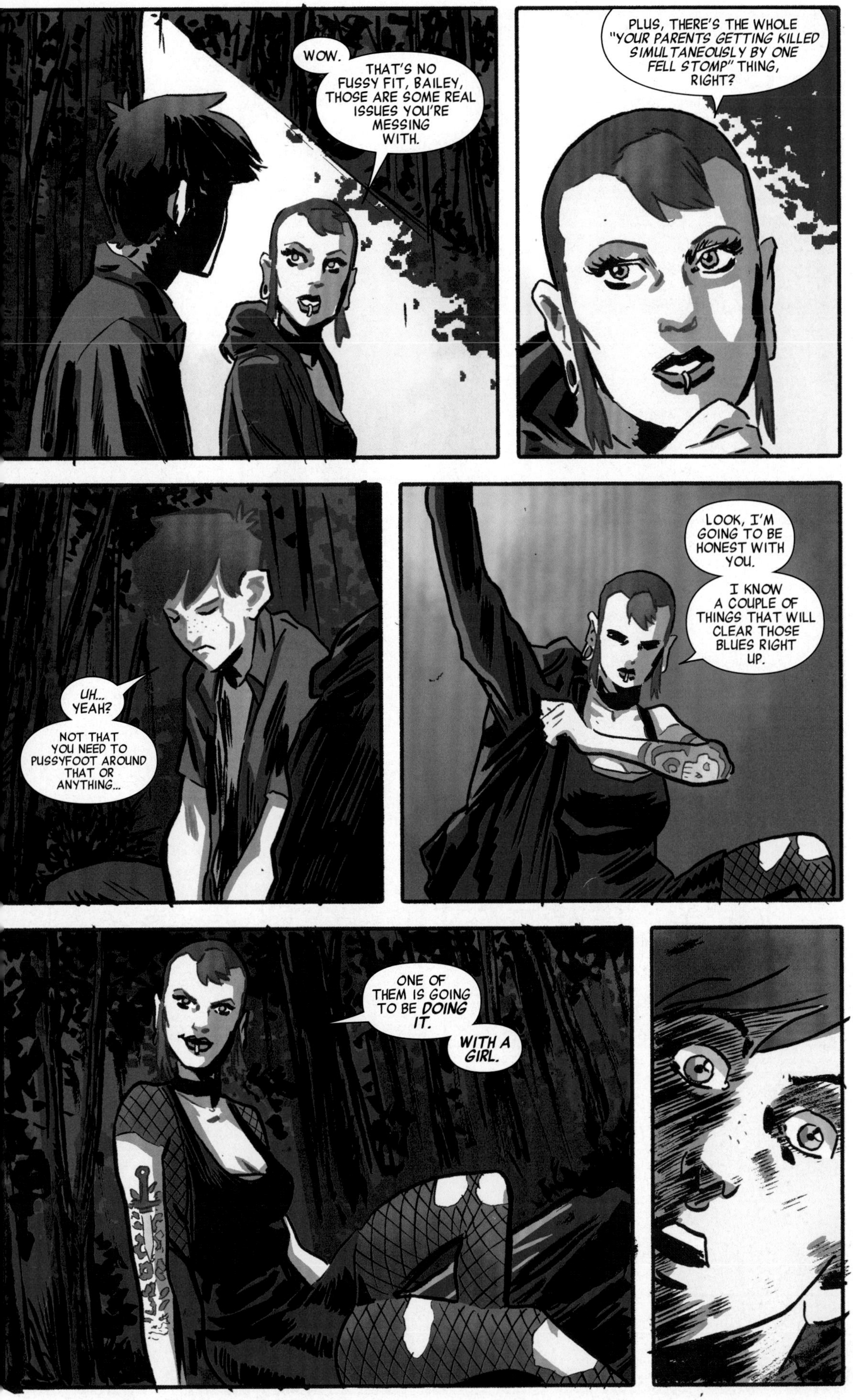
WOW.
THAT'S NO FUSSY FIT, BAILEY, THOSE ARE SOME REAL ISSUES YOU'RE MESSING WITH.
PLUS, THERE'S THE WHOLE "YOUR PARENTS GETTING KILLED SIMULTANEOUSLY BY ONE FELL STOMP" THING, RIGHT?
UH... YEAH?
NOT THAT YOU NEED TO PUSSYFOOT AROUND THAT OR ANYTHING...
LOOK, I'M GOING TO BE HONEST WITH YOU.
I KNOW A COUPLE OF THINGS THAT WILL CLEAR THOSE BLUES RIGHT UP.
ONE OF THEM IS GOING TO BE *DOING IT.*
WITH A GIRL.

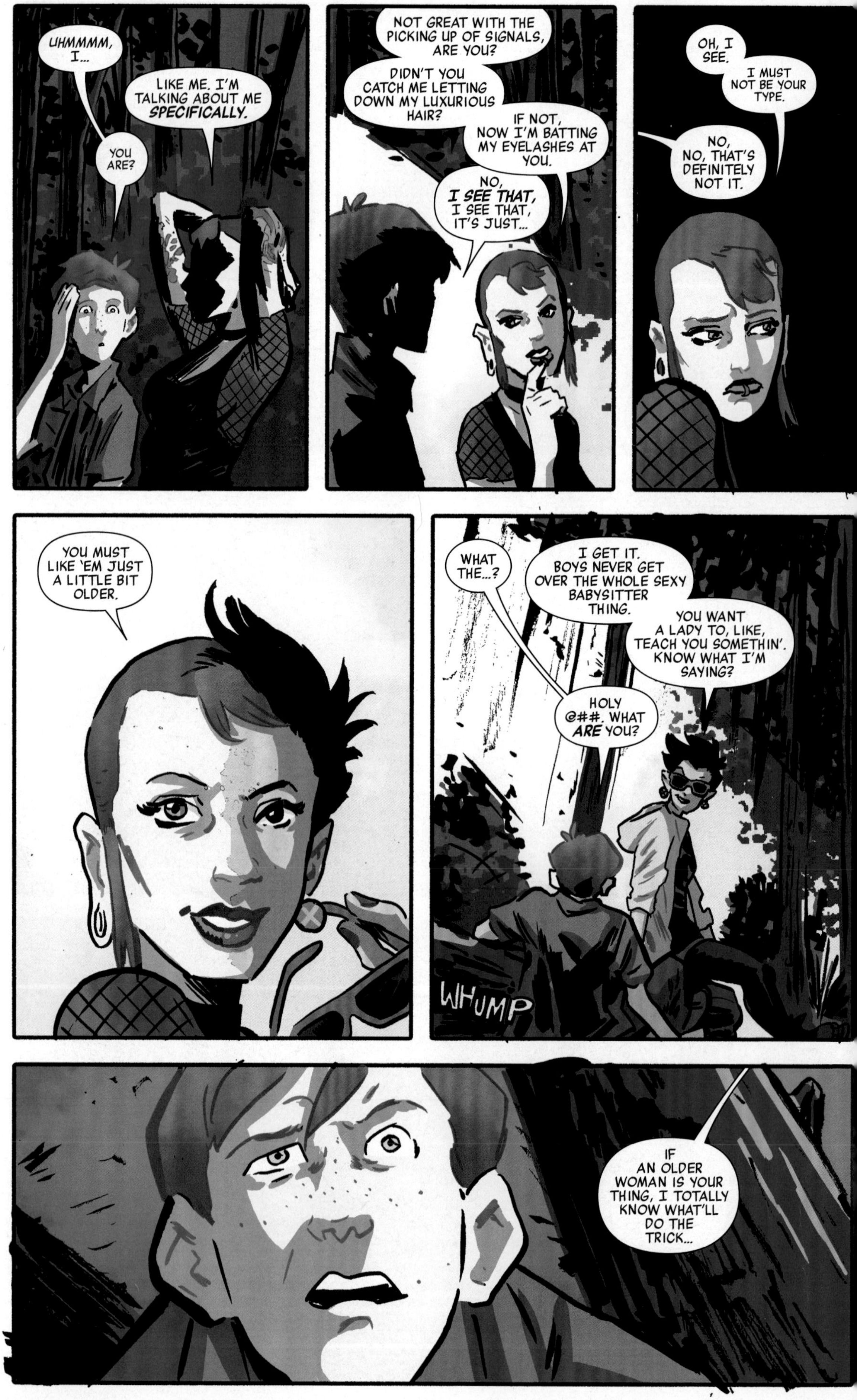
UHMMMM, I...
LIKE ME. I'M TALKING ABOUT ME SPECIFICALLY.
YOU ARE?
NOT GREAT WITH THE PICKING UP OF SIGNALS, ARE YOU?
DIDN'T YOU CATCH ME LETTING DOWN MY LUXURIOUS HAIR?
IF NOT, NOW I'M BATTING MY EYELASHES AT YOU.
NO, I SEE THAT, I SEE THAT, IT'S JUST...
OH, I SEE.
I MUST NOT BE YOUR TYPE.
NO, NO, THAT'S DEFINITELY NOT IT.
YOU MUST LIKE 'EM JUST A LITTLE BIT OLDER.
WHAT THE...?
I GET IT. BOYS NEVER GET OVER THE WHOLE SEXY BABYSITTER THING.
YOU WANT A LADY TO, LIKE, TEACH YOU SOMETHIN'. KNOW WHAT I'M SAYING?
HOLY @##. WHAT ARE YOU?
WHUMP
IF AN OLDER WOMAN IS YOUR THING, I TOTALLY KNOW WHAT'LL DO THE TRICK...

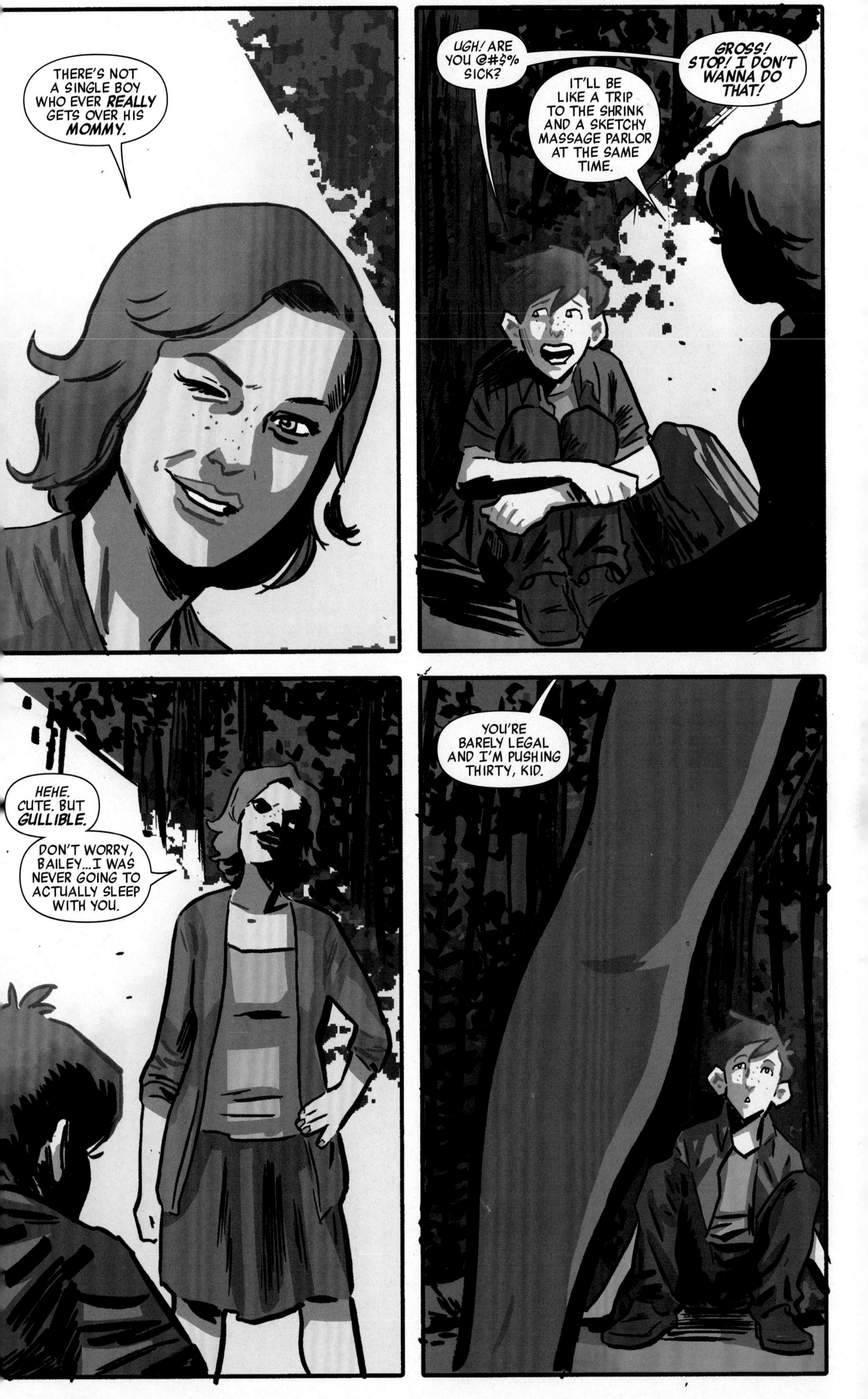
THERE'S NOT A SINGLE BOY WHO EVER **REALLY** GETS OVER HIS **MOMMY.**
UGH! ARE YOU @#$% SICK?
IT'LL BE LIKE A TRIP TO THE SHRINK AND A SKETCHY MASSAGE PARLOR AT THE SAME TIME.
GROSS! STOP! I DON'T WANNA DO THAT!
HEHE. CUTE. BUT **GULLIBLE.**
DON'T WORRY, BAILEY...I WAS NEVER GOING TO ACTUALLY SLEEP WITH YOU.
YOU'RE BARELY LEGAL AND I'M PUSHING THIRTY, KID.

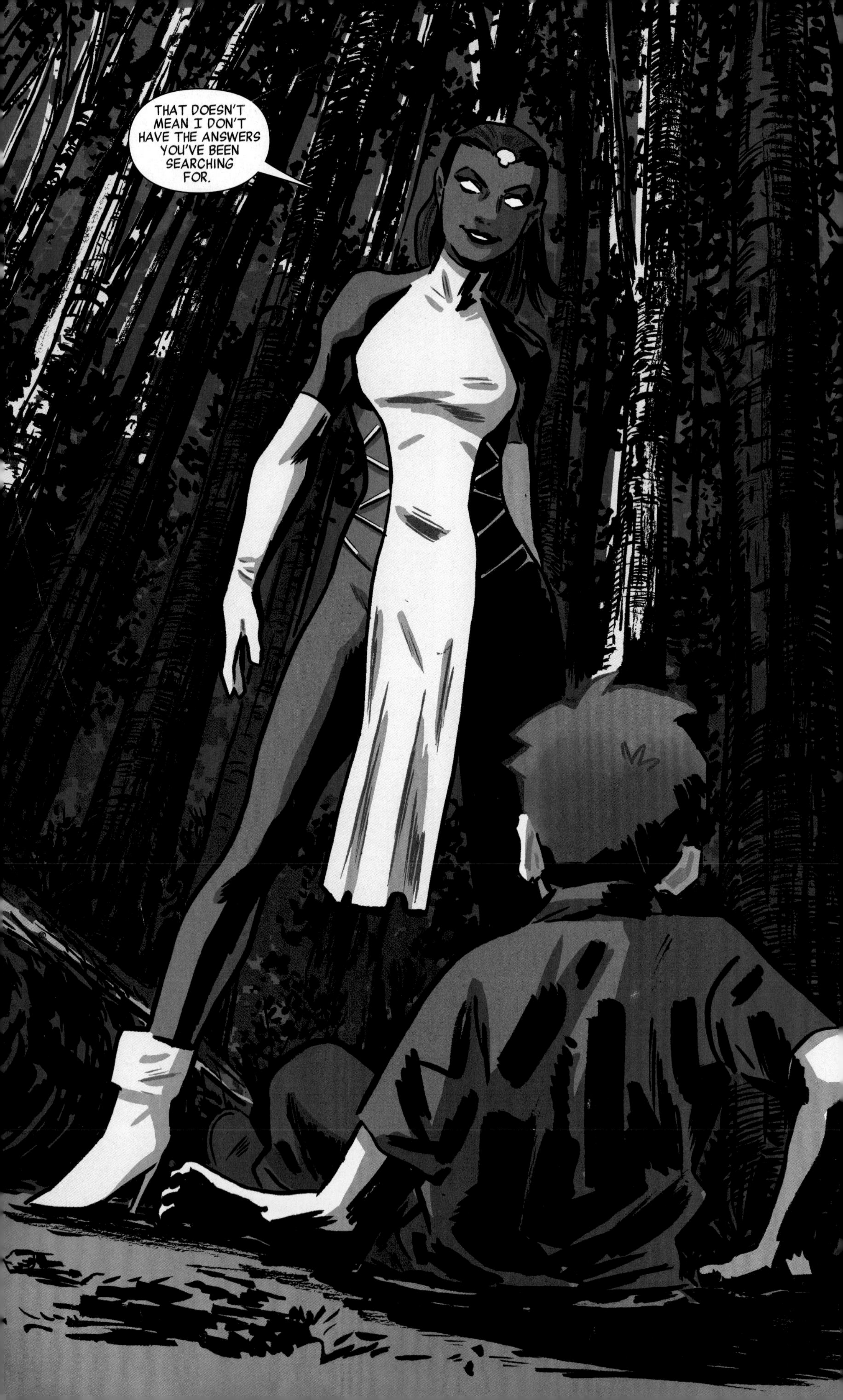
THAT DOESN'T MEAN I DON'T HAVE THE ANSWERS YOU'VE BEEN SEARCHING FOR.

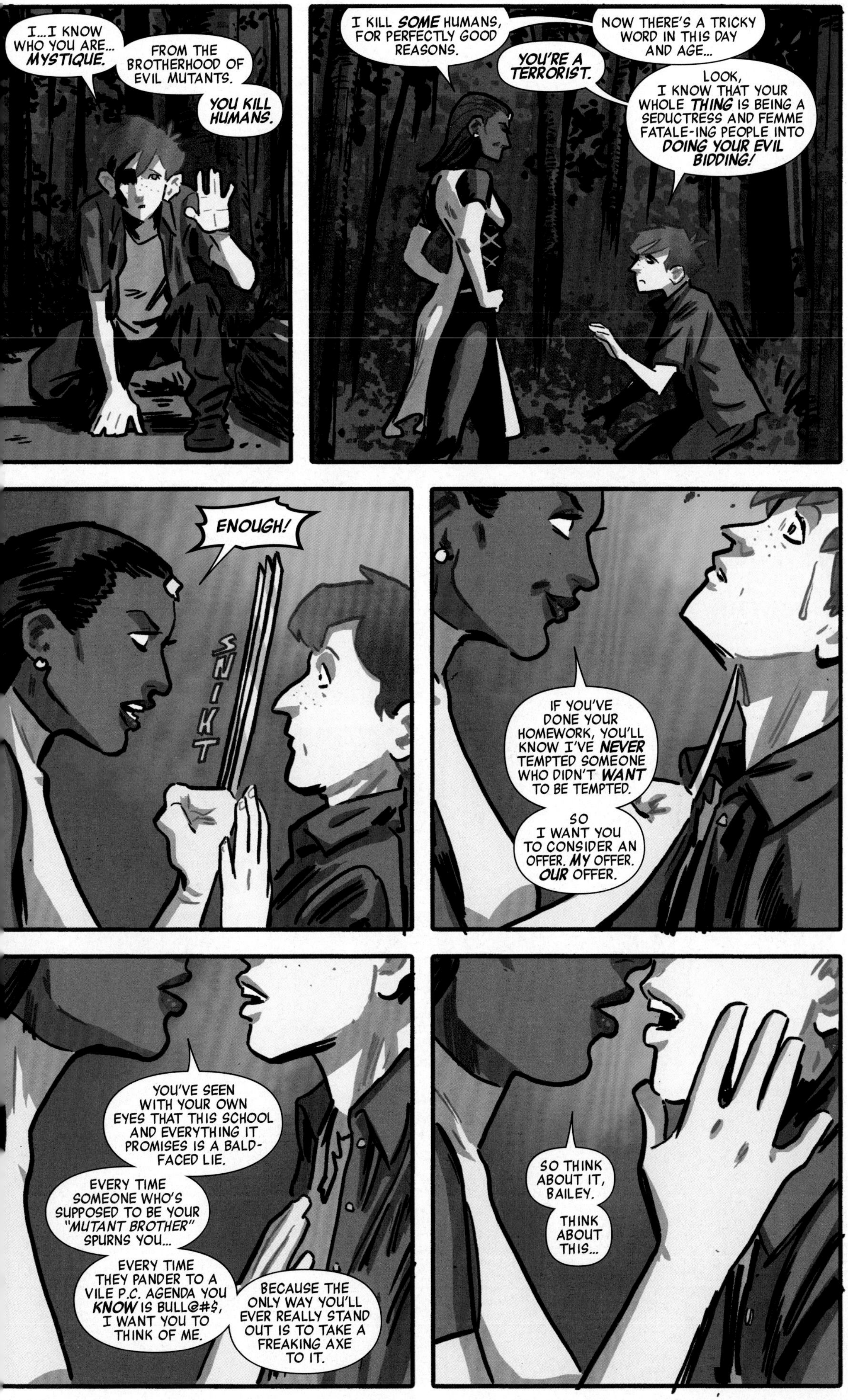

I...I KNOW WHO YOU ARE... MYSTIQUE.
FROM THE BROTHERHOOD OF EVIL MUTANTS.
YOU KILL HUMANS.
I KILL SOME HUMANS, FOR PERFECTLY GOOD REASONS.
YOU'RE A TERRORIST.
NOW THERE'S A TRICKY WORD IN THIS DAY AND AGE...
LOOK, I KNOW THAT YOUR WHOLE THING IS BEING A SEDUCTRESS AND FEMME FATALE-ING PEOPLE INTO DOING YOUR EVIL BIDDING!
ENOUGH!
SNIKT
IF YOU'VE DONE YOUR HOMEWORK, YOU'LL KNOW I'VE NEVER TEMPTED SOMEONE WHO DIDN'T WANT TO BE TEMPTED.
SO I WANT YOU TO CONSIDER AN OFFER. MY OFFER. OUR OFFER.
YOU'VE SEEN WITH YOUR OWN EYES THAT THIS SCHOOL AND EVERYTHING IT PROMISES IS A BALD-FACED LIE.
EVERY TIME SOMEONE WHO'S SUPPOSED TO BE YOUR "MUTANT BROTHER" SPURNS YOU...
EVERY TIME THEY PANDER TO A VILE P.C. AGENDA YOU KNOW IS BULL@#$, I WANT YOU TO THINK OF ME.
BECAUSE THE ONLY WAY YOU'LL EVER REALLY STAND OUT IS TO TAKE A FREAKING AXE TO IT.
SO THINK ABOUT IT, BAILEY.
THINK ABOUT THIS...

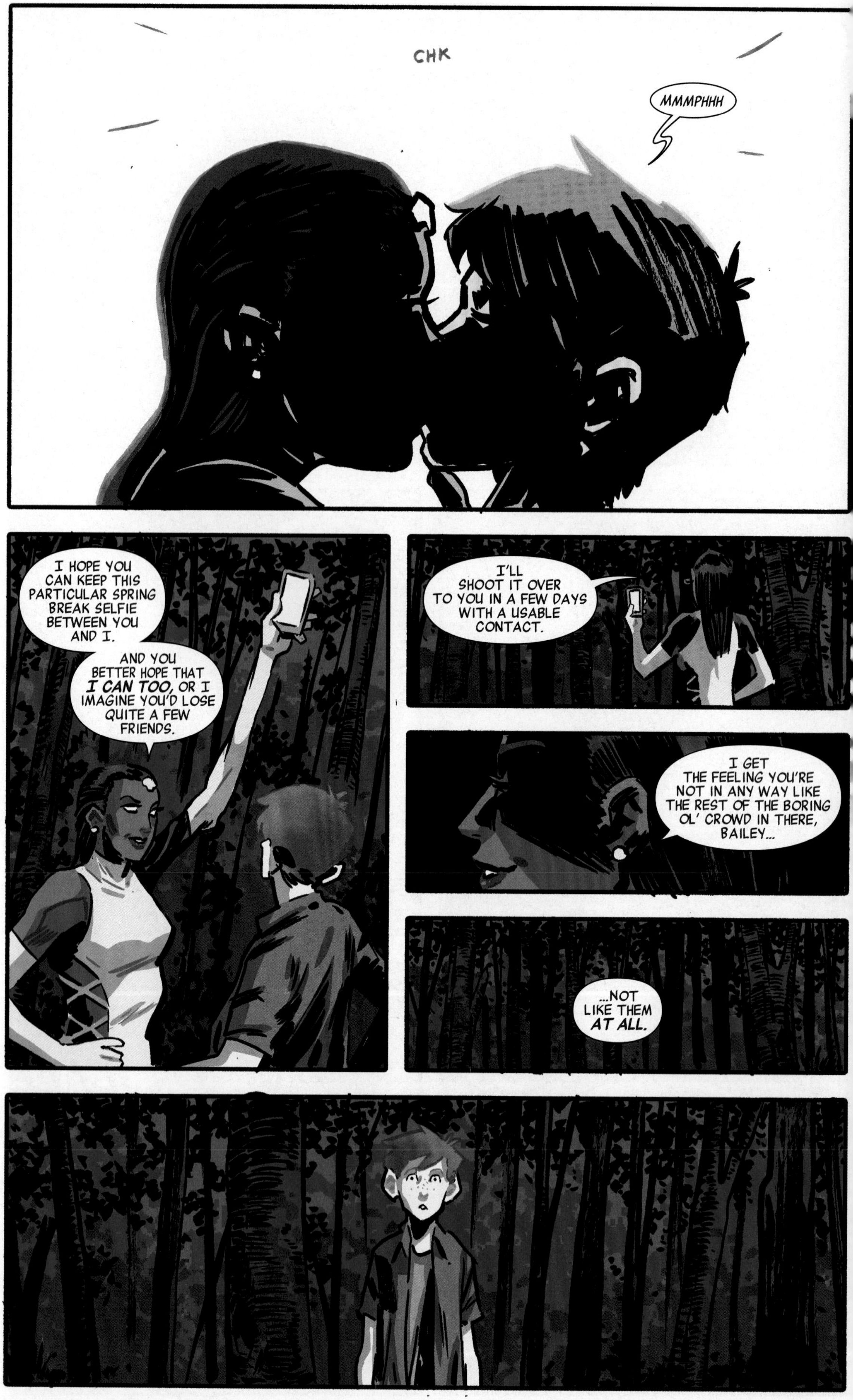
CHK
MMMPHHH
I HOPE YOU CAN KEEP THIS PARTICULAR SPRING BREAK SELFIE BETWEEN YOU AND I.
AND YOU BETTER HOPE THAT ***I CAN TOO,*** OR I IMAGINE YOU'D LOSE QUITE A FEW FRIENDS.
I'LL SHOOT IT OVER TO YOU IN A FEW DAYS WITH A USABLE CONTACT.
I GET THE FEELING YOU'RE NOT IN ANY WAY LIKE THE REST OF THE BORING OL' CROWD IN THERE, BAILEY...
...NOT LIKE THEM ***AT ALL.***

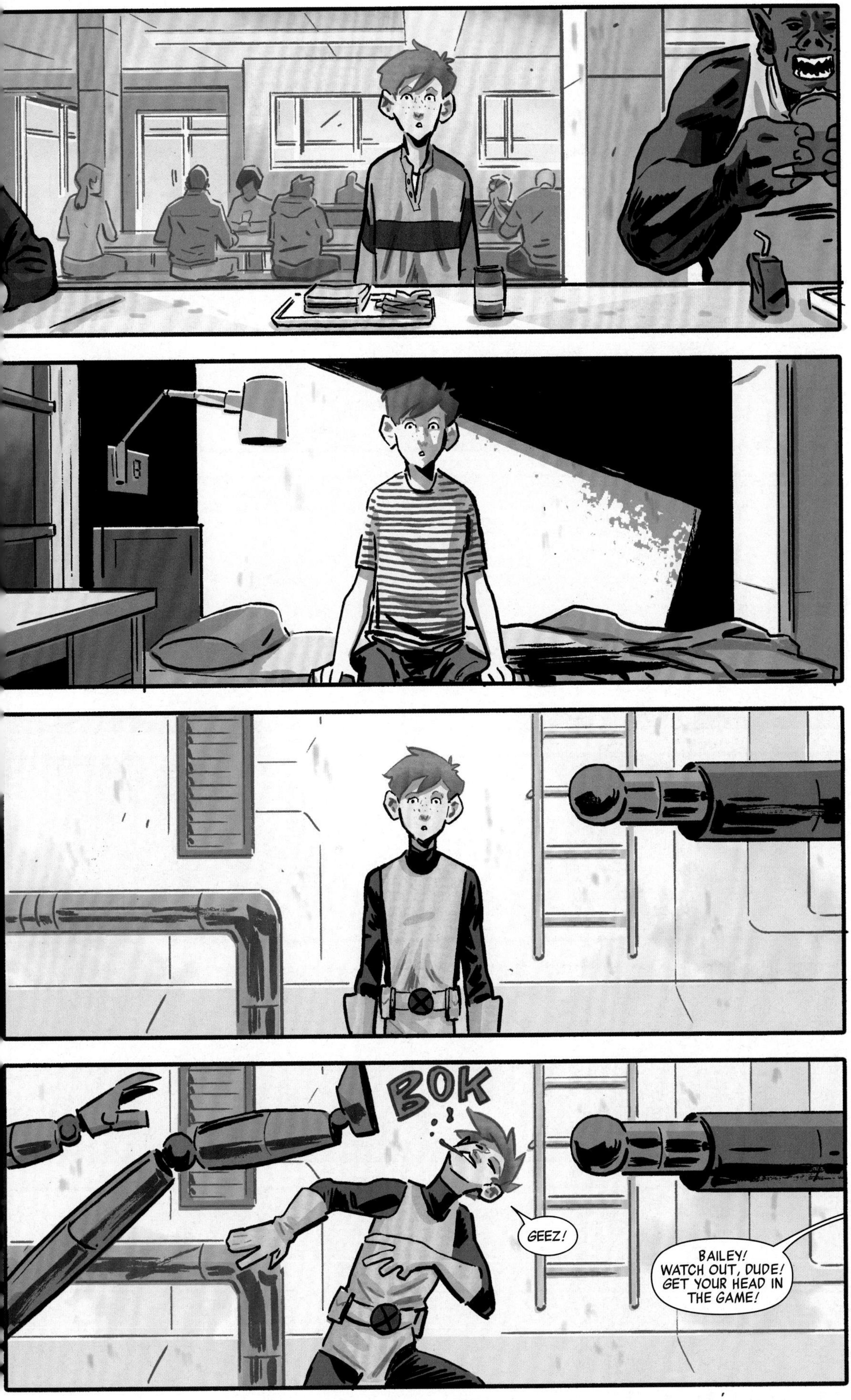
BOK
GEEZ!
BAILEY! WATCH OUT, DUDE! GET YOUR HEAD IN THE GAME!

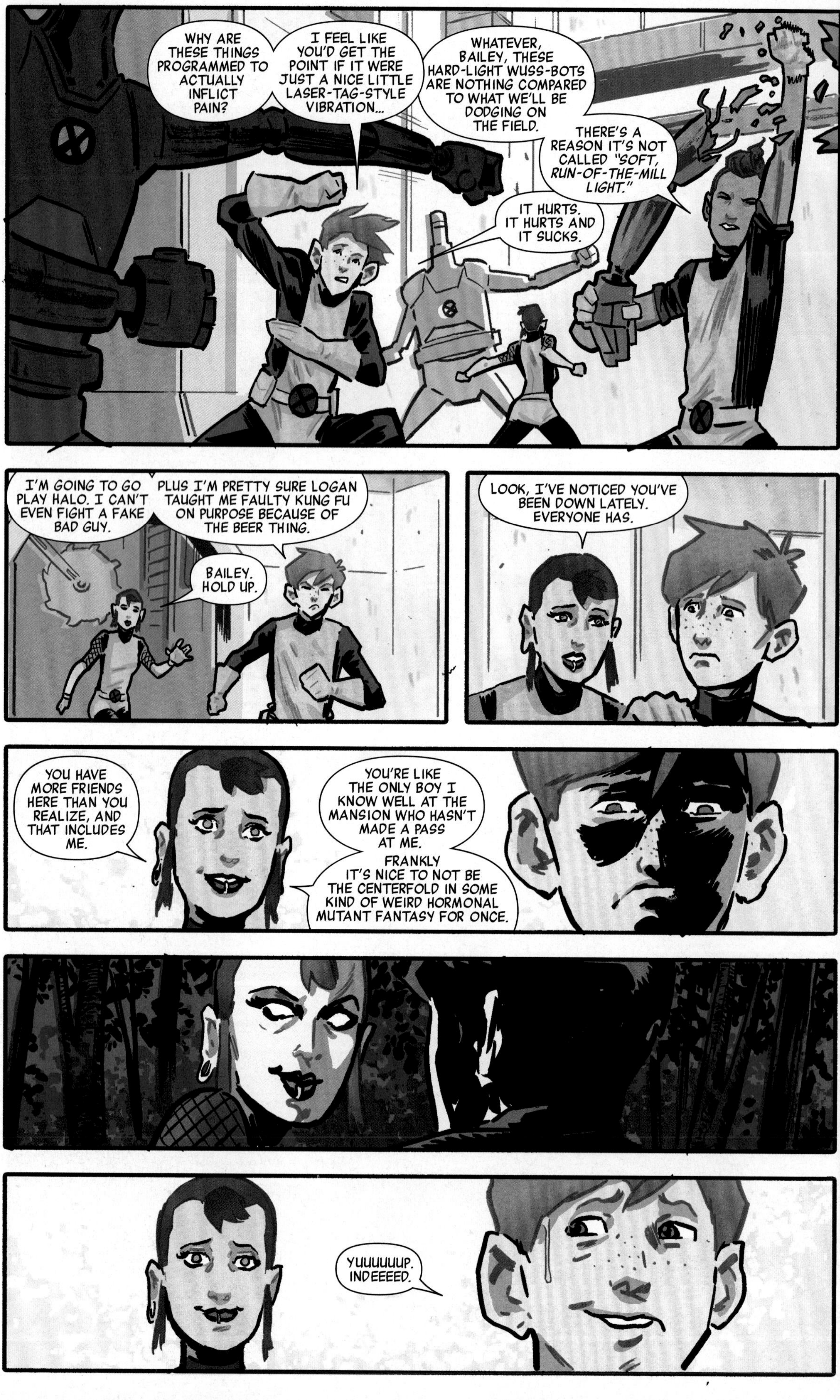
WHY ARE THESE THINGS PROGRAMMED TO ACTUALLY INFLICT PAIN?
I FEEL LIKE YOU'D GET THE POINT IF IT WERE JUST A NICE LITTLE LASER-TAG-STYLE VIBRATION...
WHATEVER, BAILEY, THESE HARD-LIGHT WUSS-BOTS ARE NOTHING COMPARED TO WHAT WE'LL BE DODGING ON THE FIELD.
THERE'S A REASON IT'S NOT CALLED "SOFT, RUN-OF-THE-MILL LIGHT."
IT HURTS. IT HURTS AND IT SUCKS.
I'M GOING TO GO PLAY HALO. I CAN'T EVEN FIGHT A FAKE BAD GUY.
PLUS I'M PRETTY SURE LOGAN TAUGHT ME FAULTY KUNG FU ON PURPOSE BECAUSE OF THE BEER THING.
BAILEY. HOLD UP.
LOOK, I'VE NOTICED YOU'VE BEEN DOWN LATELY. EVERYONE HAS.
YOU HAVE MORE FRIENDS HERE THAN YOU REALIZE, AND THAT INCLUDES ME.
YOU'RE LIKE THE ONLY BOY I KNOW WELL AT THE MANSION WHO HASN'T MADE A PASS AT ME.
FRANKLY IT'S NICE TO NOT BE THE CENTERFOLD IN SOME KIND OF WEIRD HORMONAL MUTANT FANTASY FOR ONCE.
YUUUUUUP. INDEEEED.

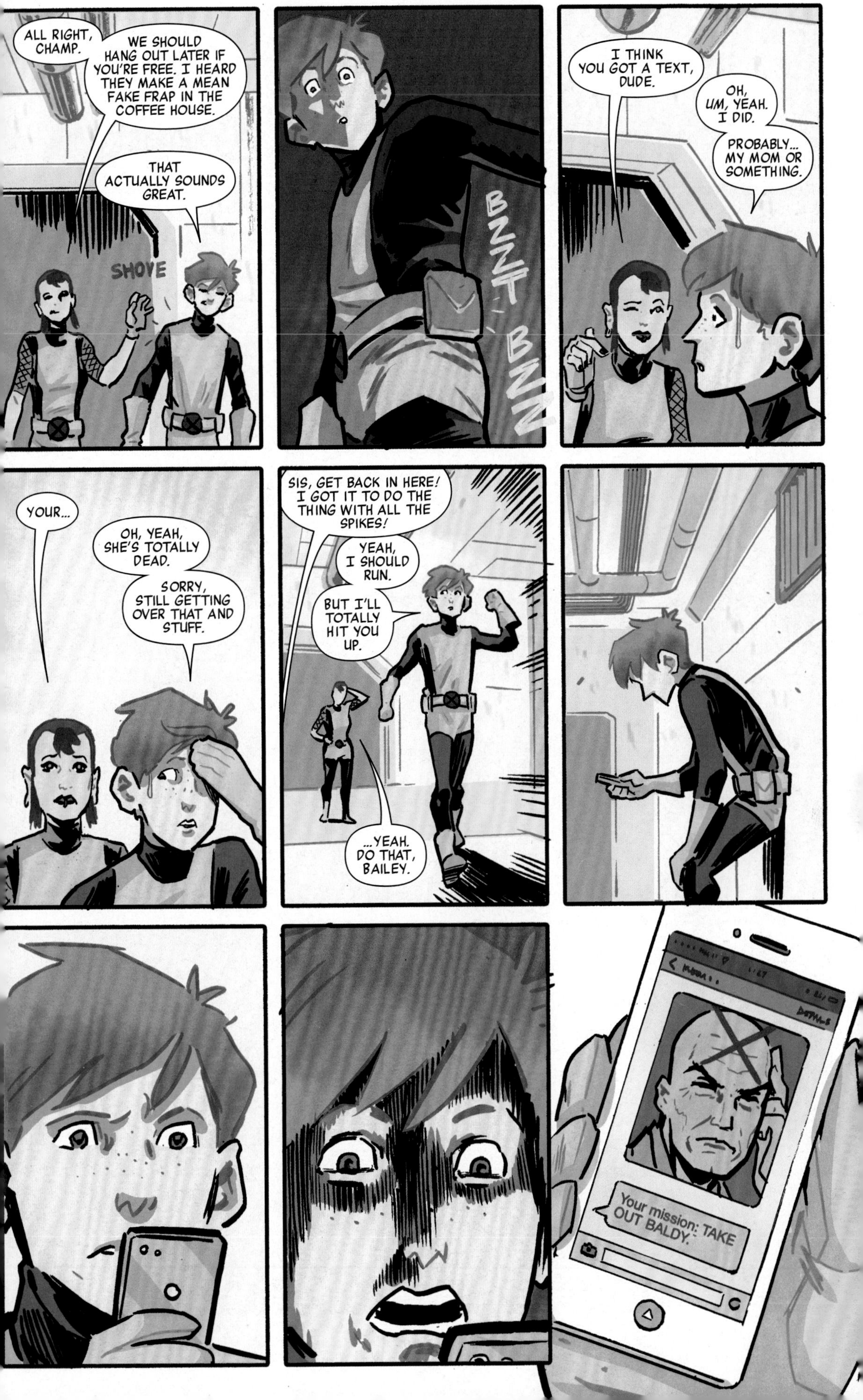
ALL RIGHT, CHAMP.
WE SHOULD HANG OUT LATER IF YOU'RE FREE. I HEARD THEY MAKE A MEAN FAKE FRAP IN THE COFFEE HOUSE.
THAT ACTUALLY SOUNDS GREAT.
SHOVE
BZZZT BZZZ
I THINK YOU GOT A TEXT, DUDE.
OH, UM, YEAH. I DID.
PROBABLY... MY MOM OR SOMETHING.
YOUR...
OH, YEAH, SHE'S TOTALLY DEAD.
SORRY, STILL GETTING OVER THAT AND STUFF.
SIS, GET BACK IN HERE! I GOT IT TO DO THE THING WITH ALL THE SPIKES!
YEAH, I SHOULD RUN.
BUT I'LL TOTALLY HIT YOU UP.
...YEAH. DO THAT, BAILEY.
Your mission: TAKE OUT BALDY.

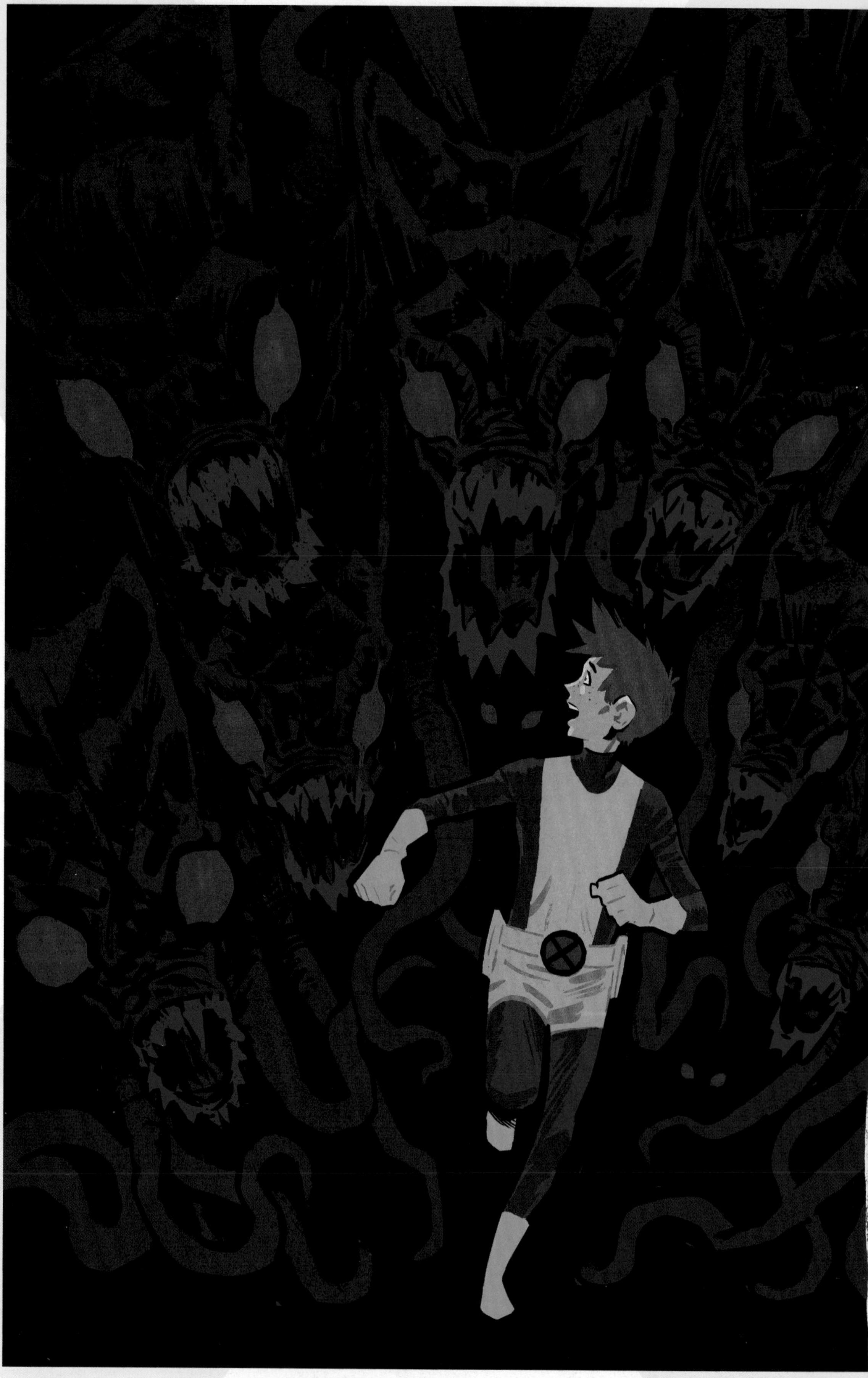

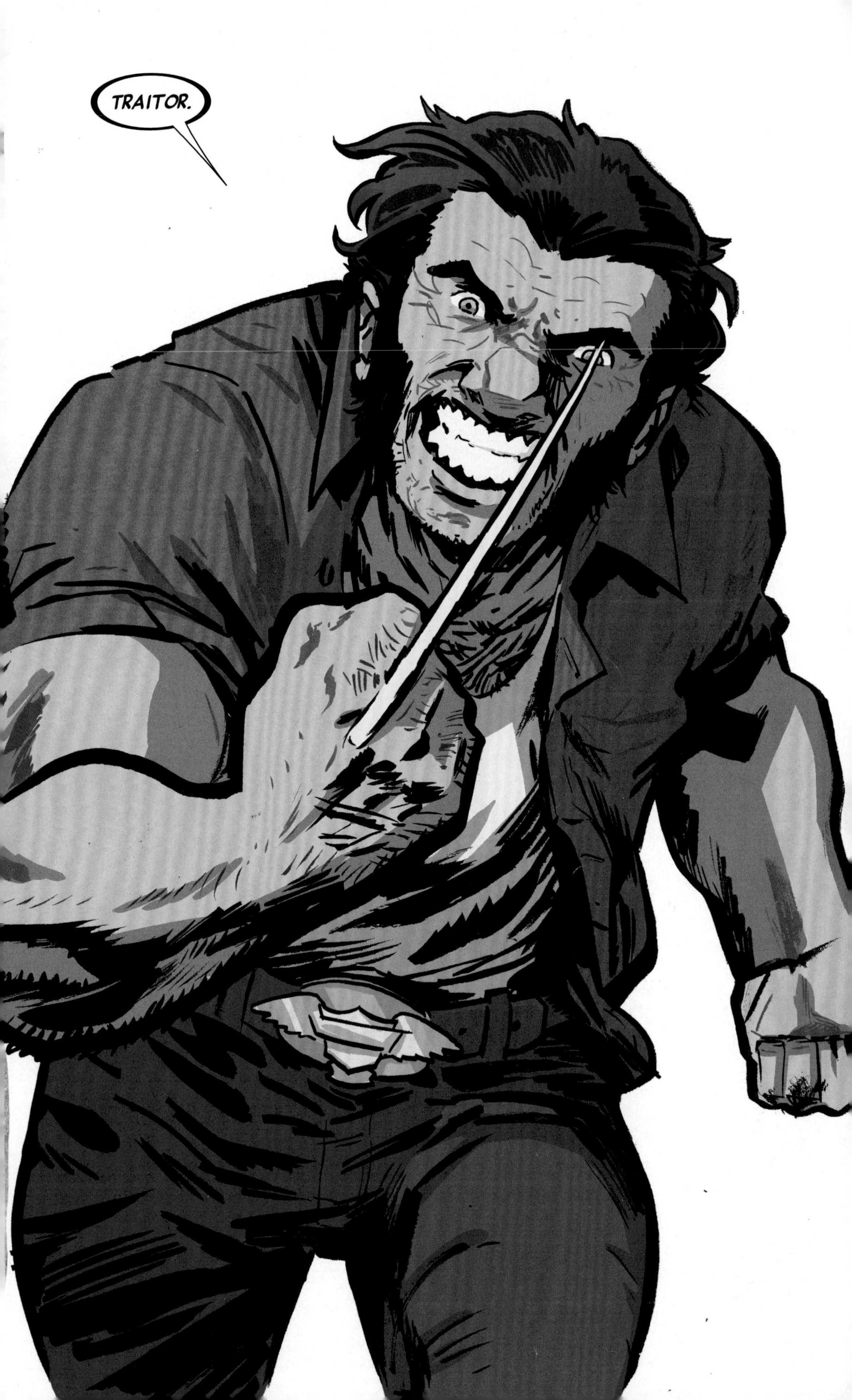
TRAITOR.

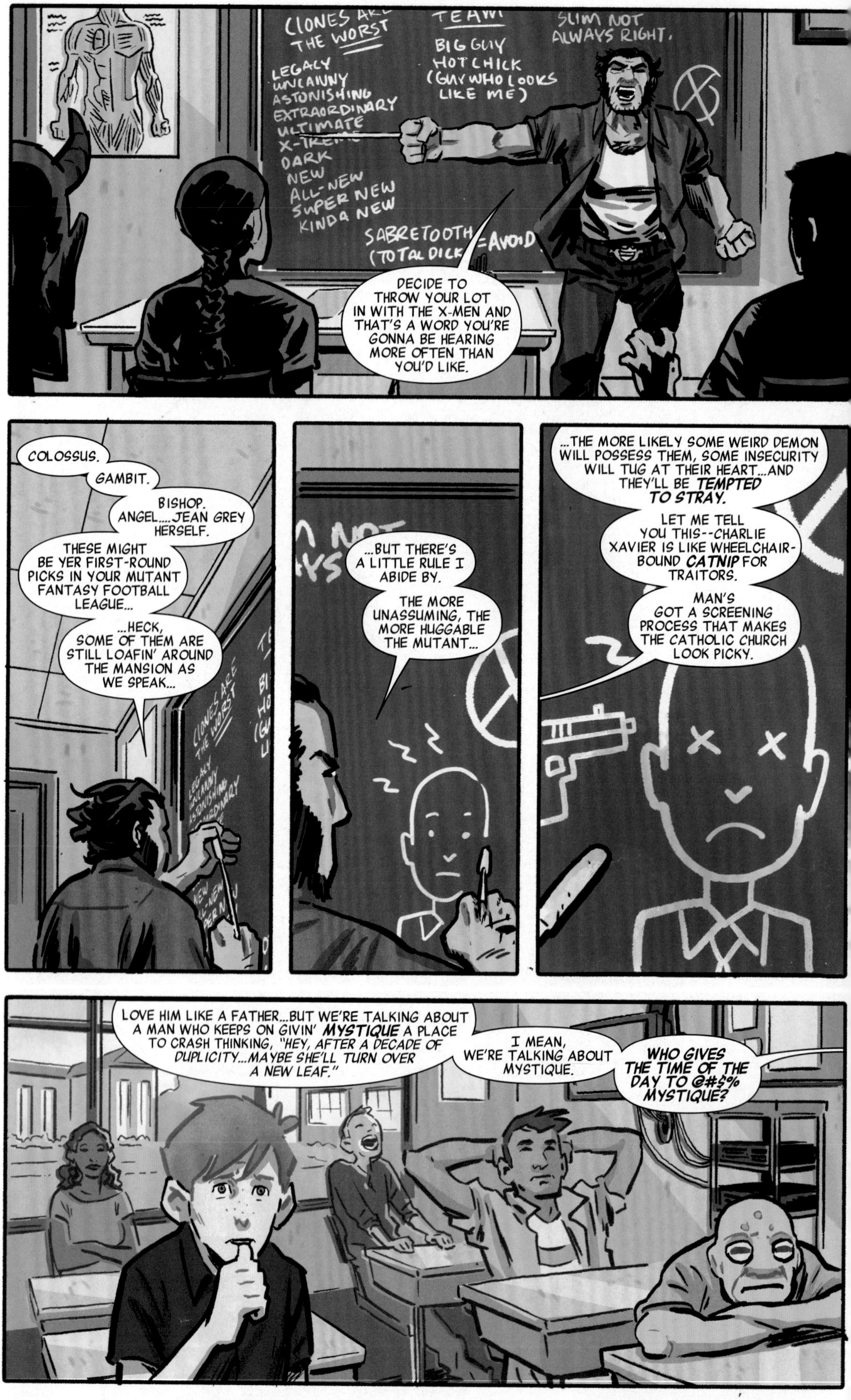
CLONES ARE THE WORST
LEGACY
UNCANNY
ASTONISHING
EXTRAORDINARY
ULTIMATE
X-TREME
DARK
NEW
ALL-NEW
SUPER NEW
KINDA NEW
BIG GUY
HOT CHICK
(GUY WHO LOOKS LIKE ME)
SLIM NOT ALWAYS RIGHT.
SABRETOOTH (TOTAL DICK) =AVOID!
DECIDE TO THROW YOUR LOT IN WITH THE X-MEN AND THAT'S A WORD YOU'RE GONNA BE HEARING MORE OFTEN THAN YOU'D LIKE.
COLOSSUS.
GAMBIT.
BISHOP. ANGEL....JEAN GREY HERSELF.
THESE MIGHT BE YER FIRST-ROUND PICKS IN YOUR MUTANT FANTASY FOOTBALL LEAGUE...
...HECK, SOME OF THEM ARE STILL LOAFIN' AROUND THE MANSION AS WE SPEAK...
...BUT THERE'S A LITTLE RULE I ABIDE BY.
THE MORE UNASSUMING, THE MORE HUGGABLE THE MUTANT...
...THE MORE LIKELY SOME WEIRD DEMON WILL POSSESS THEM, SOME INSECURITY WILL TUG AT THEIR HEART...AND THEY'LL BE TEMPTED TO STRAY.
LET ME TELL YOU THIS--CHARLIE XAVIER IS LIKE WHEELCHAIR-BOUND CATNIP FOR TRAITORS.
MAN'S GOT A SCREENING PROCESS THAT MAKES THE CATHOLIC CHURCH LOOK PICKY.
LOVE HIM LIKE A FATHER...BUT WE'RE TALKING ABOUT A MAN WHO KEEPS ON GIVIN' MYSTIQUE A PLACE TO CRASH THINKING, "HEY, AFTER A DECADE OF DUPLICITY...MAYBE SHE'LL TURN OVER A NEW LEAF."
I MEAN, WE'RE TALKING ABOUT MYSTIQUE.
WHO GIVES THE TIME OF THE DAY TO @#$% MYSTIQUE?

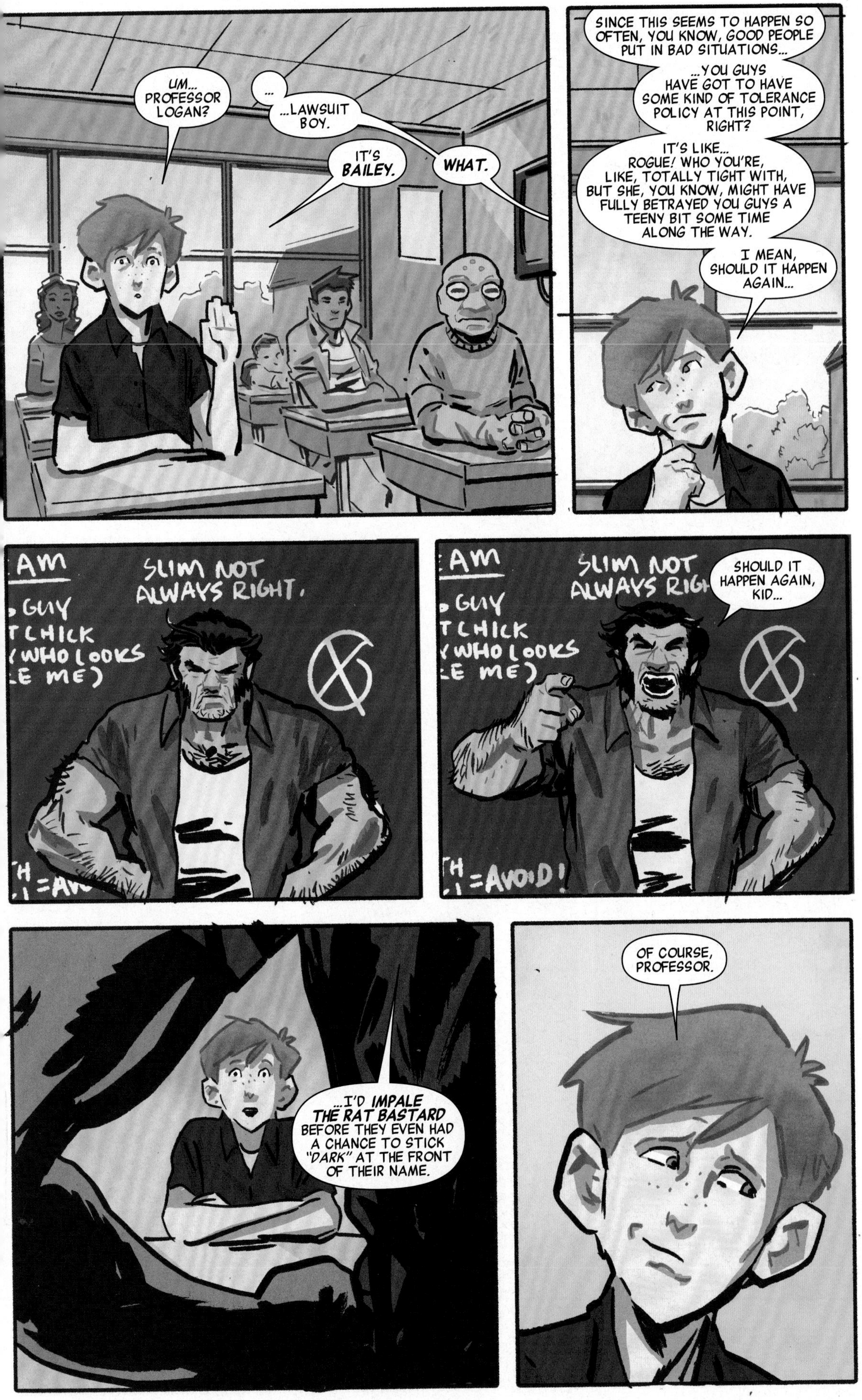
UM... PROFESSOR LOGAN?
...
...LAWSUIT BOY.
IT'S BAILEY.
WHAT.
SINCE THIS SEEMS TO HAPPEN SO OFTEN, YOU KNOW, GOOD PEOPLE PUT IN BAD SITUATIONS...
...YOU GUYS HAVE GOT TO HAVE SOME KIND OF TOLERANCE POLICY AT THIS POINT, RIGHT?
IT'S LIKE... ROGUE! WHO YOU'RE, LIKE, TOTALLY TIGHT WITH, BUT SHE, YOU KNOW, MIGHT HAVE FULLY BETRAYED YOU GUYS A TEENY BIT SOME TIME ALONG THE WAY.
I MEAN, SHOULD IT HAPPEN AGAIN...
SLIM NOT ALWAYS RIGHT.
SHOULD IT HAPPEN AGAIN, KID...
=AVOID!
...I'D IMPALE THE RAT BASTARD BEFORE THEY EVEN HAD A CHANCE TO STICK "DARK" AT THE FRONT OF THEIR NAME.
OF COURSE, PROFESSOR.

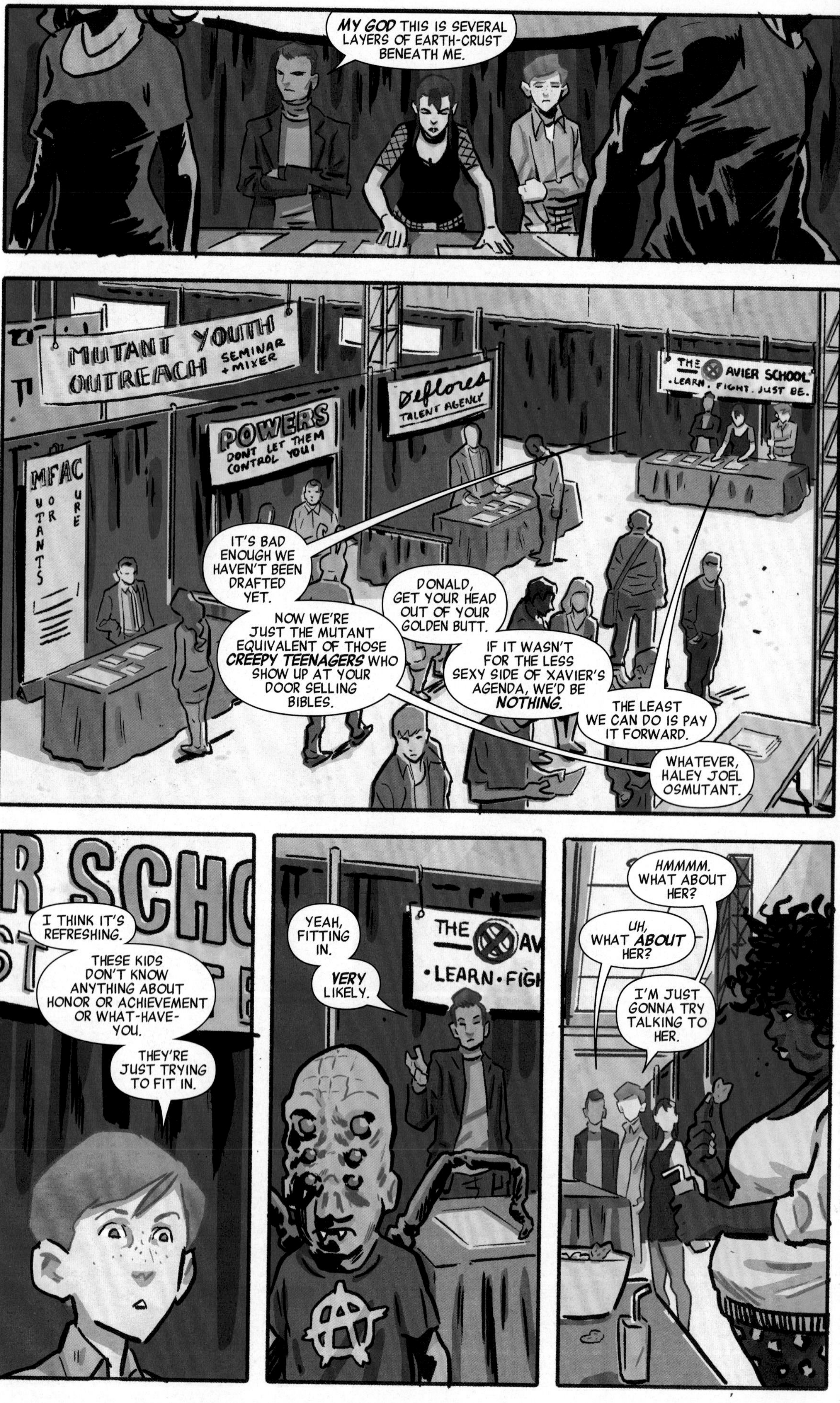
MY GOD THIS IS SEVERAL LAYERS OF EARTH-CRUST BENEATH ME.
MUTANT YOUTH OUTREACH SEMINAR + MIXER
POWERS DONT LET THEM CONTROL YOU!
Deflores TALENT AGENCY
THE XAVIER SCHOOL .LEARN. FIGHT. JUST BE.
MFAC
IT'S BAD ENOUGH WE HAVEN'T BEEN DRAFTED YET.
NOW WE'RE JUST THE MUTANT EQUIVALENT OF THOSE CREEPY TEENAGERS WHO SHOW UP AT YOUR DOOR SELLING BIBLES.
DONALD, GET YOUR HEAD OUT OF YOUR GOLDEN BUTT.
IF IT WASN'T FOR THE LESS SEXY SIDE OF XAVIER'S AGENDA, WE'D BE NOTHING.
THE LEAST WE CAN DO IS PAY IT FORWARD.
WHATEVER, HALEY JOEL OSMUTANT.
I THINK IT'S REFRESHING.
THESE KIDS DON'T KNOW ANYTHING ABOUT HONOR OR ACHIEVEMENT OR WHAT-HAVE-YOU.
THEY'RE JUST TRYING TO FIT IN.
YEAH, FITTING IN.
VERY LIKELY.
HMMMM. WHAT ABOUT HER?
UH, WHAT ABOUT HER?
I'M JUST GONNA TRY TALKING TO HER.

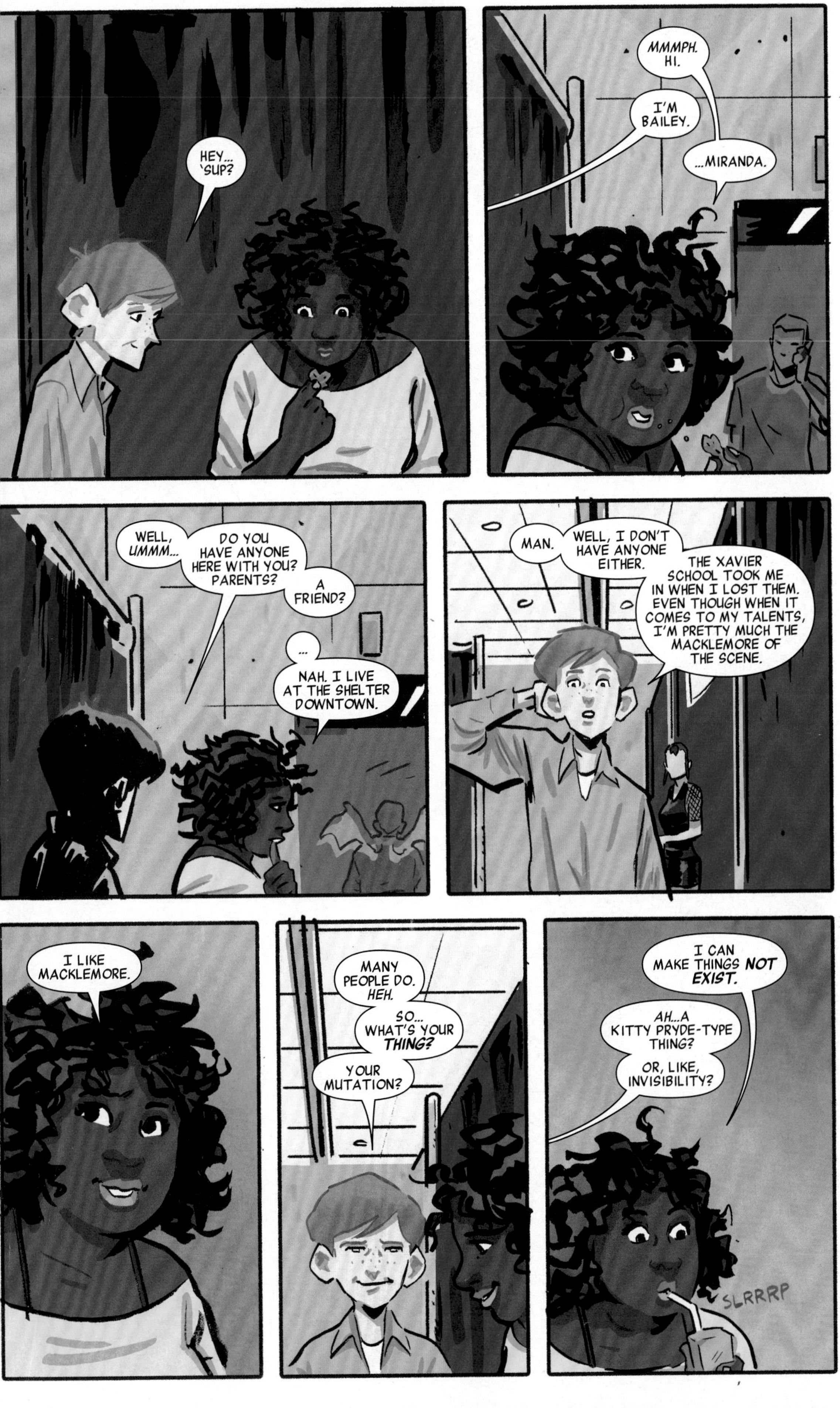
HEY... 'SUP?
MMMPH. HI.
I'M BAILEY.
...MIRANDA.
WELL, UMMM...
DO YOU HAVE ANYONE HERE WITH YOU? PARENTS?
A FRIEND?
...
NAH. I LIVE AT THE SHELTER DOWNTOWN.
MAN.
WELL, I DON'T HAVE ANYONE EITHER.
THE XAVIER SCHOOL TOOK ME IN WHEN I LOST THEM. EVEN THOUGH WHEN IT COMES TO MY TALENTS, I'M PRETTY MUCH THE MACKLEMORE OF THE SCENE.
I LIKE MACKLEMORE.
MANY PEOPLE DO. HEH.
SO... WHAT'S YOUR THING?
YOUR MUTATION?
I CAN MAKE THINGS NOT EXIST.
AH...A KITTY PRYDE-TYPE THING?
OR, LIKE, INVISIBILITY?
SLRRRP

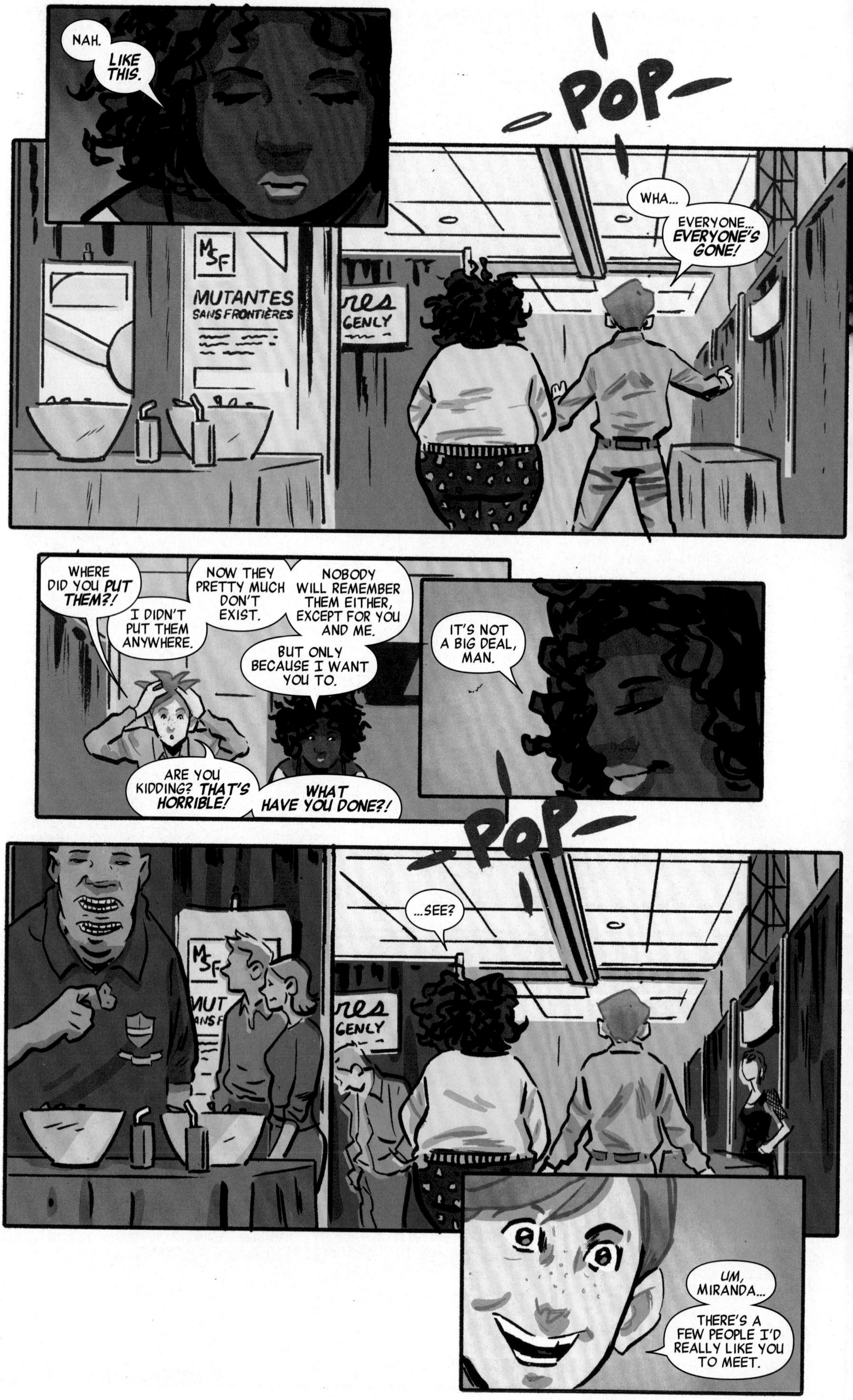

NAH.
LIKE THIS.
POP
WHA...
EVERYONE... EVERYONE'S GONE!
MUTANTES SANS FRONTIÈRES
WHERE DID YOU PUT THEM?!
I DIDN'T PUT THEM ANYWHERE.
NOW THEY PRETTY MUCH DON'T EXIST.
NOBODY WILL REMEMBER THEM EITHER, EXCEPT FOR YOU AND ME.
BUT ONLY BECAUSE I WANT YOU TO.
IT'S NOT A BIG DEAL, MAN.
ARE YOU KIDDING? THAT'S HORRIBLE!
WHAT HAVE YOU DONE?!
POP
...SEE?
UM, MIRANDA...
THERE'S A FEW PEOPLE I'D REALLY LIKE YOU TO MEET.

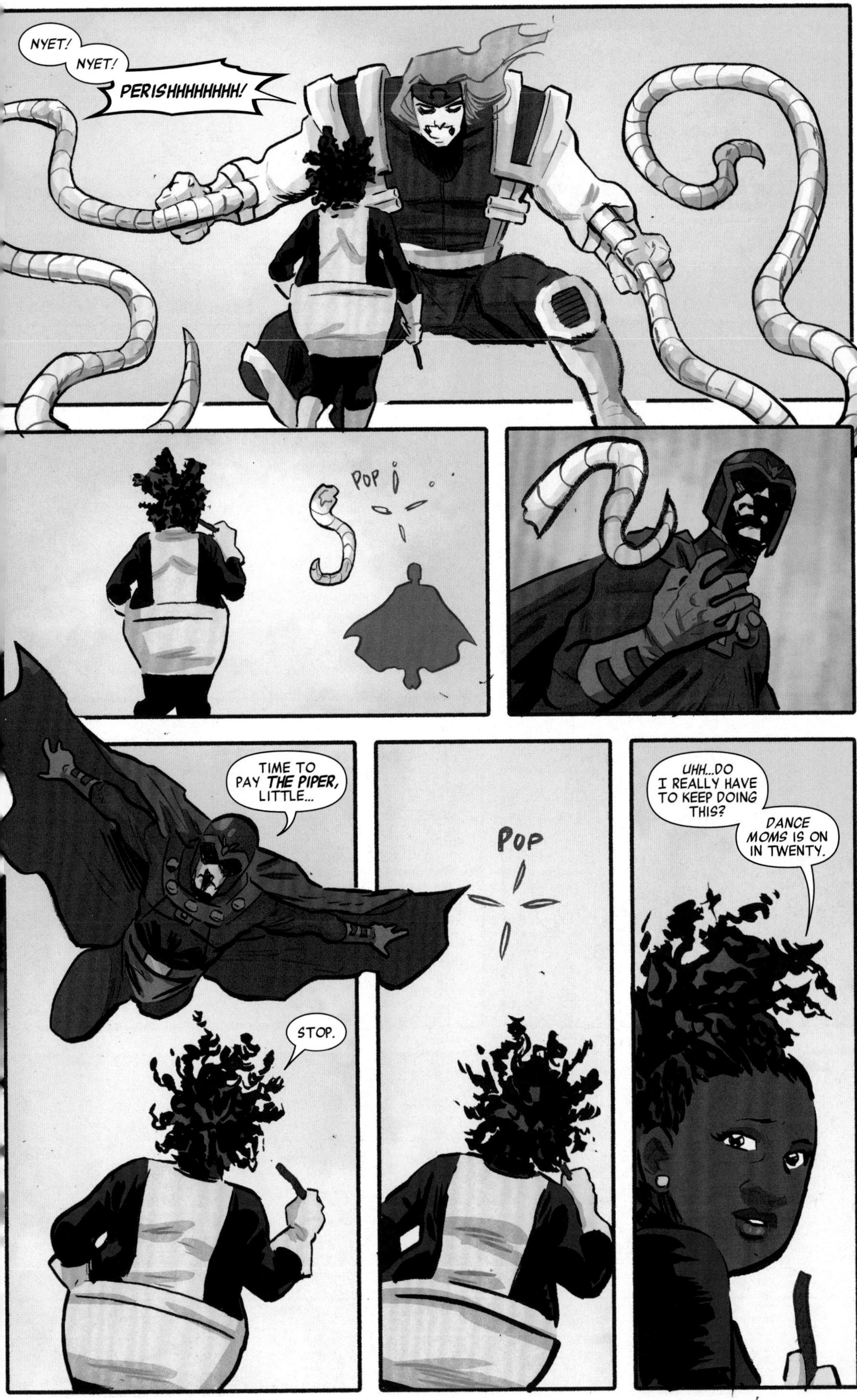

NYET!
NYET!
PERISHHHHHHHH!
POP
TIME TO PAY THE PIPER, LITTLE...
STOP.
POP
UHH...DO I REALLY HAVE TO KEEP DOING THIS?
DANCE MOMS IS ON IN TWENTY.

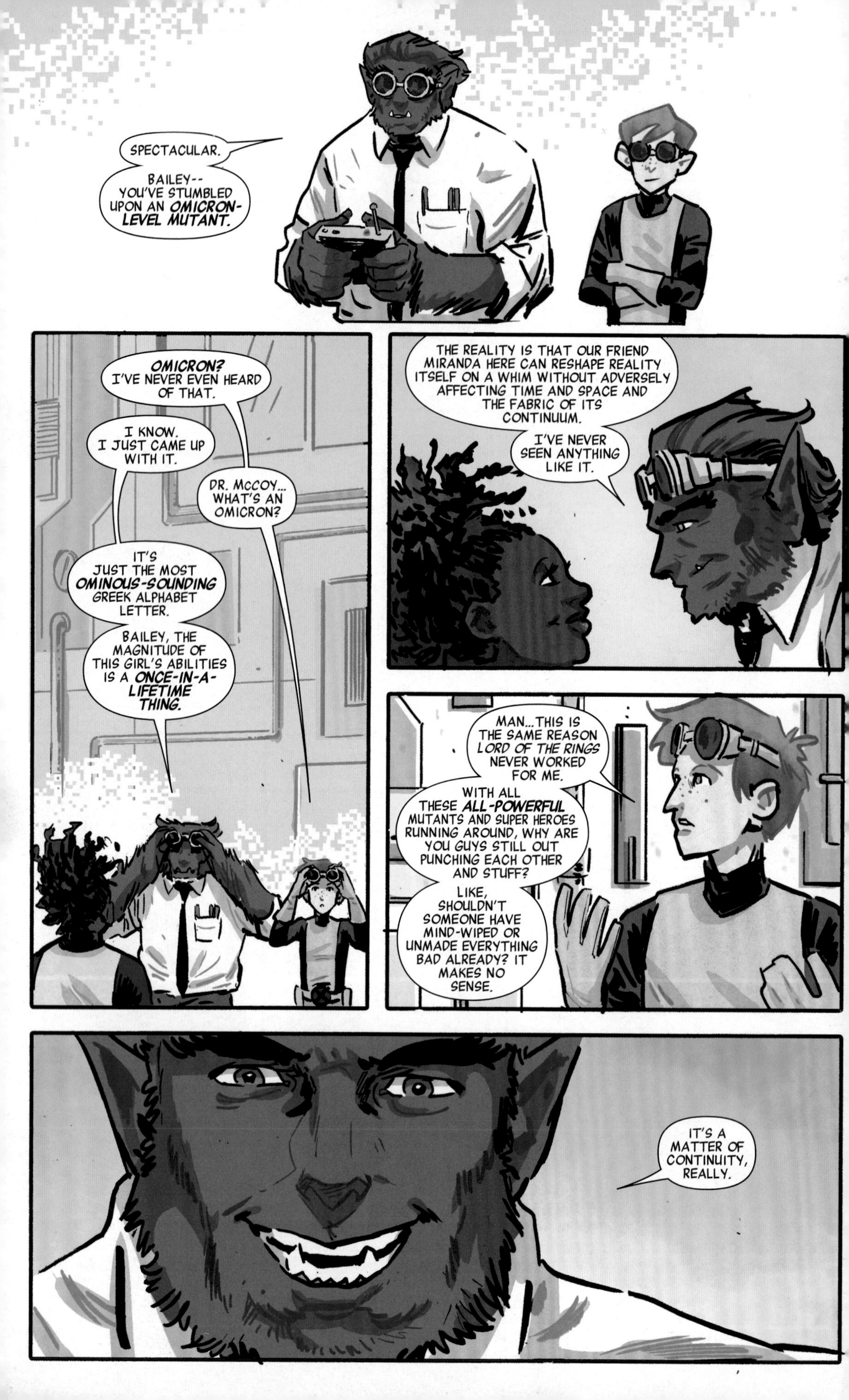

SPECTACULAR.
BAILEY-- YOU'VE STUMBLED UPON AN OMICRON-LEVEL MUTANT.
OMICRON? I'VE NEVER EVEN HEARD OF THAT.
I KNOW. I JUST CAME UP WITH IT.
DR. McCOY... WHAT'S AN OMICRON?
IT'S JUST THE MOST OMINOUS-SOUNDING GREEK ALPHABET LETTER.
BAILEY, THE MAGNITUDE OF THIS GIRL'S ABILITIES IS A ONCE-IN-A-LIFETIME THING.
THE REALITY IS THAT OUR FRIEND MIRANDA HERE CAN RESHAPE REALITY ITSELF ON A WHIM WITHOUT ADVERSELY AFFECTING TIME AND SPACE AND THE FABRIC OF ITS CONTINUUM.
I'VE NEVER SEEN ANYTHING LIKE IT.
MAN...THIS IS THE SAME REASON LORD OF THE RINGS NEVER WORKED FOR ME.
WITH ALL THESE ALL-POWERFUL MUTANTS AND SUPER HEROES RUNNING AROUND, WHY ARE YOU GUYS STILL OUT PUNCHING EACH OTHER AND STUFF?
LIKE, SHOULDN'T SOMEONE HAVE MIND-WIPED OR UNMADE EVERYTHING BAD ALREADY? IT MAKES NO SENSE.
IT'S A MATTER OF CONTINUITY, REALLY.

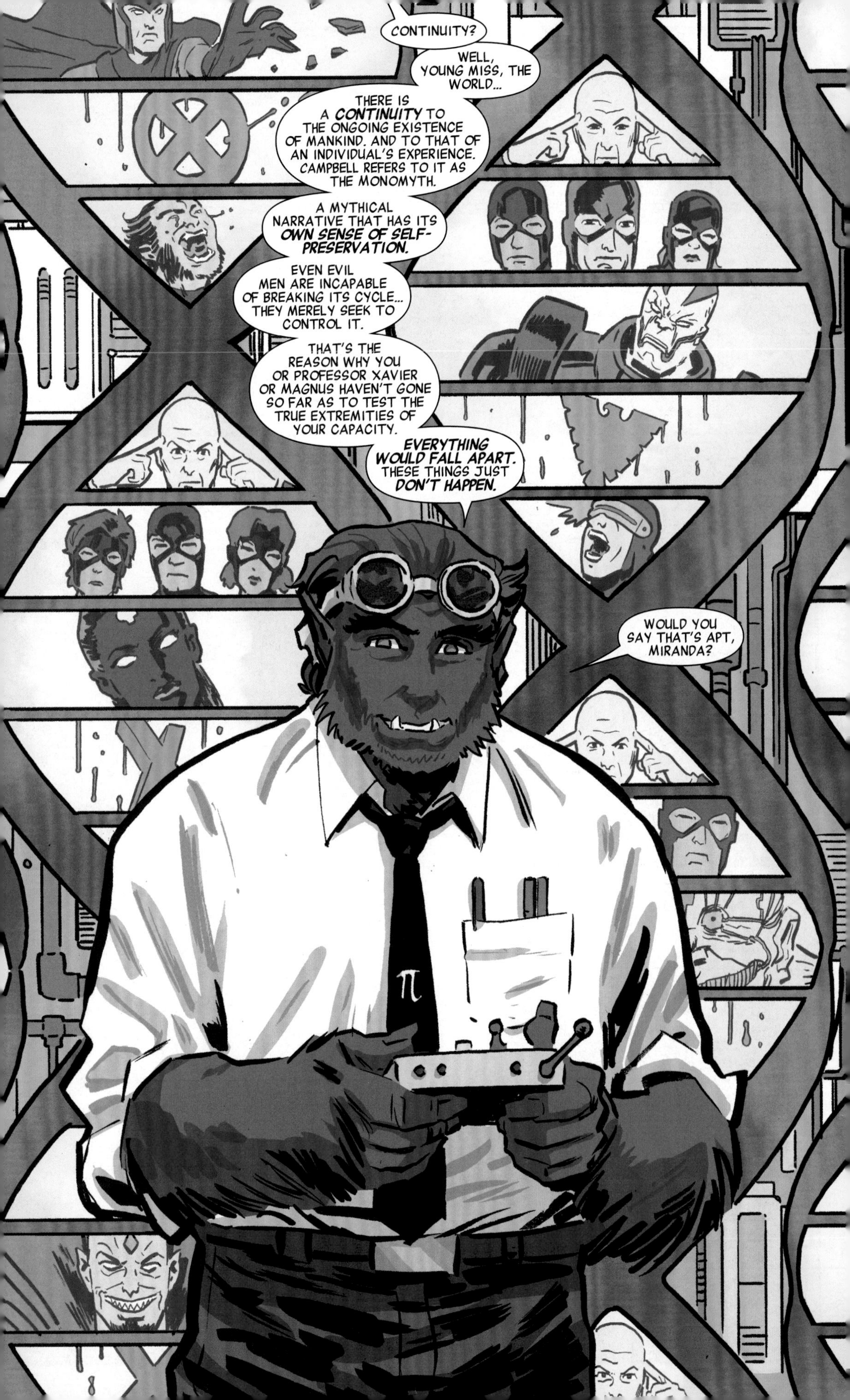
CONTINUITY?
WELL, YOUNG MISS, THE WORLD...
THERE IS A **CONTINUITY** TO THE ONGOING EXISTENCE OF MANKIND. AND TO THAT OF AN INDIVIDUAL'S EXPERIENCE. CAMPBELL REFERS TO IT AS THE MONOMYTH.
A MYTHICAL NARRATIVE THAT HAS ITS ***OWN SENSE OF SELF-PRESERVATION.***
EVEN EVIL MEN ARE INCAPABLE OF BREAKING ITS CYCLE... THEY MERELY SEEK TO CONTROL IT.
THAT'S THE REASON WHY YOU OR PROFESSOR XAVIER OR MAGNUS HAVEN'T GONE SO FAR AS TO TEST THE TRUE EXTREMITIES OF YOUR CAPACITY.
EVERYTHING WOULD FALL APART. THESE THINGS JUST ***DON'T HAPPEN.***
WOULD YOU SAY THAT'S APT, MIRANDA?

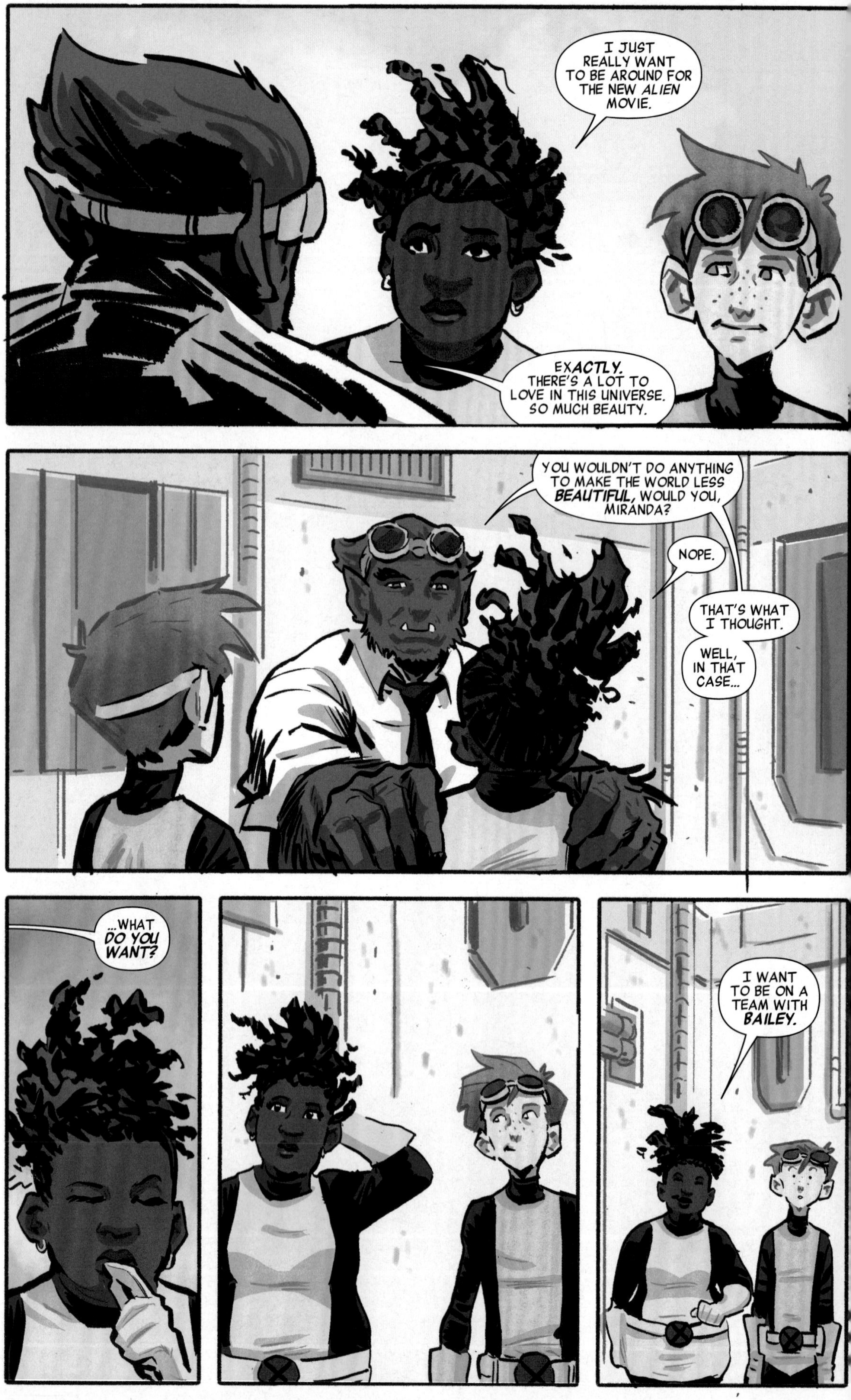
I JUST REALLY WANT TO BE AROUND FOR THE NEW ALIEN MOVIE.
EXACTLY. THERE'S A LOT TO LOVE IN THIS UNIVERSE. SO MUCH BEAUTY.
YOU WOULDN'T DO ANYTHING TO MAKE THE WORLD LESS BEAUTIFUL, WOULD YOU, MIRANDA?
NOPE.
THAT'S WHAT I THOUGHT.
WELL, IN THAT CASE...
...WHAT DO YOU WANT?
I WANT TO BE ON A TEAM WITH BAILEY.

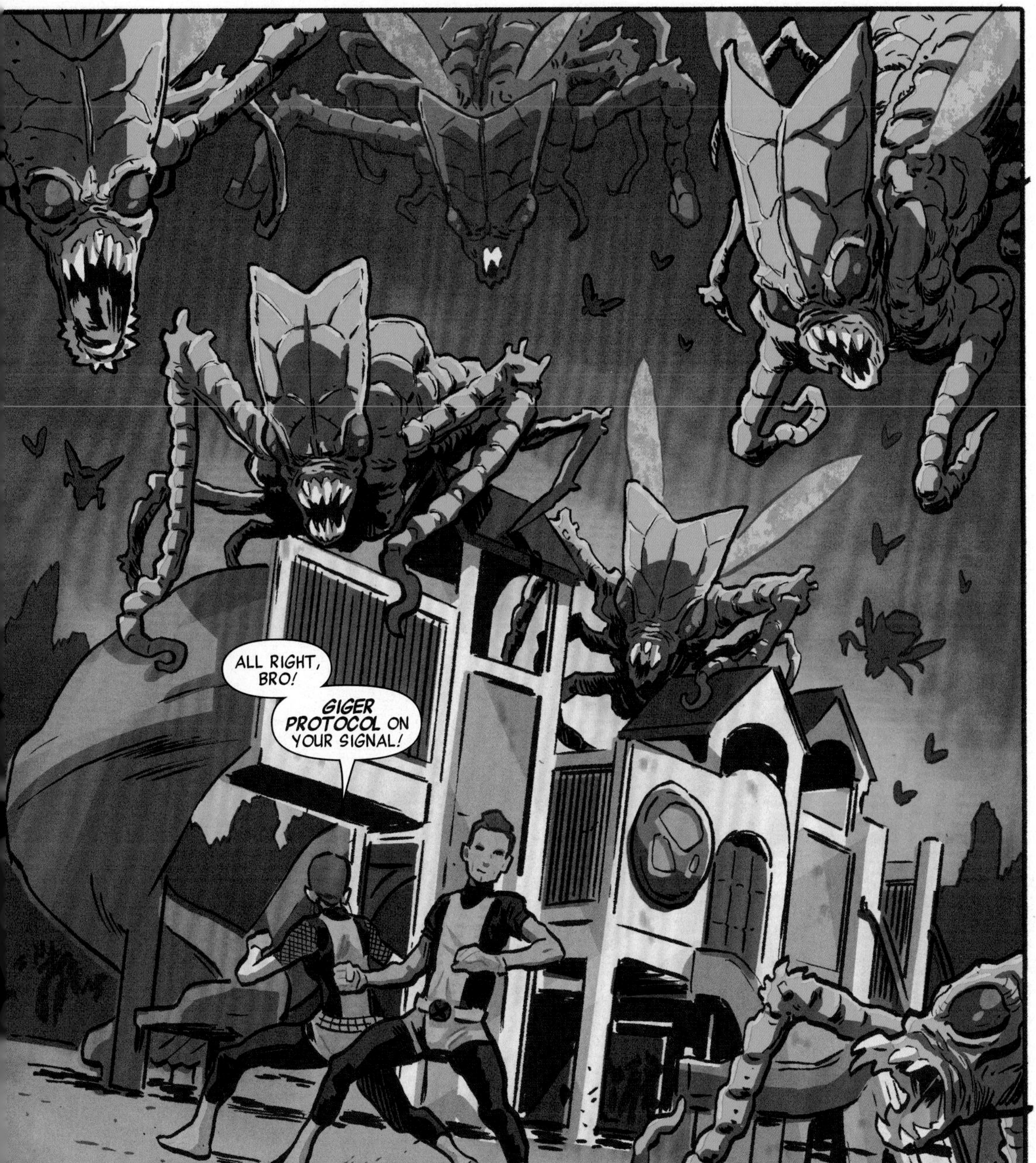
ALL RIGHT, BRO!
GIGER PROTOCOL ON YOUR SIGNAL!

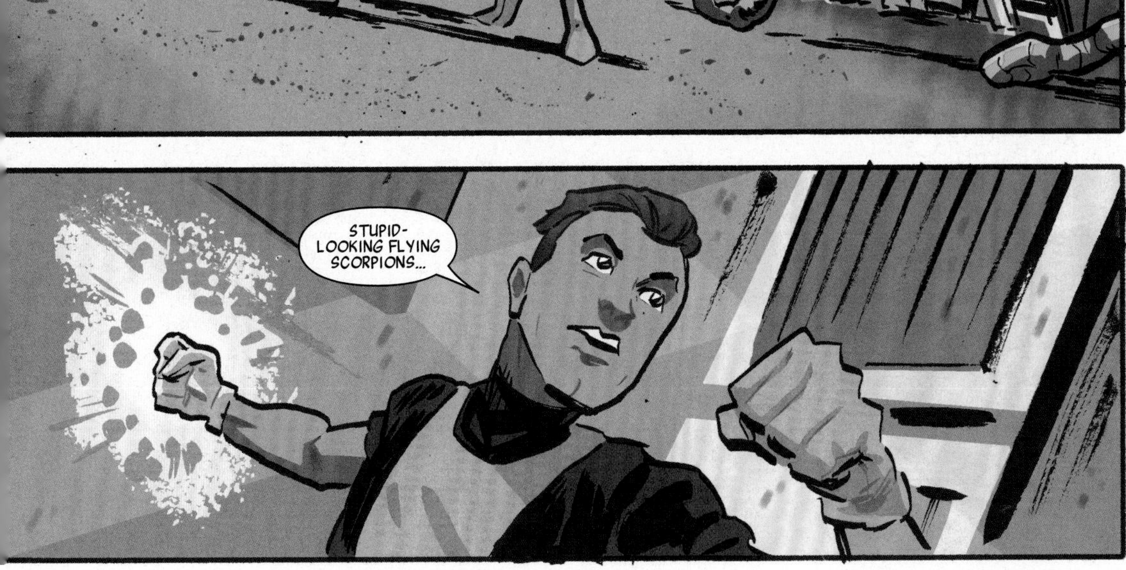
STUPID-LOOKING FLYING SCORPIONS...

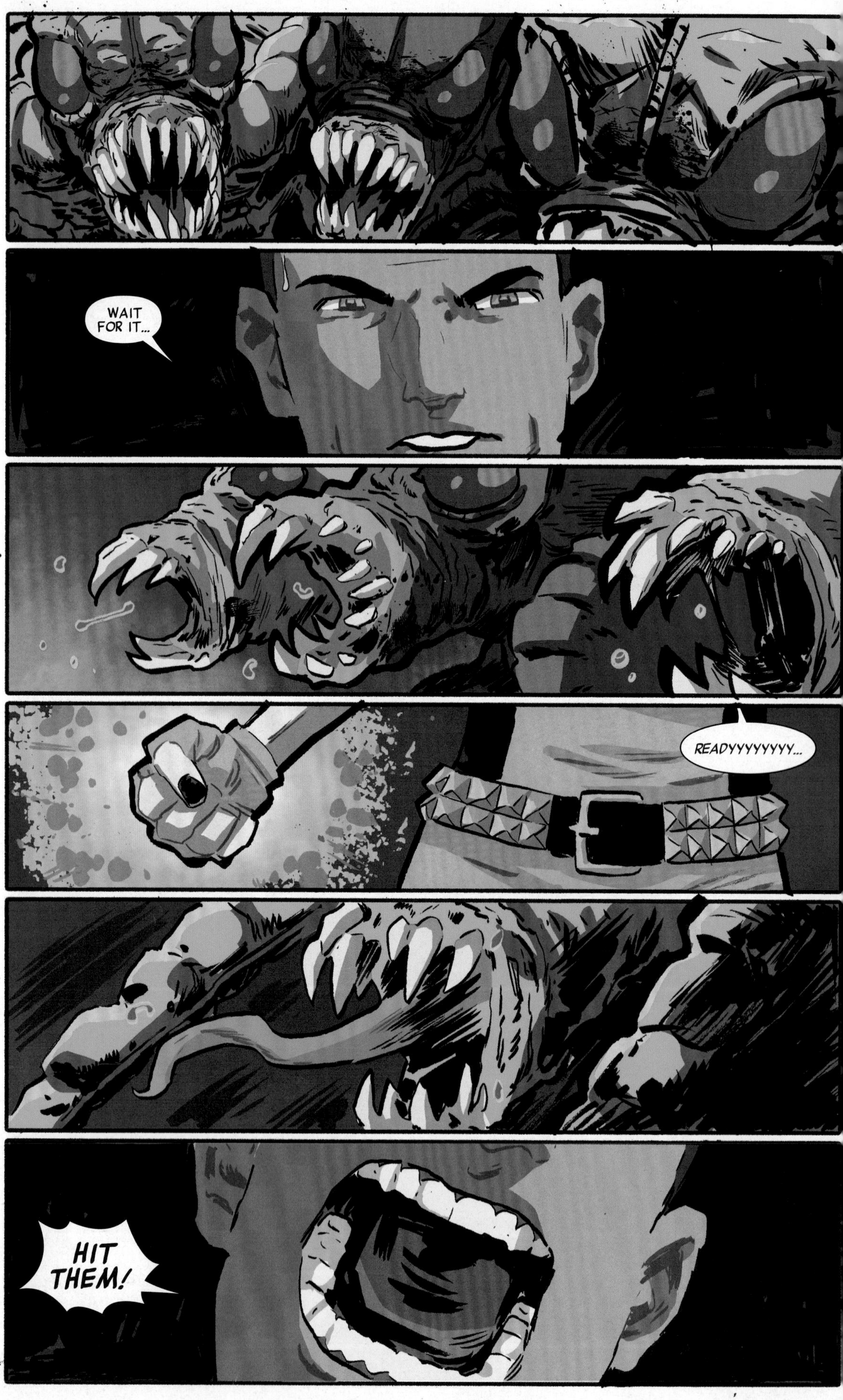
WAIT FOR IT...
READYYYYYYYYY...
HIT THEM!

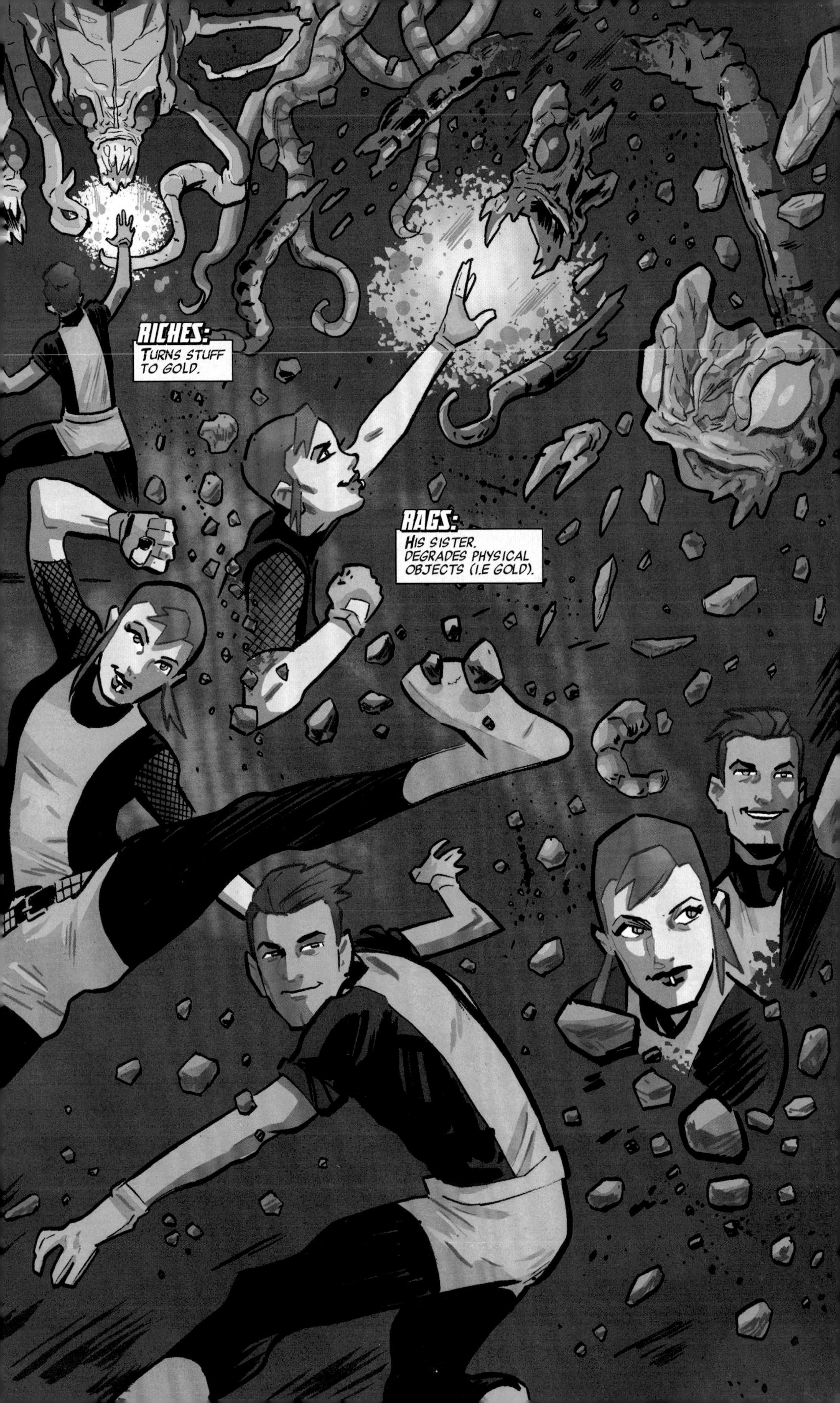
RICHES:
TURNS STUFF TO GOLD.
RAGS:
HIS SISTER. DEGRADES PHYSICAL OBJECTS (I.E GOLD).

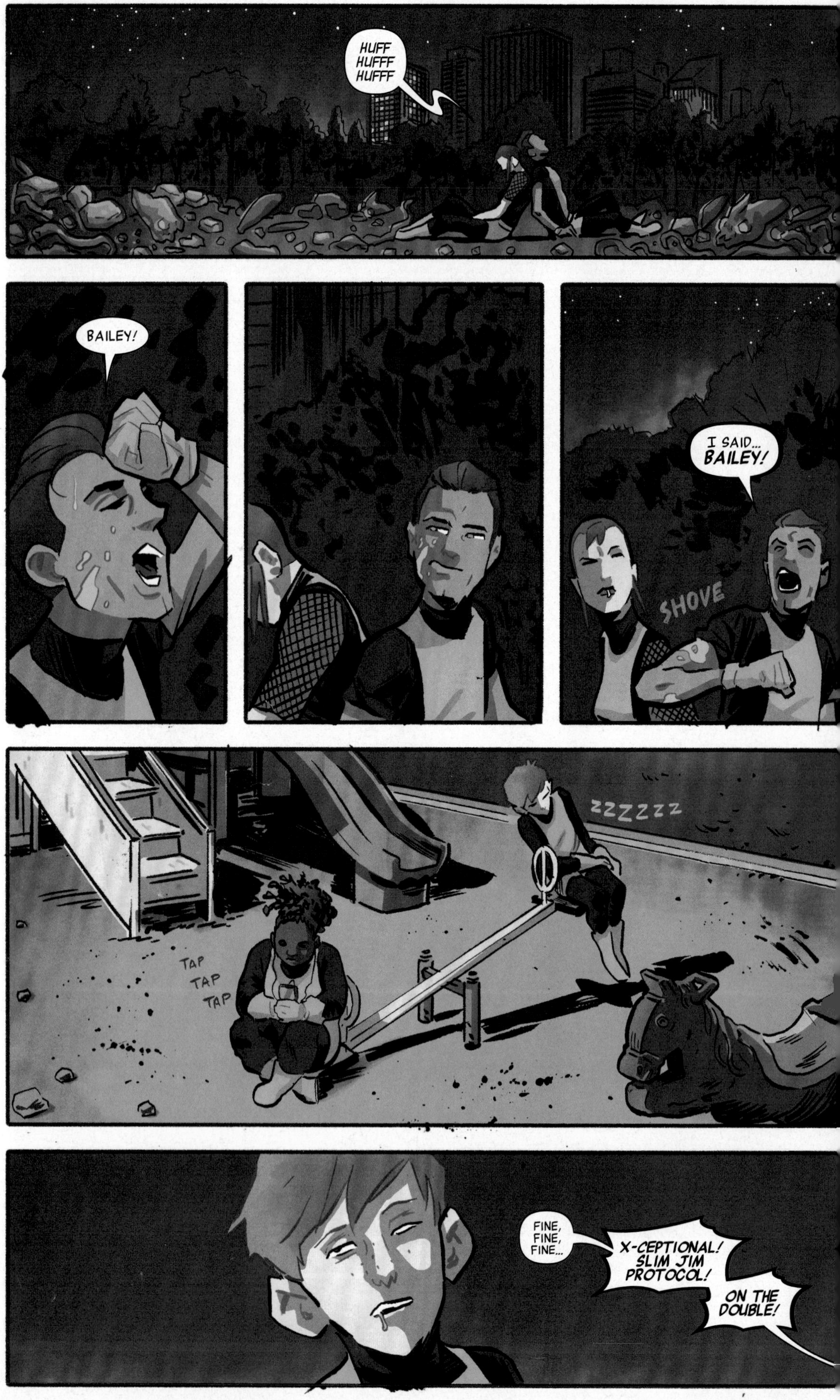
HUFF
HUFFF
HUFFF
BAILEY!
I SAID... BAILEY!
SHOVE
ZZZZZZ
TAP
TAP
TAP
FINE, FINE, FINE...
X-CEPTIONAL! SLIM JIM PROTOCOL!
ON THE DOUBLE!

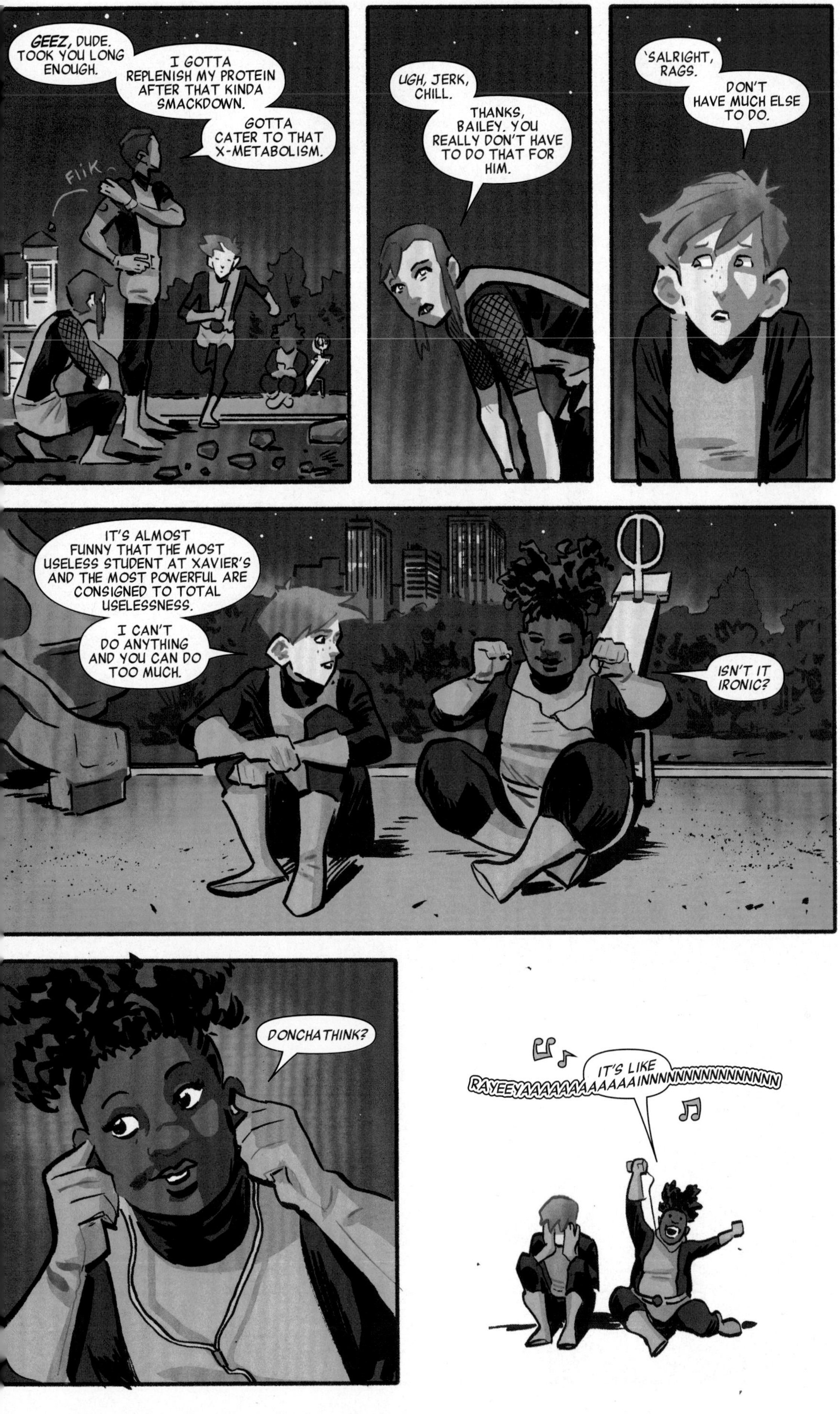
GEEZ, DUDE. TOOK YOU LONG ENOUGH.
I GOTTA REPLENISH MY PROTEIN AFTER THAT KINDA SMACKDOWN.
GOTTA CATER TO THAT X-METABOLISM.
FLIK
UGH, JERK, CHILL.
THANKS, BAILEY. YOU REALLY DON'T HAVE TO DO THAT FOR HIM.
'SALRIGHT, RAGS.
DON'T HAVE MUCH ELSE TO DO.
IT'S ALMOST FUNNY THAT THE MOST USELESS STUDENT AT XAVIER'S AND THE MOST POWERFUL ARE CONSIGNED TO TOTAL USELESSNESS.
I CAN'T DO ANYTHING AND YOU CAN DO TOO MUCH.
ISN'T IT IRONIC?
DONCHATHINK?
IT'S LIKE
RAYEEYAAAAAAAAAAAAINNNNNNNNNNNNNNN

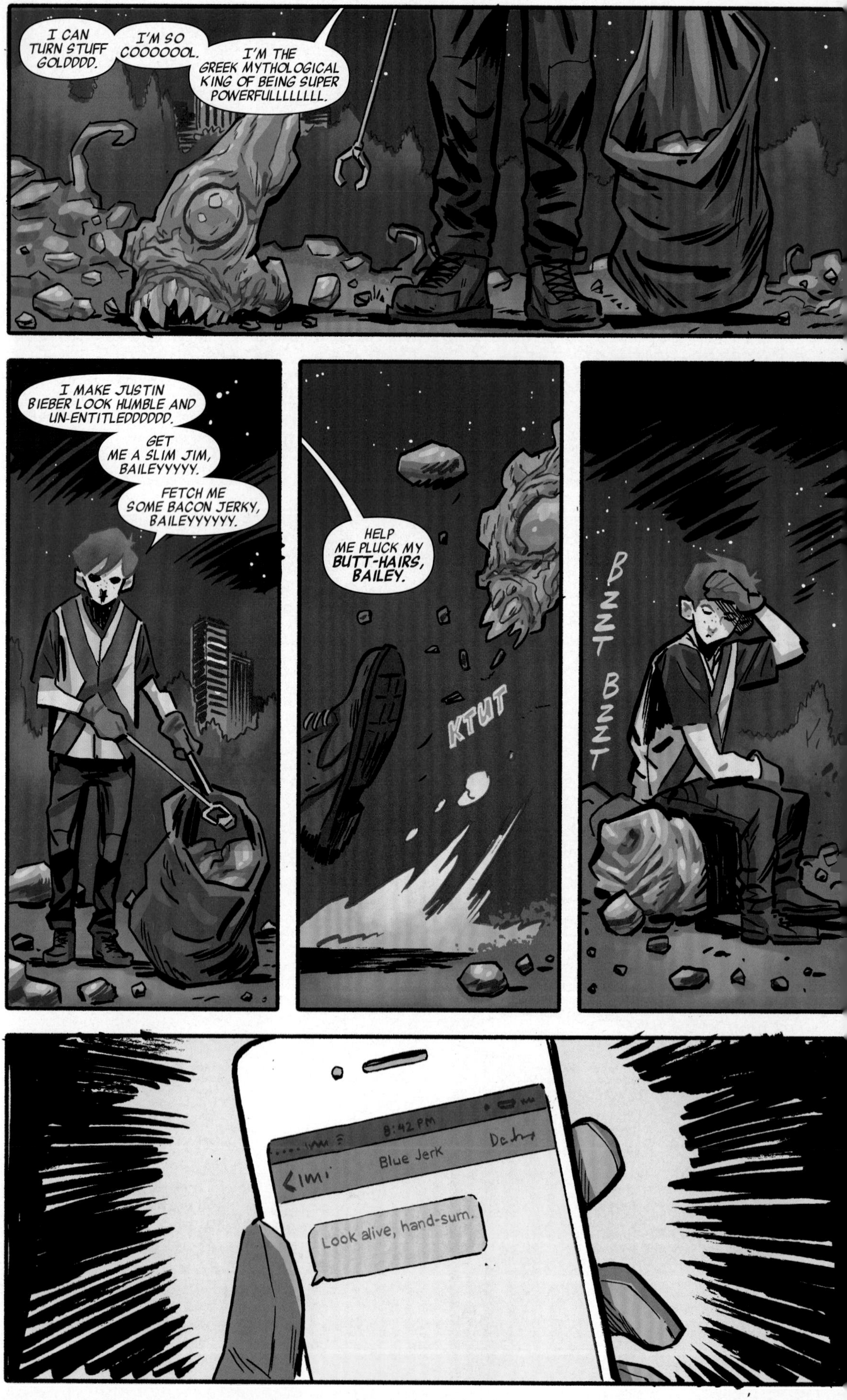
I CAN TURN STUFF GOLDDDD.
I'M SO COOOOOOL.
I'M THE GREEK MYTHOLOGICAL KING OF BEING SUPER POWERFULLLLLLLL.
I MAKE JUSTIN BIEBER LOOK HUMBLE AND UN-ENTITLEDDDDDD.
GET ME A SLIM JIM, BAILEYYYYY.
FETCH ME SOME BACON JERKY, BAILEYYYYYY.
HELP ME PLUCK MY BUTT-HAIRS, BAILEY.
KTUT
BZZT BZZT
8:42 PM
Blue Jerk
Look alive, hand-sum.

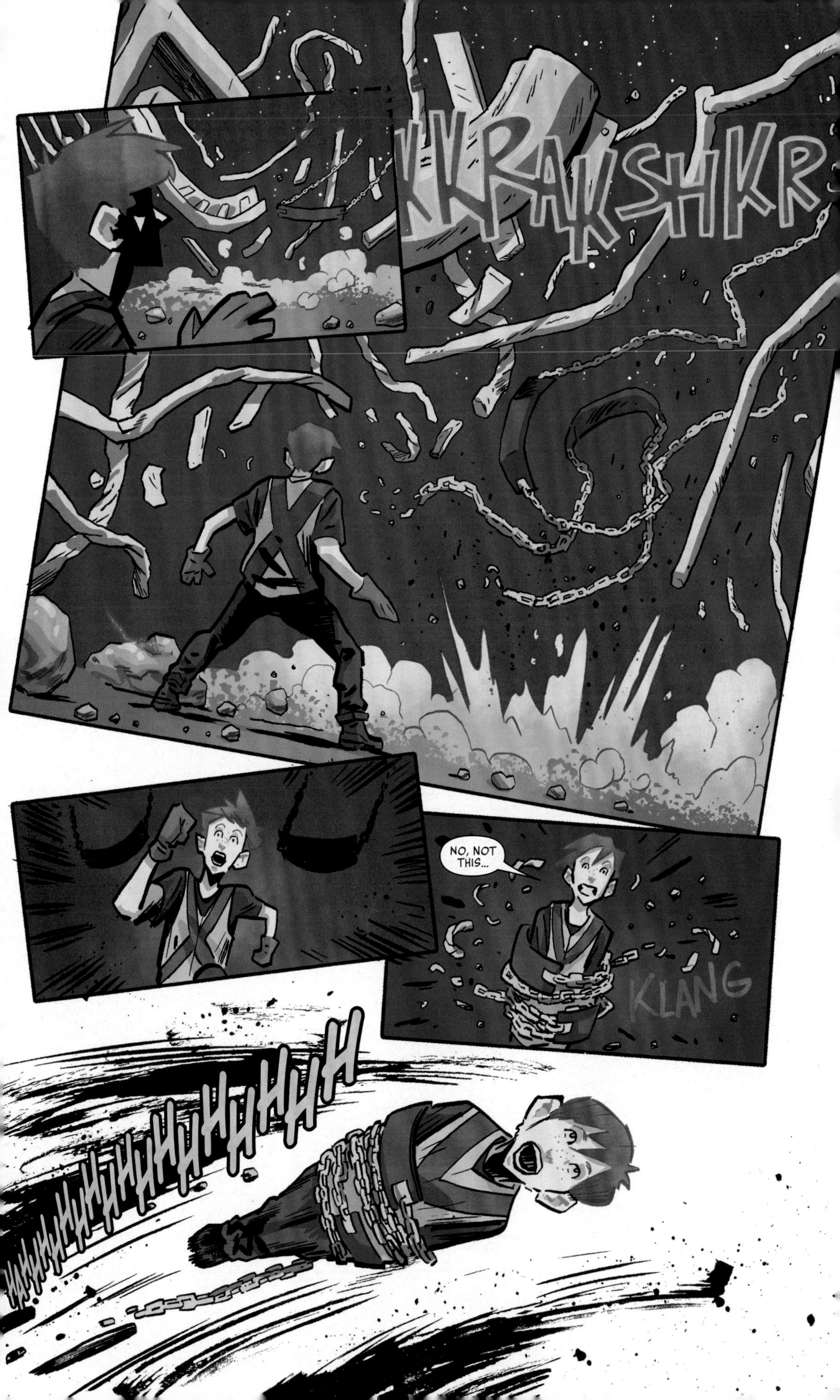
KKRAKSHKR
NO, NOT THIS...
KLANG
HAAAAAAAHHHHHHHHHHHHH

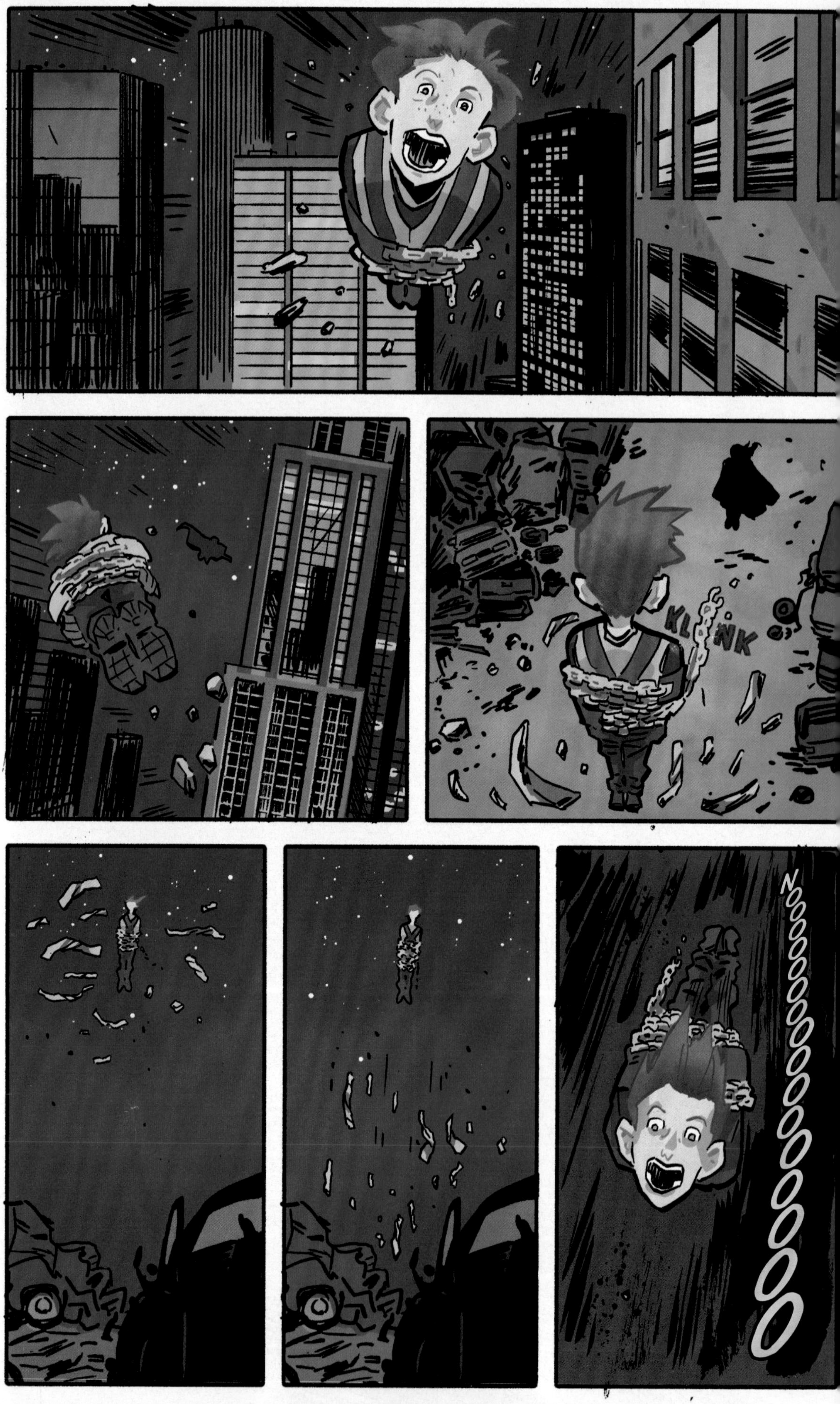
KLINK
NOOOOOOOOOOOOOOOO

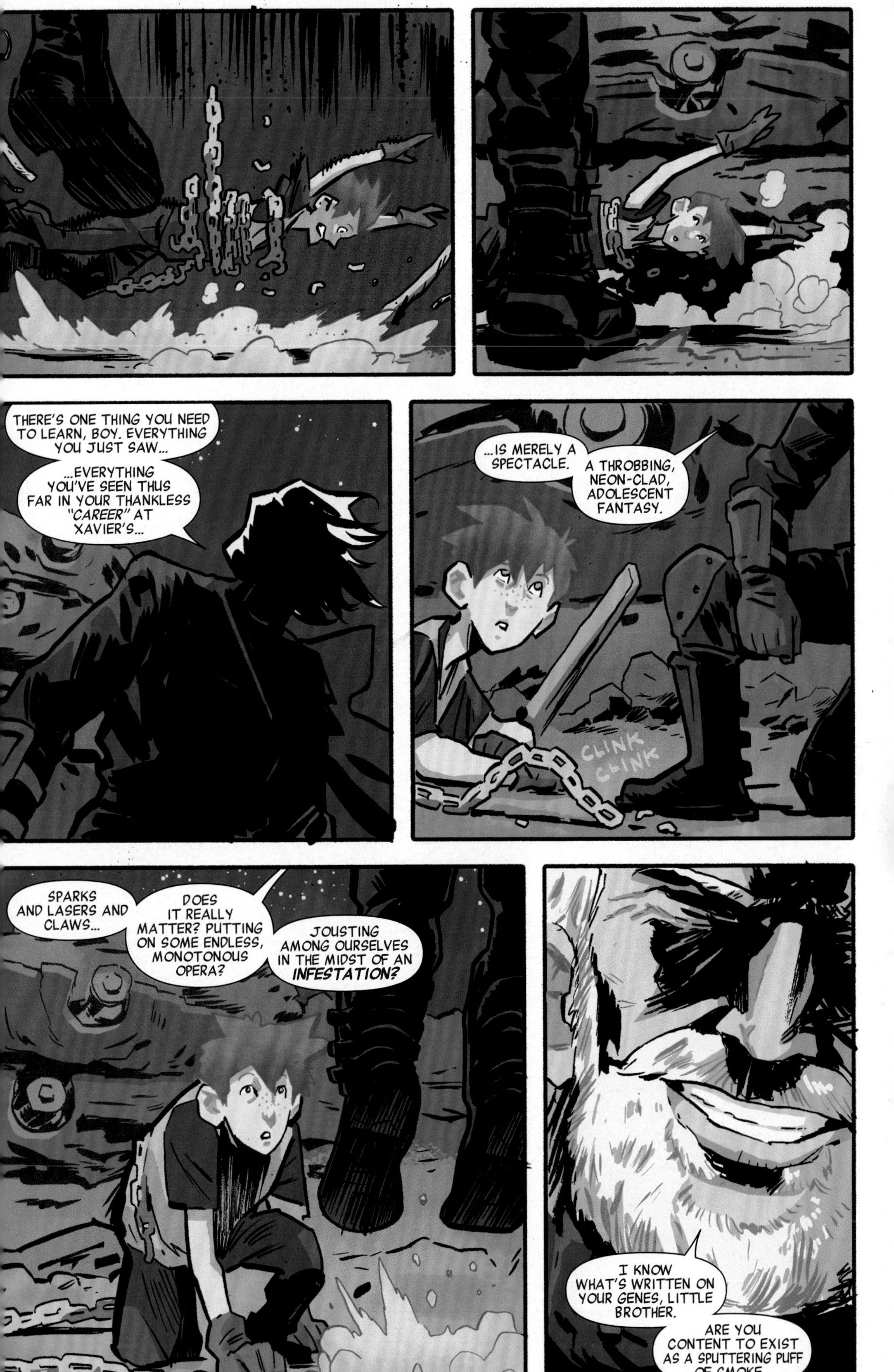
THERE'S ONE THING YOU NEED TO LEARN, BOY. EVERYTHING YOU JUST SAW...
...EVERYTHING YOU'VE SEEN THUS FAR IN YOUR THANKLESS "CAREER" AT XAVIER'S...
...IS MERELY A SPECTACLE.
A THROBBING, NEON-CLAD, ADOLESCENT FANTASY.
CLINK CLINK
SPARKS AND LASERS AND CLAWS...
DOES IT REALLY MATTER? PUTTING ON SOME ENDLESS, MONOTONOUS OPERA?
JOUSTING AMONG OURSELVES IN THE MIDST OF AN INFESTATION?
I KNOW WHAT'S WRITTEN ON YOUR GENES, LITTLE BROTHER.
ARE YOU CONTENT TO EXIST AS A SPUTTERING PUFF OF SMOKE...

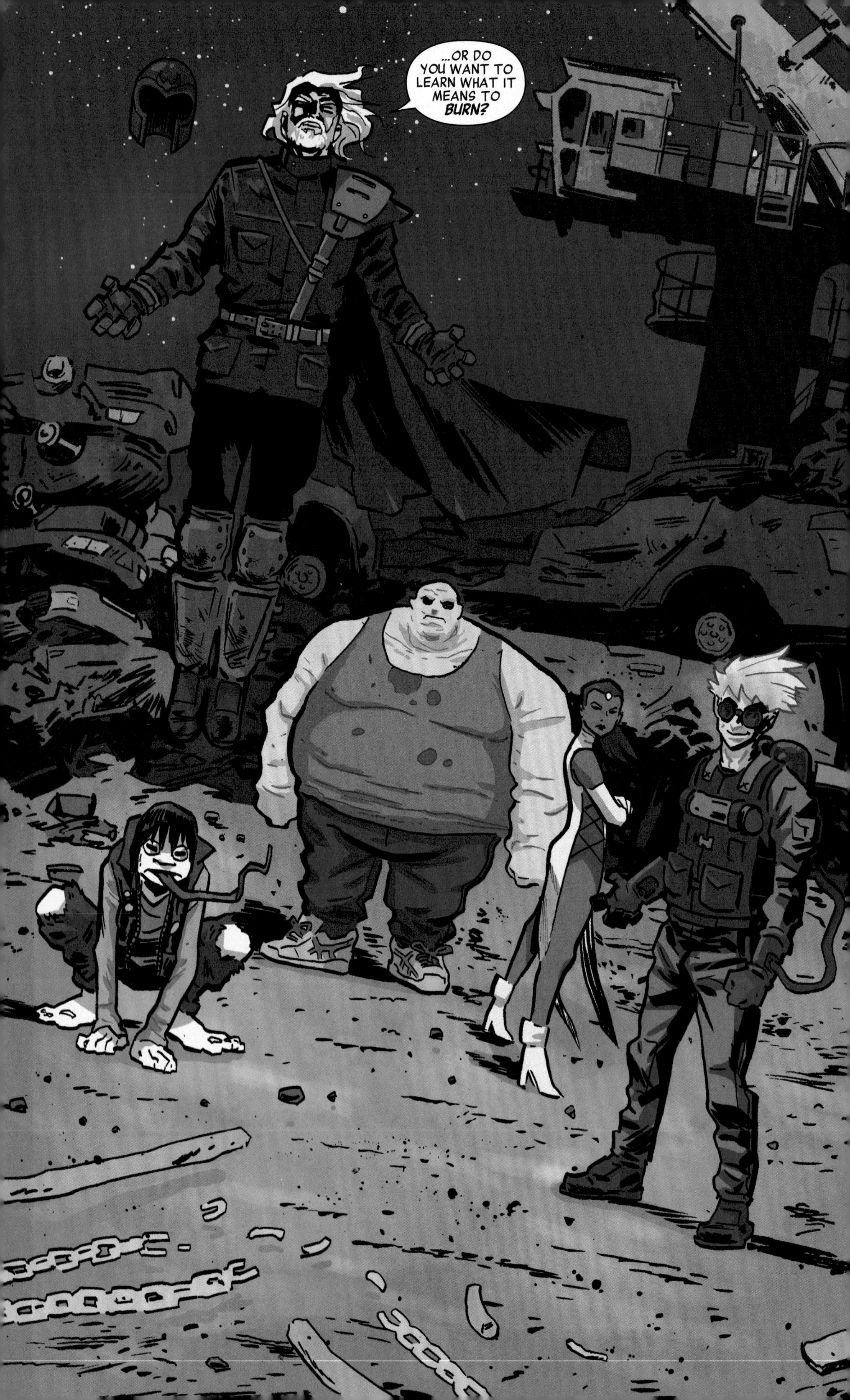
...OR DO YOU WANT TO LEARN WHAT IT MEANS TO *BURN?*

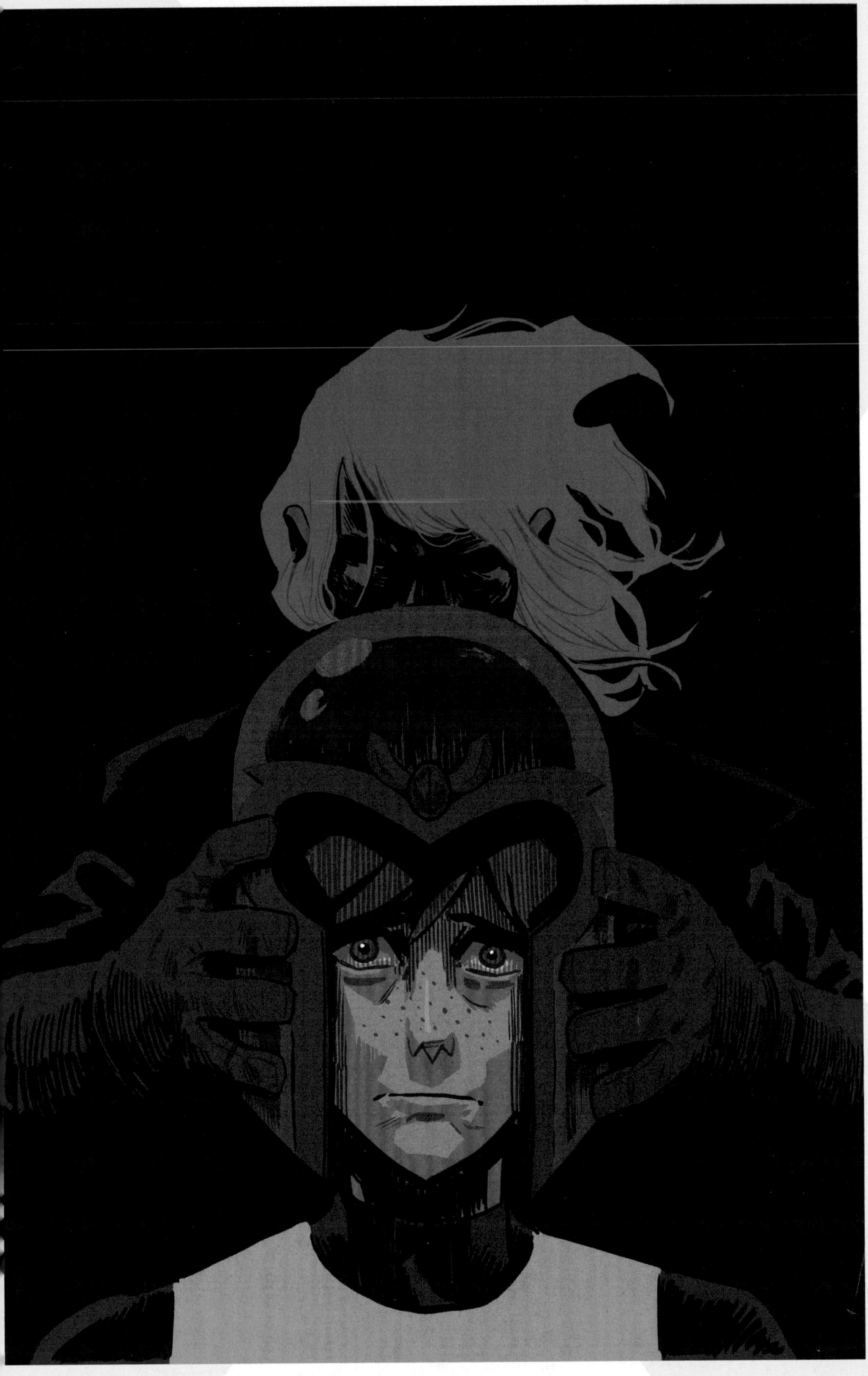

4

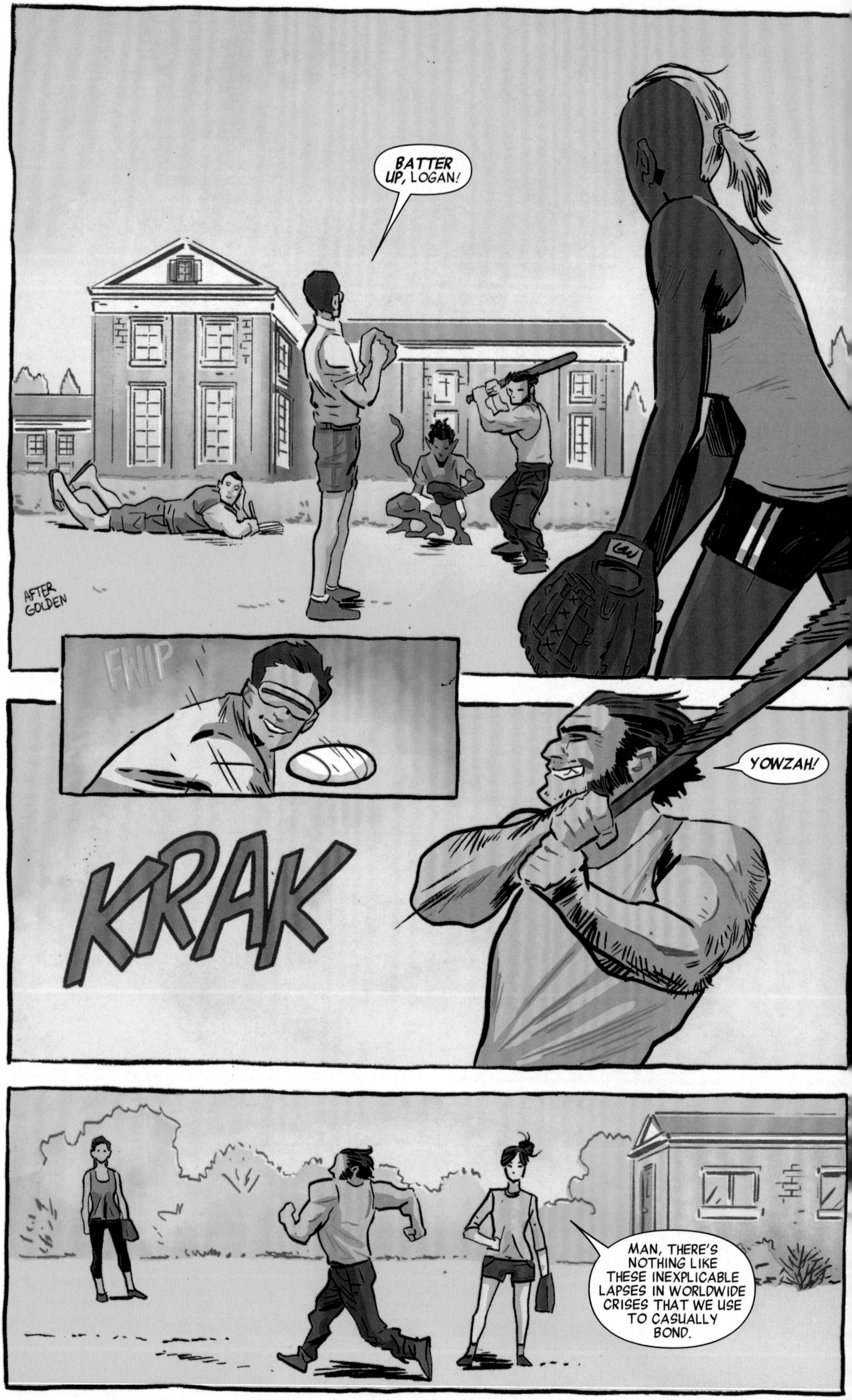
BATTER UP, LOGAN!
AFTER GOLDEN
FWIP
YOWZAH!
KRAK
MAN, THERE'S NOTHING LIKE THESE INEXPLICABLE LAPSES IN WORLDWIDE CRISES THAT WE USE TO CASUALLY BOND.

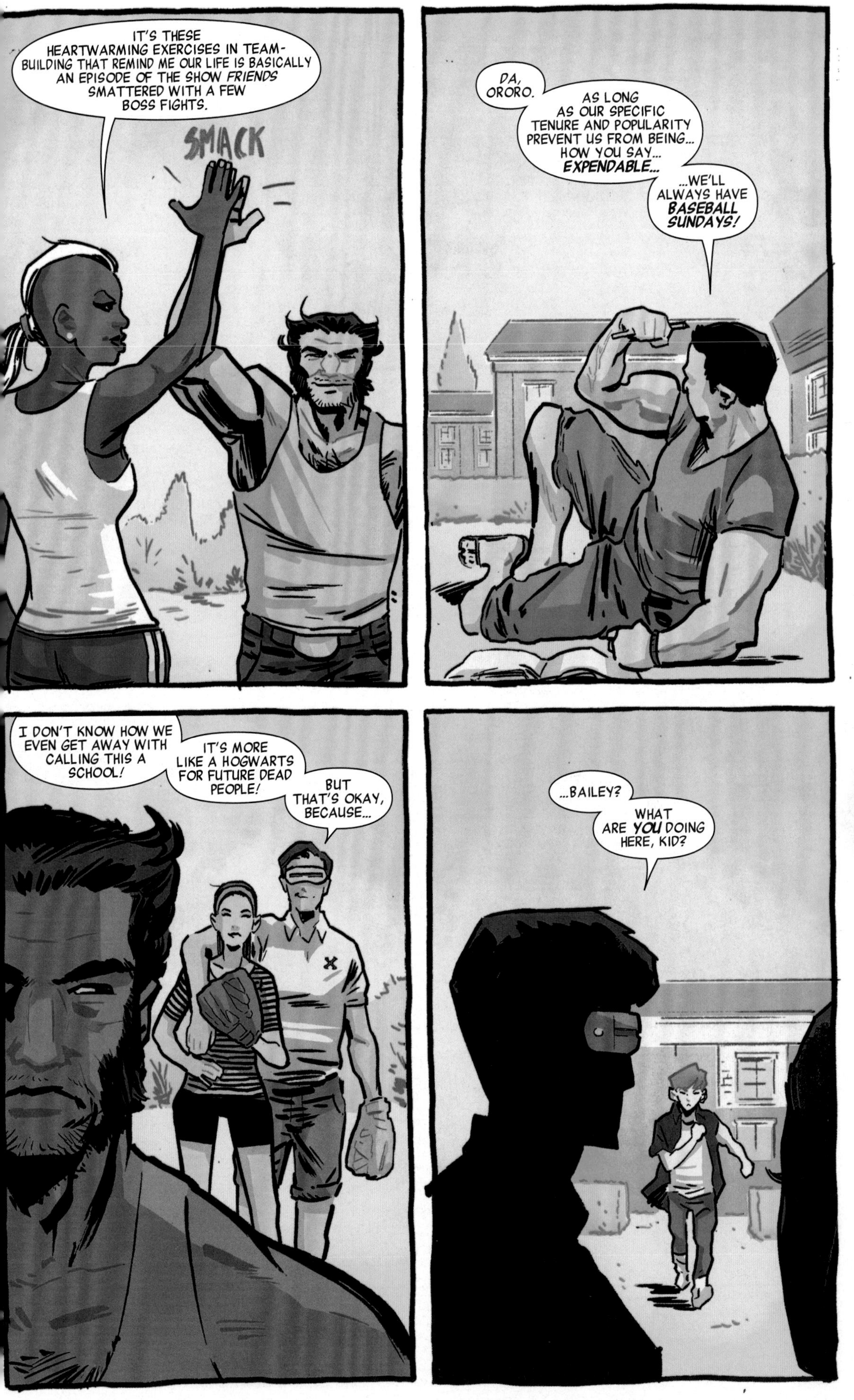
IT'S THESE HEARTWARMING EXERCISES IN TEAM-BUILDING THAT REMIND ME OUR LIFE IS BASICALLY AN EPISODE OF THE SHOW *FRIENDS* SMATTERED WITH A FEW BOSS FIGHTS.
SMACK
DA, ORORO.
AS LONG AS OUR SPECIFIC TENURE AND POPULARITY PREVENT US FROM BEING... HOW YOU SAY... ***EXPENDABLE...***
...WE'LL ALWAYS HAVE ***BASEBALL SUNDAYS!***
I DON'T KNOW HOW WE EVEN GET AWAY WITH CALLING THIS A SCHOOL!
IT'S MORE LIKE A HOGWARTS FOR FUTURE DEAD PEOPLE!
BUT THAT'S OKAY, BECAUSE...
...BAILEY?
WHAT ARE ***YOU*** DOING HERE, KID?

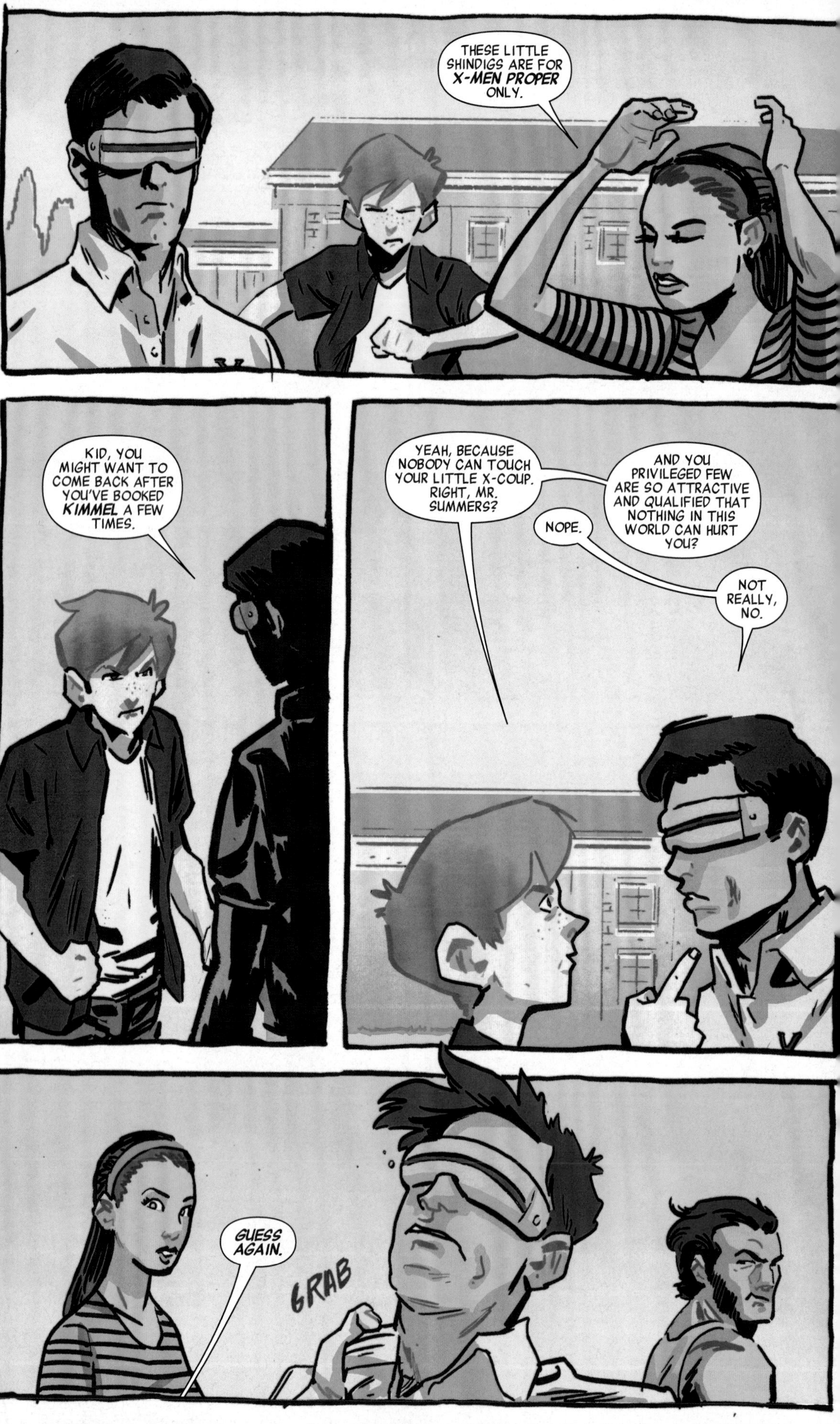

THESE LITTLE SHINDIGS ARE FOR *X-MEN PROPER* ONLY.
KID, YOU MIGHT WANT TO COME BACK AFTER YOU'VE BOOKED *KIMMEL* A FEW TIMES.
YEAH, BECAUSE NOBODY CAN TOUCH YOUR LITTLE X-COUP. RIGHT, MR. SUMMERS?
AND YOU PRIVILEGED FEW ARE SO ATTRACTIVE AND QUALIFIED THAT NOTHING IN THIS WORLD CAN HURT YOU?
NOPE.
NOT REALLY, NO.
GUESS AGAIN.
GRAB

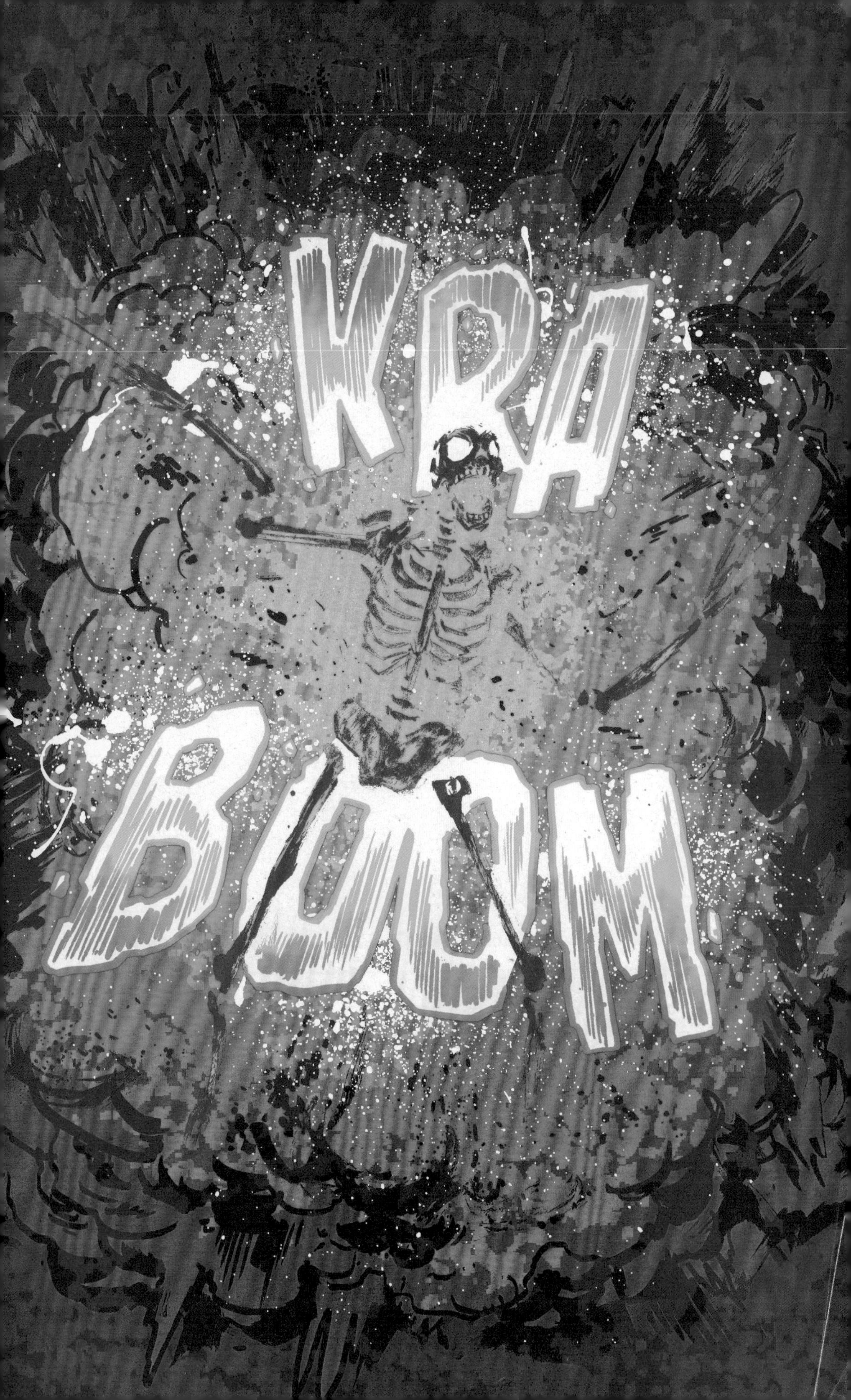
KRA
BOOM

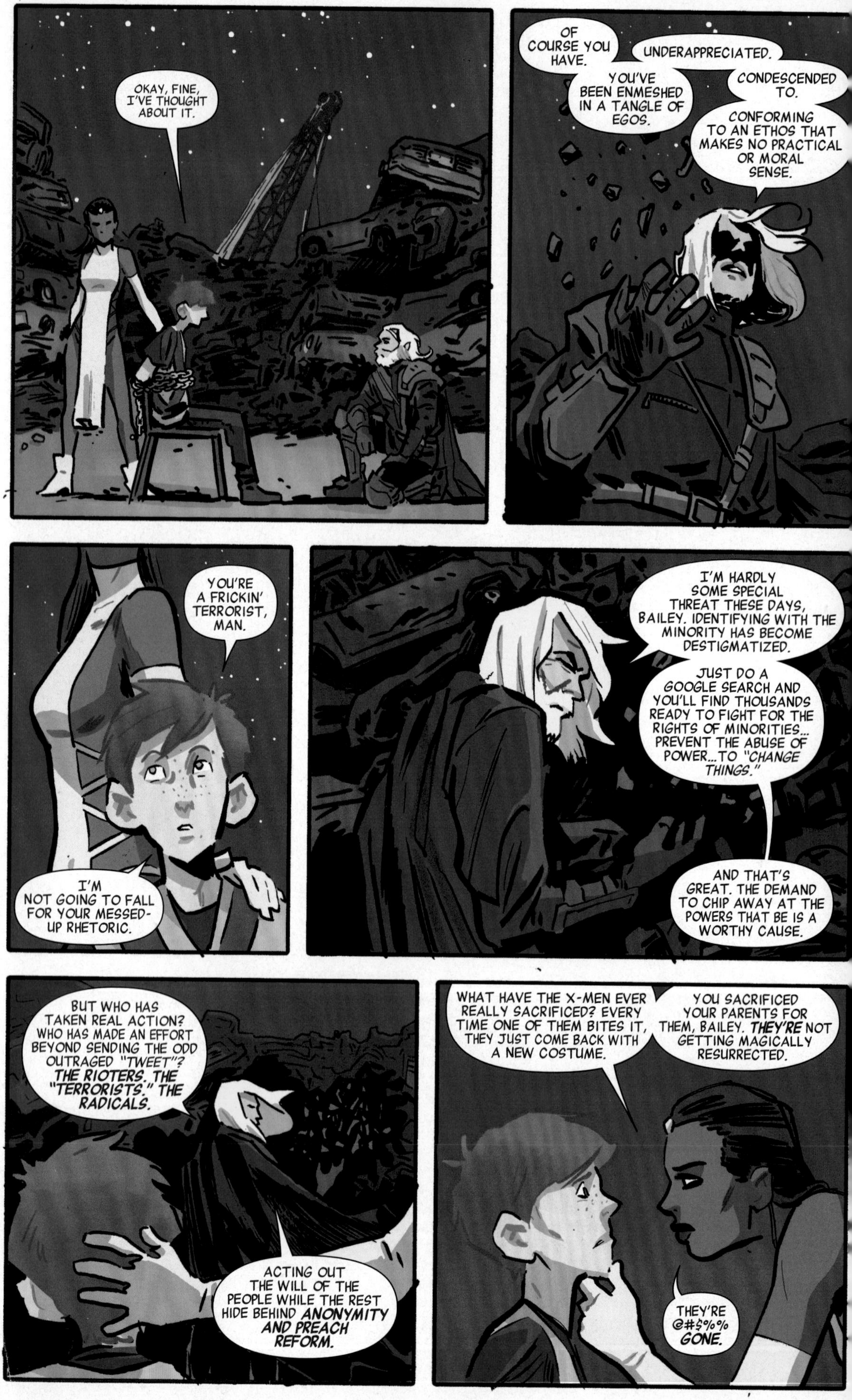
OKAY, FINE, I'VE THOUGHT ABOUT IT.
OF COURSE YOU HAVE.
UNDERAPPRECIATED.
YOU'VE BEEN ENMESHED IN A TANGLE OF EGOS.
CONDESCENDED TO.
CONFORMING TO AN ETHOS THAT MAKES NO PRACTICAL OR MORAL SENSE.
YOU'RE A FRICKIN' TERRORIST, MAN.
I'M NOT GOING TO FALL FOR YOUR MESSED-UP RHETORIC.
I'M HARDLY SOME SPECIAL THREAT THESE DAYS, BAILEY. IDENTIFYING WITH THE MINORITY HAS BECOME DESTIGMATIZED.
JUST DO A GOOGLE SEARCH AND YOU'LL FIND THOUSANDS READY TO FIGHT FOR THE RIGHTS OF MINORITIES... PREVENT THE ABUSE OF POWER...TO "CHANGE THINGS."
AND THAT'S GREAT. THE DEMAND TO CHIP AWAY AT THE POWERS THAT BE IS A WORTHY CAUSE.
BUT WHO HAS TAKEN REAL ACTION? WHO HAS MADE AN EFFORT BEYOND SENDING THE ODD OUTRAGED "TWEET"? THE RIOTERS. THE "TERRORISTS." THE RADICALS.
ACTING OUT THE WILL OF THE PEOPLE WHILE THE REST HIDE BEHIND ANONYMITY AND PREACH REFORM.
WHAT HAVE THE X-MEN EVER REALLY SACRIFICED? EVERY TIME ONE OF THEM BITES IT, THEY JUST COME BACK WITH A NEW COSTUME.
YOU SACRIFICED YOUR PARENTS FOR THEM, BAILEY. THEY'RE NOT GETTING MAGICALLY RESURRECTED.
THEY'RE @#$%% GONE.

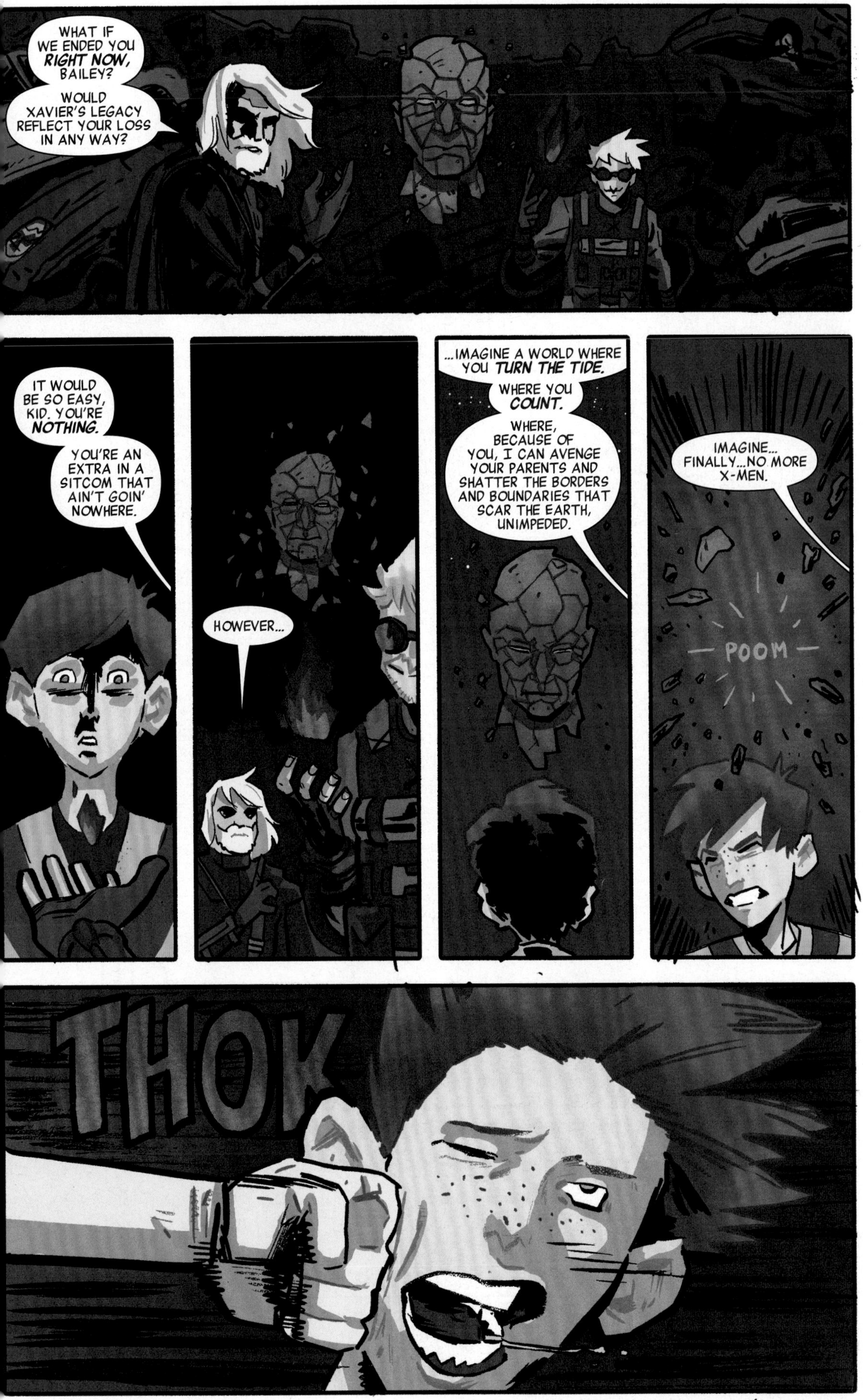
WHAT IF WE ENDED YOU RIGHT NOW, BAILEY?
WOULD XAVIER'S LEGACY REFLECT YOUR LOSS IN ANY WAY?
IT WOULD BE SO EASY, KID. YOU'RE NOTHING.
YOU'RE AN EXTRA IN A SITCOM THAT AIN'T GOIN' NOWHERE.
HOWEVER...
...IMAGINE A WORLD WHERE YOU TURN THE TIDE.
WHERE YOU COUNT.
WHERE, BECAUSE OF YOU, I CAN AVENGE YOUR PARENTS AND SHATTER THE BORDERS AND BOUNDARIES THAT SCAR THE EARTH, UNIMPEDED.
IMAGINE... FINALLY...NO MORE X-MEN.
POOM
THOK

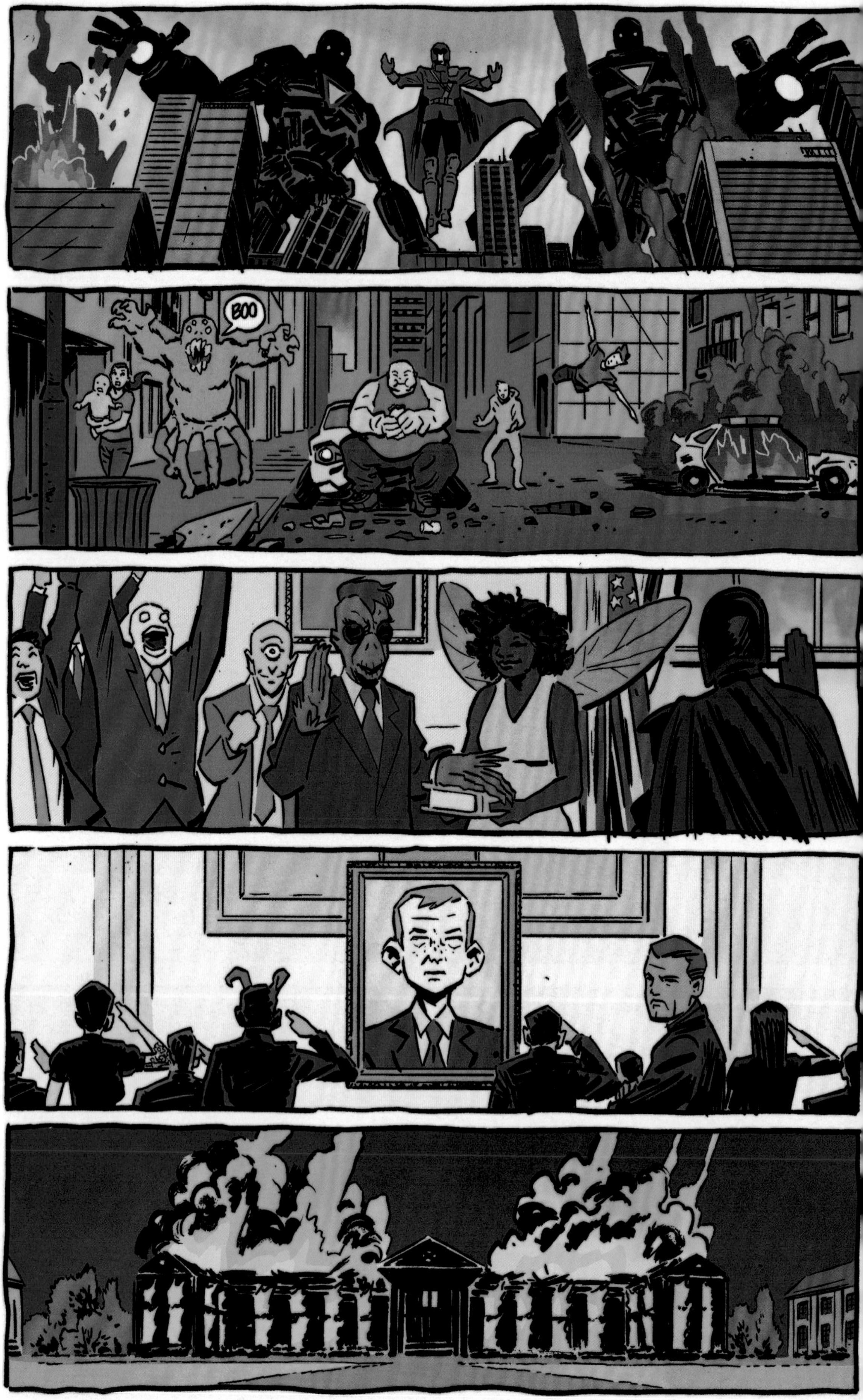
BOO

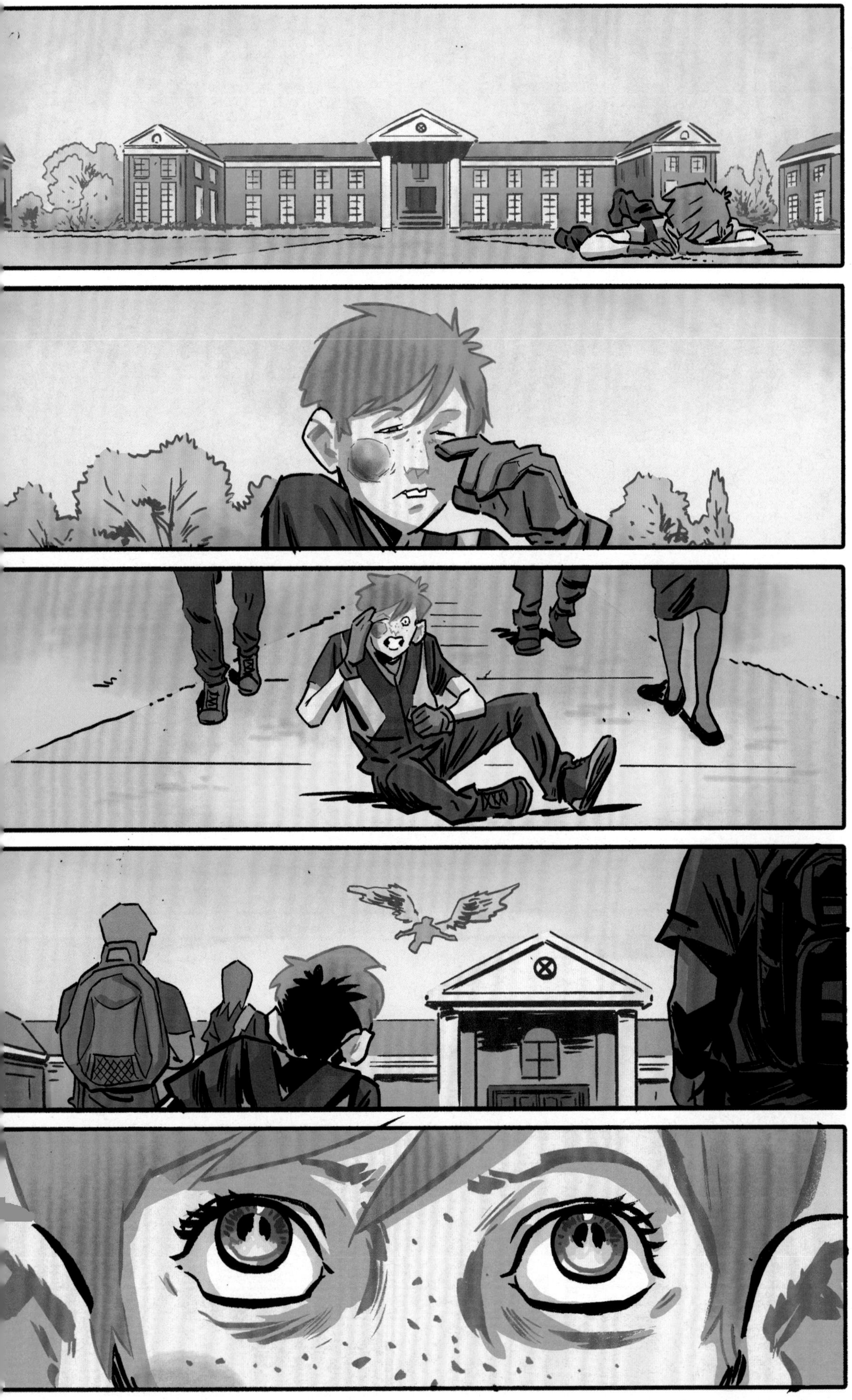

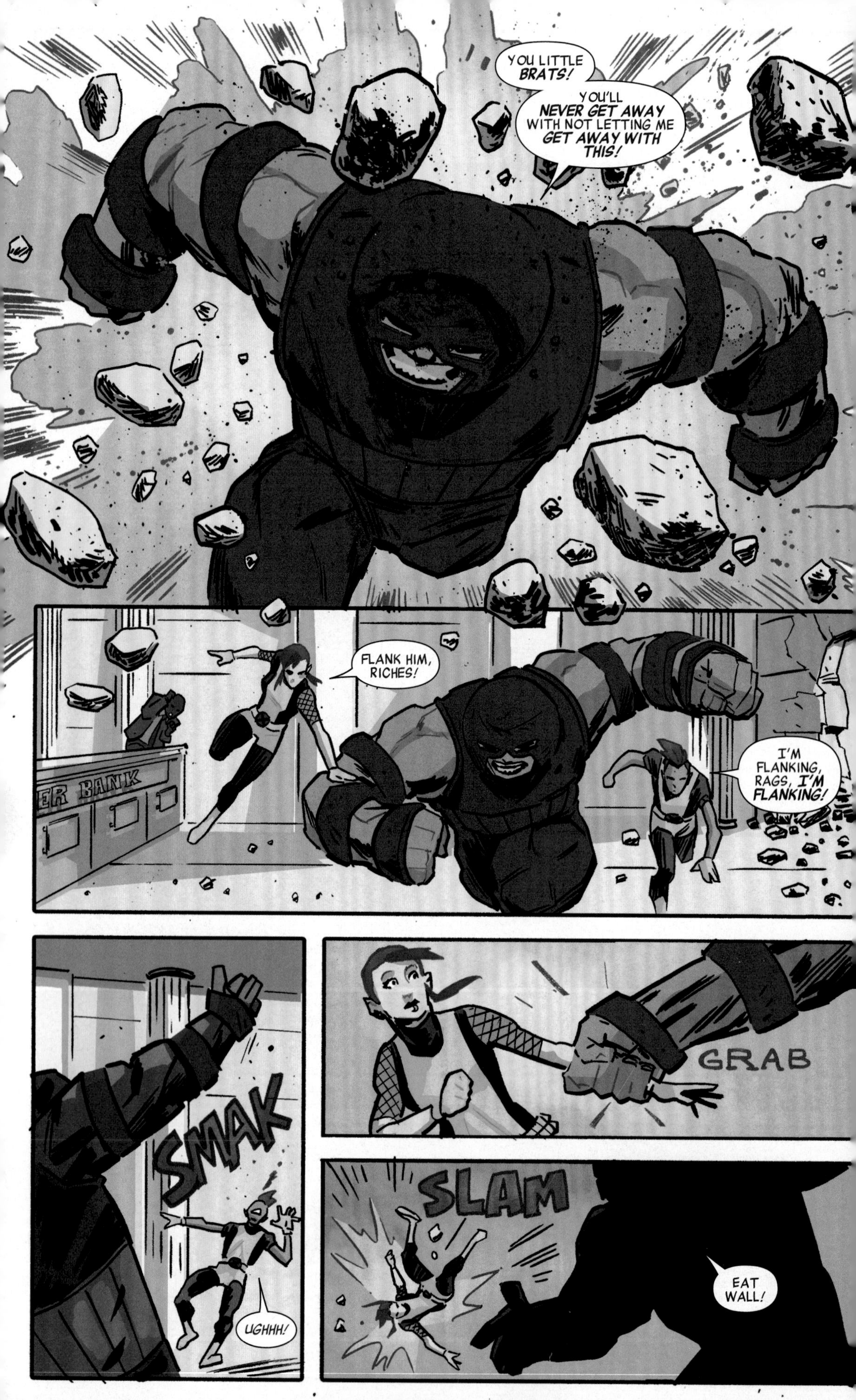
YOU LITTLE BRATS!
YOU'LL NEVER GET AWAY WITH NOT LETTING ME GET AWAY WITH THIS!
FLANK HIM, RICHES!
I'M FLANKING, RAGS, I'M FLANKING!
ER BANK
SMAK
UGHHH!
GRAB
SLAM
EAT WALL!

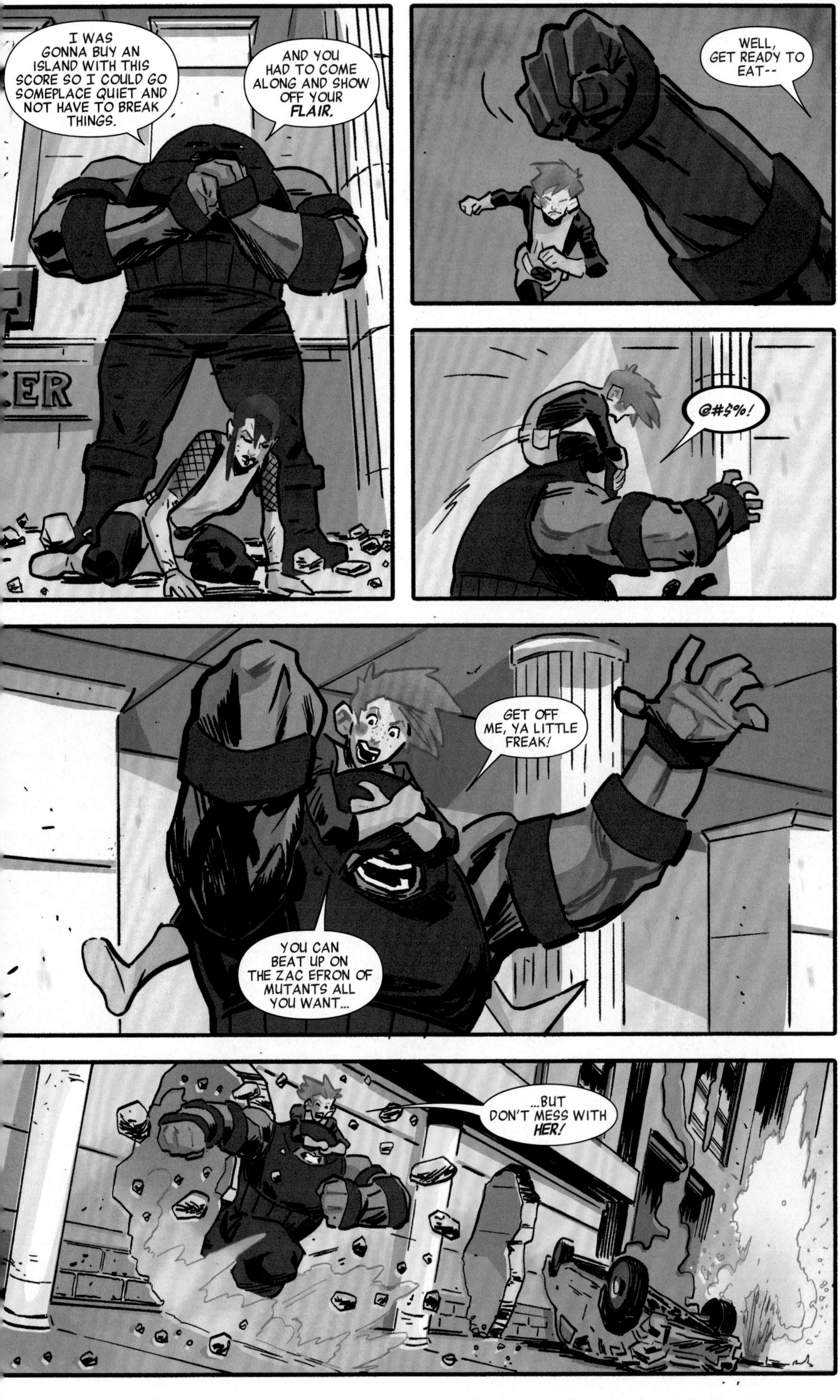
I WAS GONNA BUY AN ISLAND WITH THIS SCORE SO I COULD GO SOMEPLACE QUIET AND NOT HAVE TO BREAK THINGS.
AND YOU HAD TO COME ALONG AND SHOW OFF YOUR **FLAIR.**
WELL, GET READY TO EAT--
@#$%!
GET OFF ME, YA LITTLE FREAK!
YOU CAN BEAT UP ON THE ZAC EFRON OF MUTANTS ALL YOU WANT...
...BUT DON'T MESS WITH ***HER!***

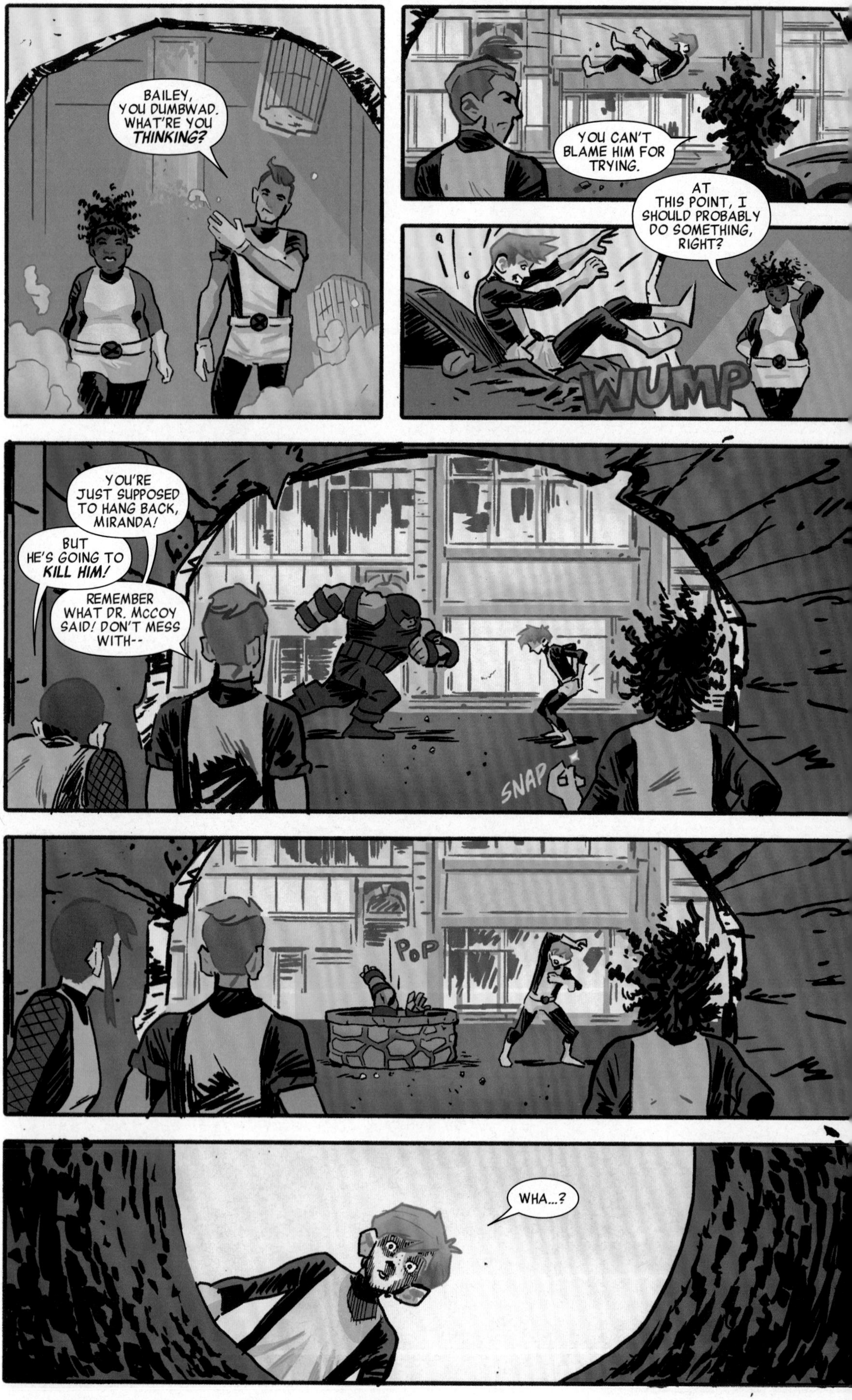

BAILEY, YOU DUMBWAD. WHAT'RE YOU THINKING?
YOU CAN'T BLAME HIM FOR TRYING.
AT THIS POINT, I SHOULD PROBABLY DO SOMETHING, RIGHT?
WUMP
YOU'RE JUST SUPPOSED TO HANG BACK, MIRANDA!
BUT HE'S GOING TO KILL HIM!
REMEMBER WHAT DR. McCOY SAID! DON'T MESS WITH--
SNAP
POP
WHA...?

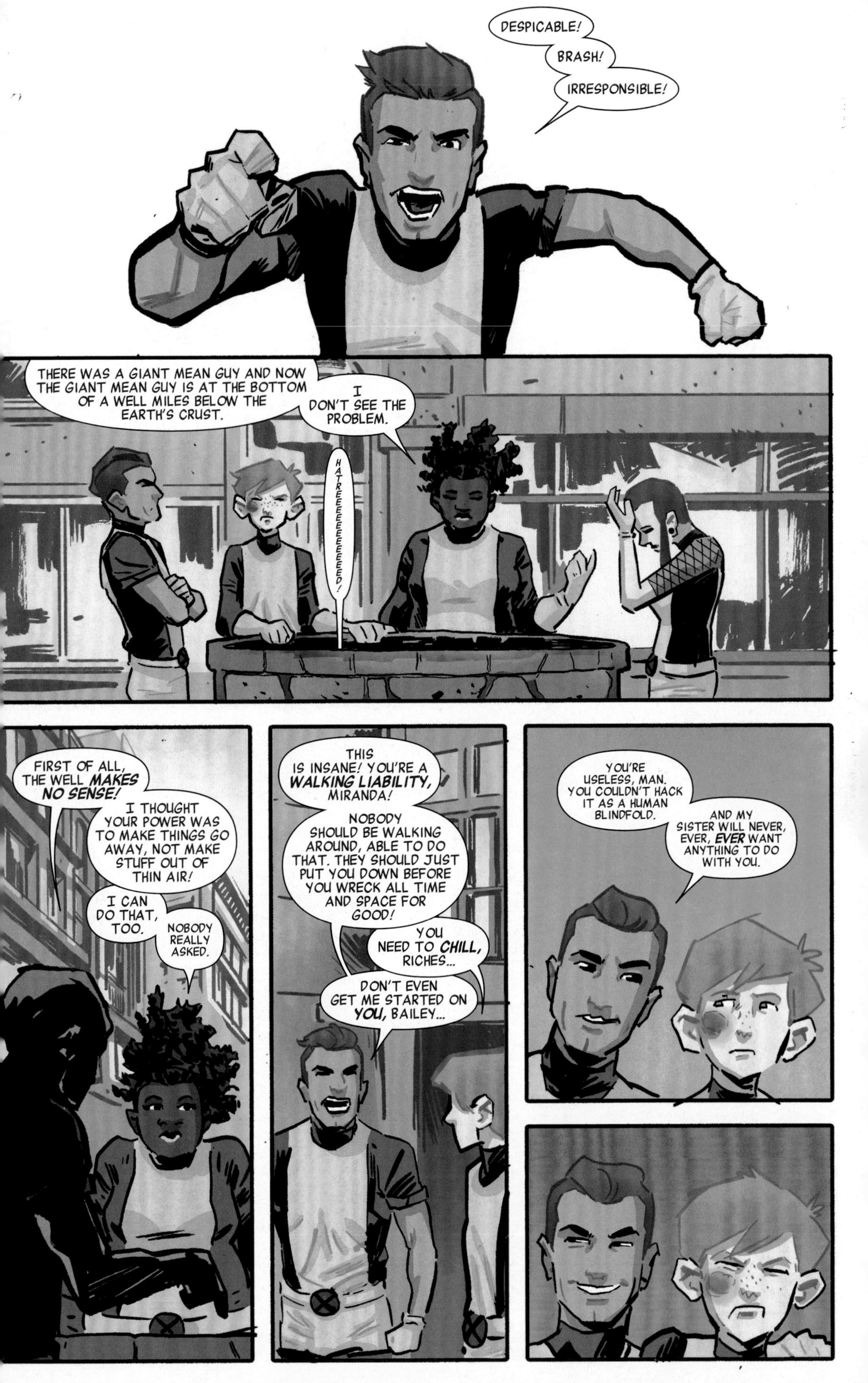
DESPICABLE!
BRASH!
IRRESPONSIBLE!
THERE WAS A GIANT MEAN GUY AND NOW THE GIANT MEAN GUY IS AT THE BOTTOM OF A WELL MILES BELOW THE EARTH'S CRUST.
I DON'T SEE THE PROBLEM.
HATREEEEEEEEEEEEEED!
FIRST OF ALL, THE WELL MAKES NO SENSE!
I THOUGHT YOUR POWER WAS TO MAKE THINGS GO AWAY, NOT MAKE STUFF OUT OF THIN AIR!
I CAN DO THAT, TOO.
NOBODY REALLY ASKED.
THIS IS INSANE! YOU'RE A WALKING LIABILITY, MIRANDA!
NOBODY SHOULD BE WALKING AROUND, ABLE TO DO THAT. THEY SHOULD JUST PUT YOU DOWN BEFORE YOU WRECK ALL TIME AND SPACE FOR GOOD!
YOU NEED TO CHILL, RICHES...
DON'T EVEN GET ME STARTED ON YOU, BAILEY...
YOU'RE USELESS, MAN. YOU COULDN'T HACK IT AS A HUMAN BLINDFOLD.
AND MY SISTER WILL NEVER, EVER, EVER WANT ANYTHING TO DO WITH YOU.

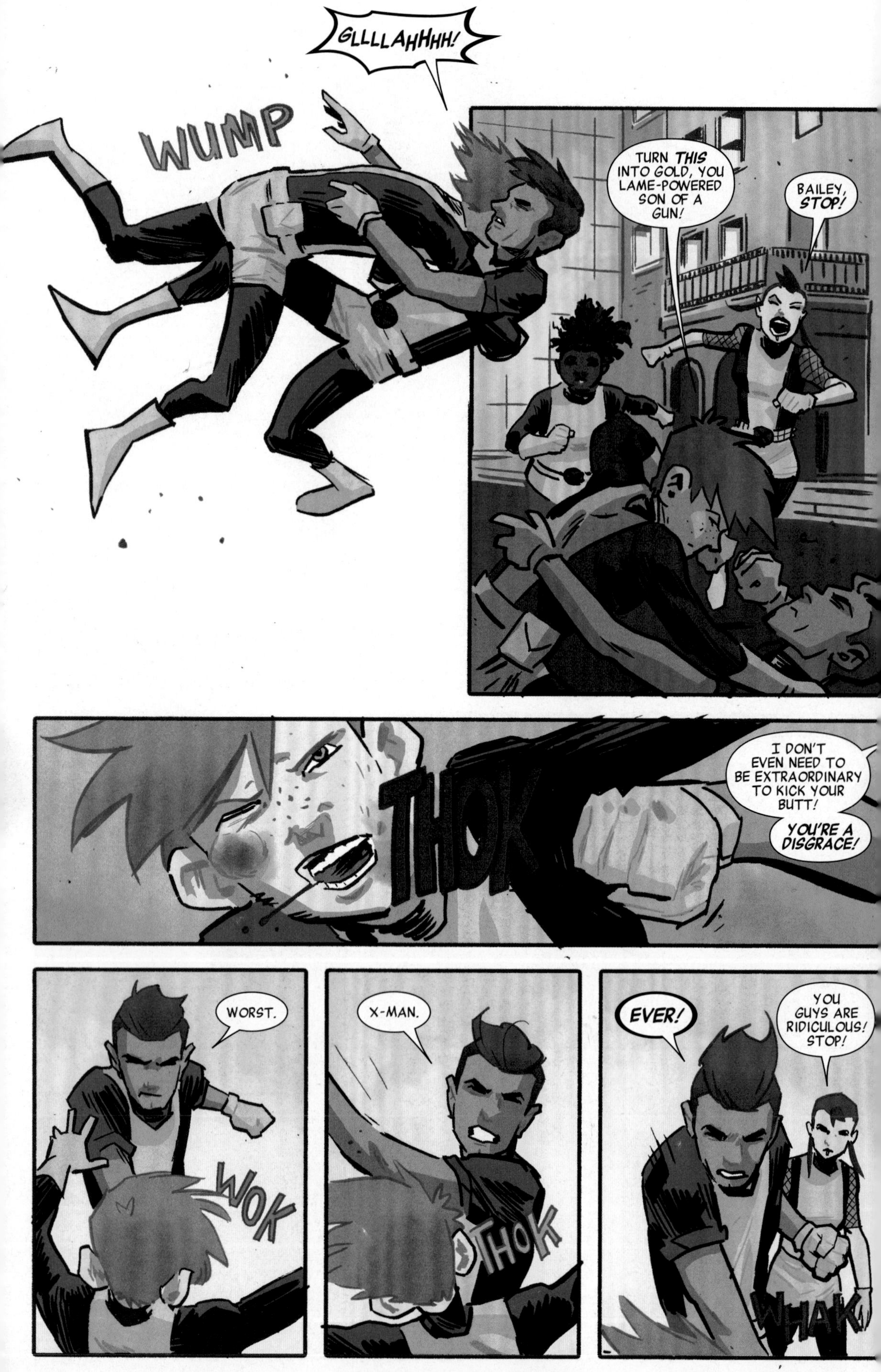
GLLLLAHHHH!
WUMP
TURN THIS INTO GOLD, YOU LAME-POWERED SON OF A GUN!
BAILEY, STOP!
I DON'T EVEN NEED TO BE EXTRAORDINARY TO KICK YOUR BUTT!
YOU'RE A DISGRACE!
THOK
WORST.
WOK
X-MAN.
THOK
EVER!
YOU GUYS ARE RIDICULOUS! STOP!
WHAK

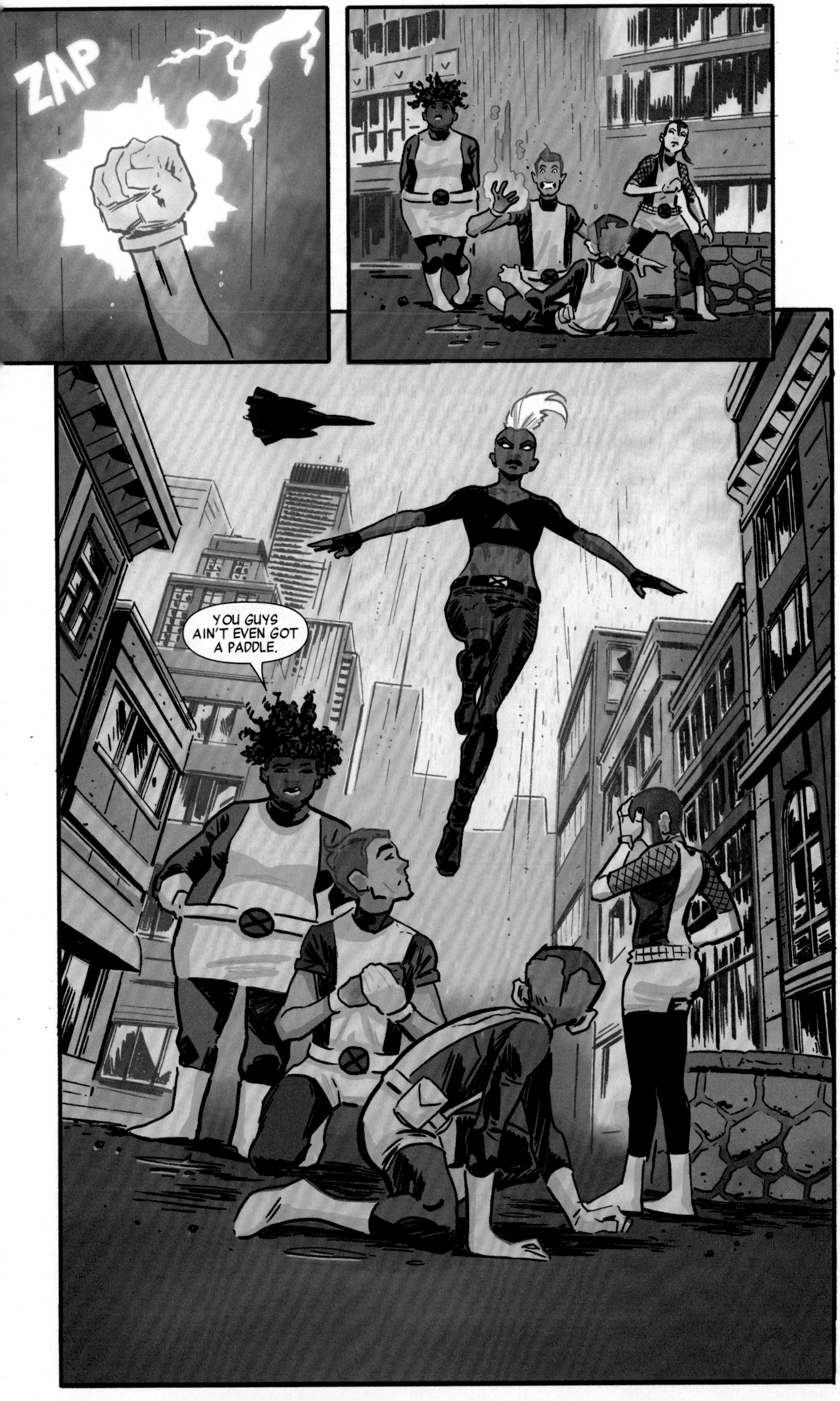
ZAP
YOU GUYS AIN'T EVEN GOT A PADDLE.

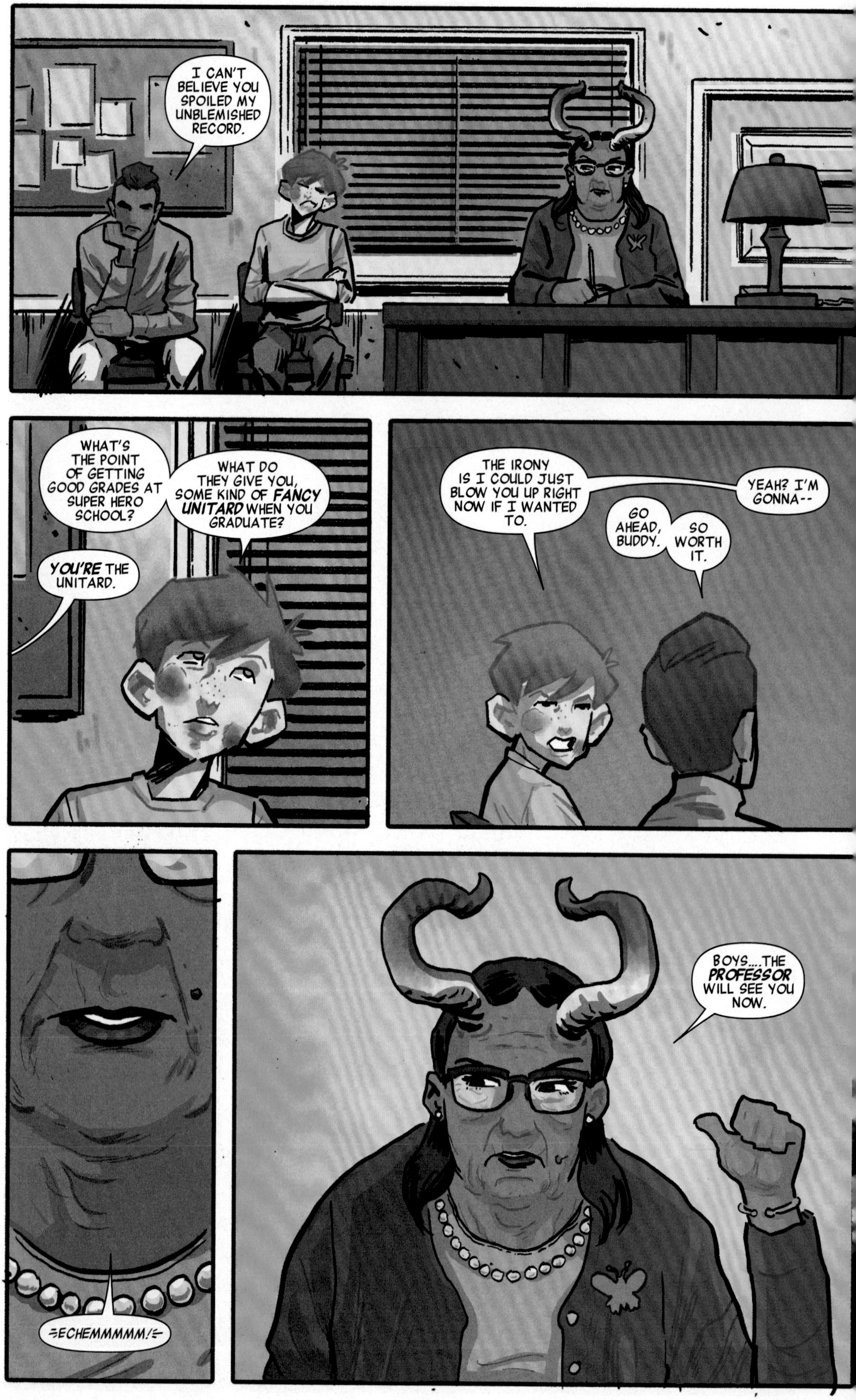
I CAN'T BELIEVE YOU SPOILED MY UNBLEMISHED RECORD.
WHAT'S THE POINT OF GETTING GOOD GRADES AT SUPER HERO SCHOOL?
WHAT DO THEY GIVE YOU, SOME KIND OF FANCY UNITARD WHEN YOU GRADUATE?
YOU'RE THE UNITARD.
THE IRONY IS I COULD JUST BLOW YOU UP RIGHT NOW IF I WANTED TO.
YEAH? I'M GONNA--
GO AHEAD, BUDDY.
SO WORTH IT.
=ECHEMMMMM!=
BOYS....THE PROFESSOR WILL SEE YOU NOW.

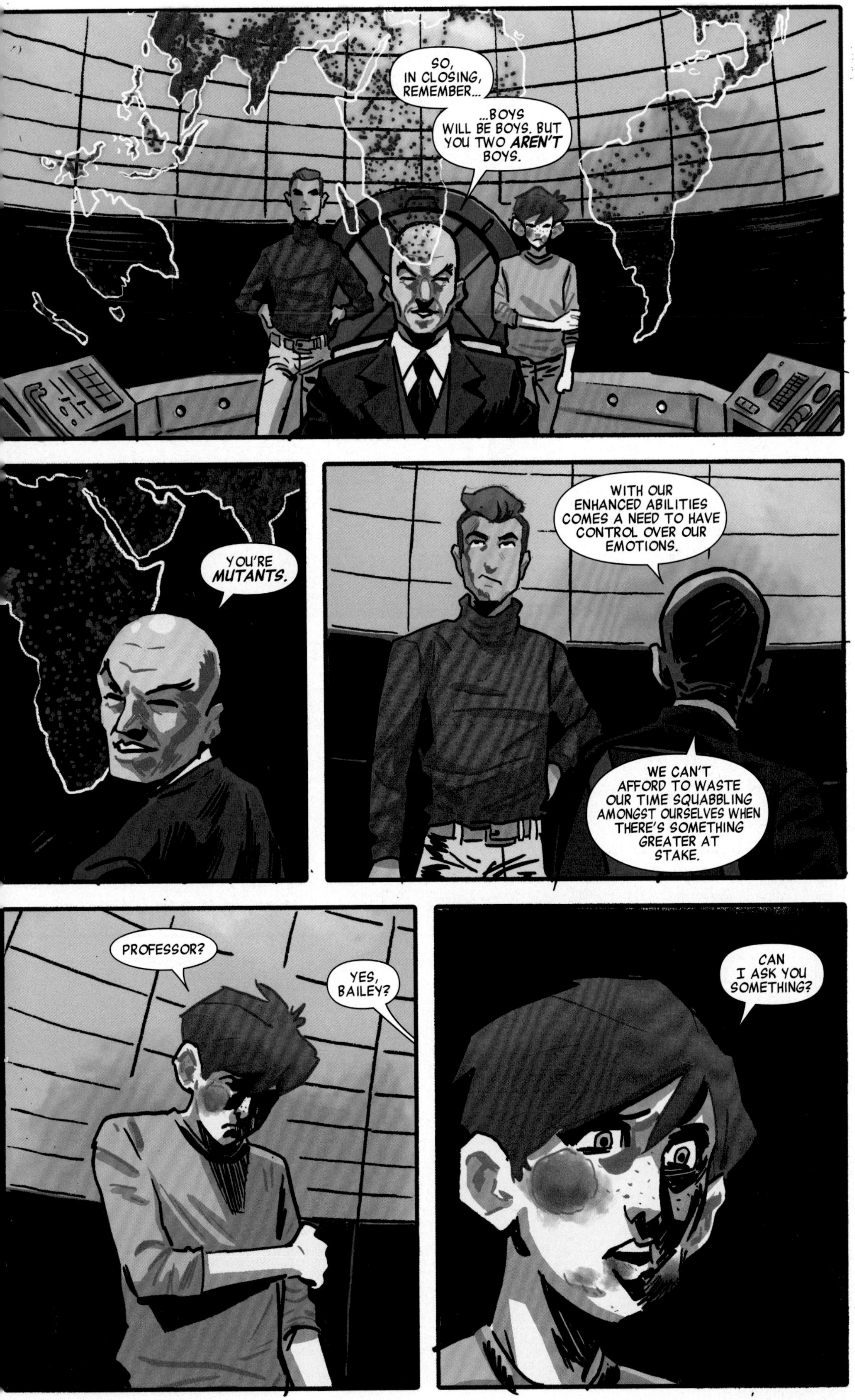
SO, IN CLOSING, REMEMBER...
...BOYS WILL BE BOYS. BUT YOU TWO AREN'T BOYS.
YOU'RE MUTANTS.
WITH OUR ENHANCED ABILITIES COMES A NEED TO HAVE CONTROL OVER OUR EMOTIONS.
WE CAN'T AFFORD TO WASTE OUR TIME SQUABBLING AMONGST OURSELVES WHEN THERE'S SOMETHING GREATER AT STAKE.
PROFESSOR?
YES, BAILEY?
CAN I ASK YOU SOMETHING?

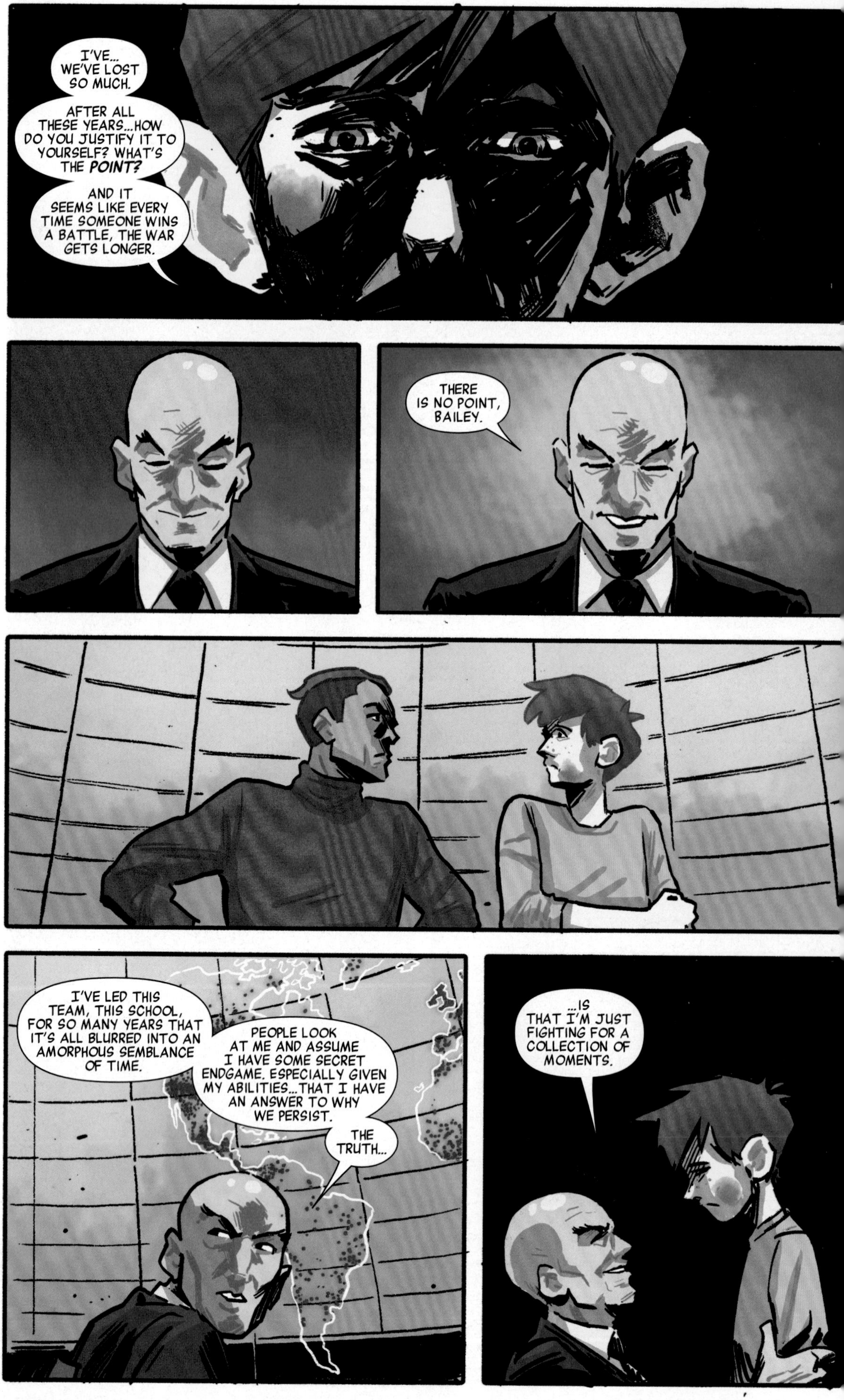
I'VE... WE'VE LOST SO MUCH.
AFTER ALL THESE YEARS...HOW DO YOU JUSTIFY IT TO YOURSELF? WHAT'S THE *POINT?*
AND IT SEEMS LIKE EVERY TIME SOMEONE WINS A BATTLE, THE WAR GETS LONGER.
THERE IS NO POINT, BAILEY.
I'VE LED THIS TEAM, THIS SCHOOL, FOR SO MANY YEARS THAT IT'S ALL BLURRED INTO AN AMORPHOUS SEMBLANCE OF TIME.
PEOPLE LOOK AT ME AND ASSUME I HAVE SOME SECRET ENDGAME. ESPECIALLY GIVEN MY ABILITIES...THAT I HAVE AN ANSWER TO WHY WE PERSIST.
THE TRUTH...
...IS THAT I'M JUST FIGHTING FOR A COLLECTION OF MOMENTS.

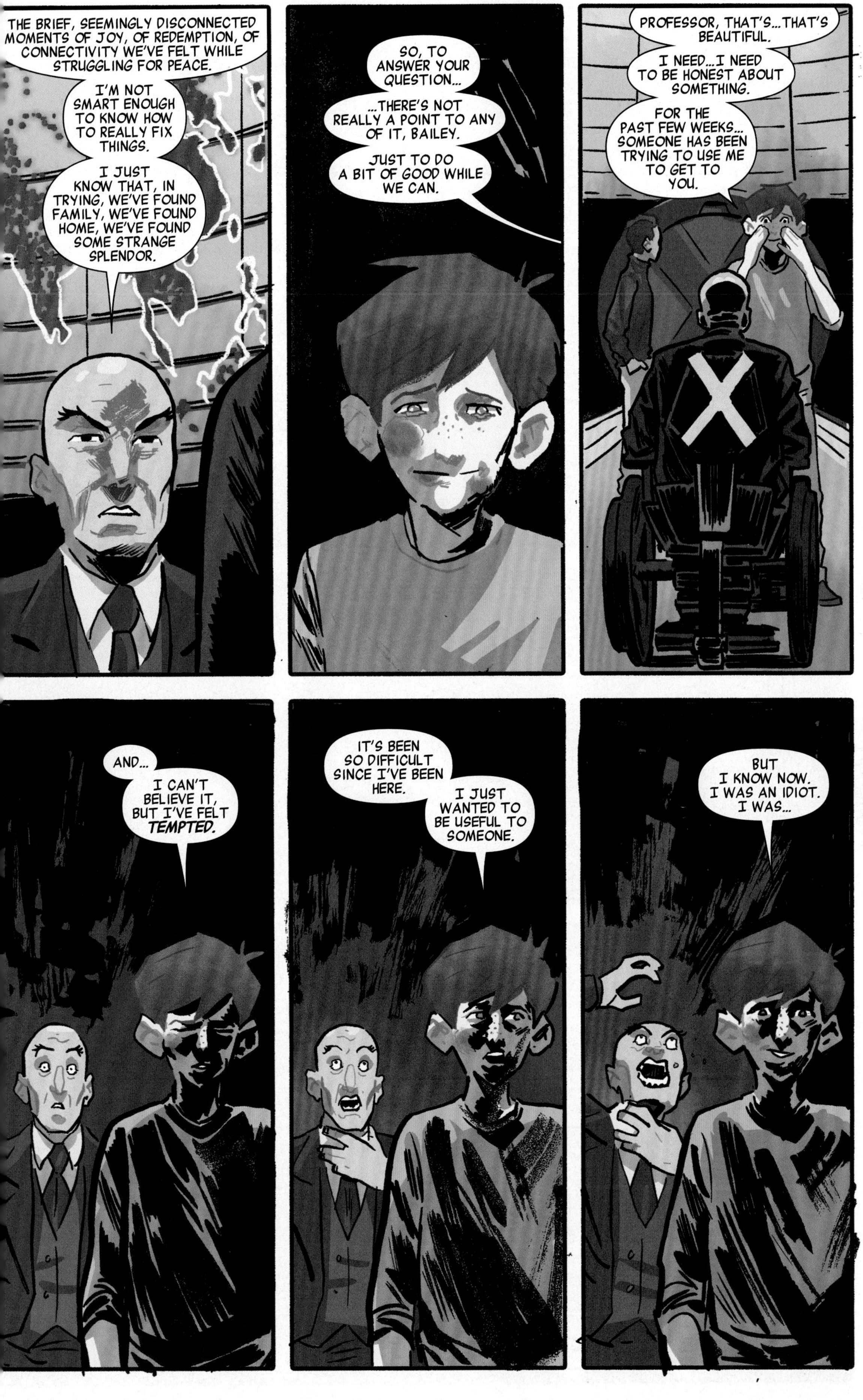
THE BRIEF, SEEMINGLY DISCONNECTED MOMENTS OF JOY, OF REDEMPTION, OF CONNECTIVITY WE'VE FELT WHILE STRUGGLING FOR PEACE.
I'M NOT SMART ENOUGH TO KNOW HOW TO REALLY FIX THINGS.
I JUST KNOW THAT, IN TRYING, WE'VE FOUND FAMILY, WE'VE FOUND HOME, WE'VE FOUND SOME STRANGE SPLENDOR.
SO, TO ANSWER YOUR QUESTION...
...THERE'S NOT REALLY A POINT TO ANY OF IT, BAILEY.
JUST TO DO A BIT OF GOOD WHILE WE CAN.
PROFESSOR, THAT'S...THAT'S BEAUTIFUL.
I NEED...I NEED TO BE HONEST ABOUT SOMETHING.
FOR THE PAST FEW WEEKS... SOMEONE HAS BEEN TRYING TO USE ME TO GET TO YOU.
AND...
I CAN'T BELIEVE IT, BUT I'VE FELT TEMPTED.
IT'S BEEN SO DIFFICULT SINCE I'VE BEEN HERE.
I JUST WANTED TO BE USEFUL TO SOMEONE.
BUT I KNOW NOW. I WAS AN IDIOT. I WAS...

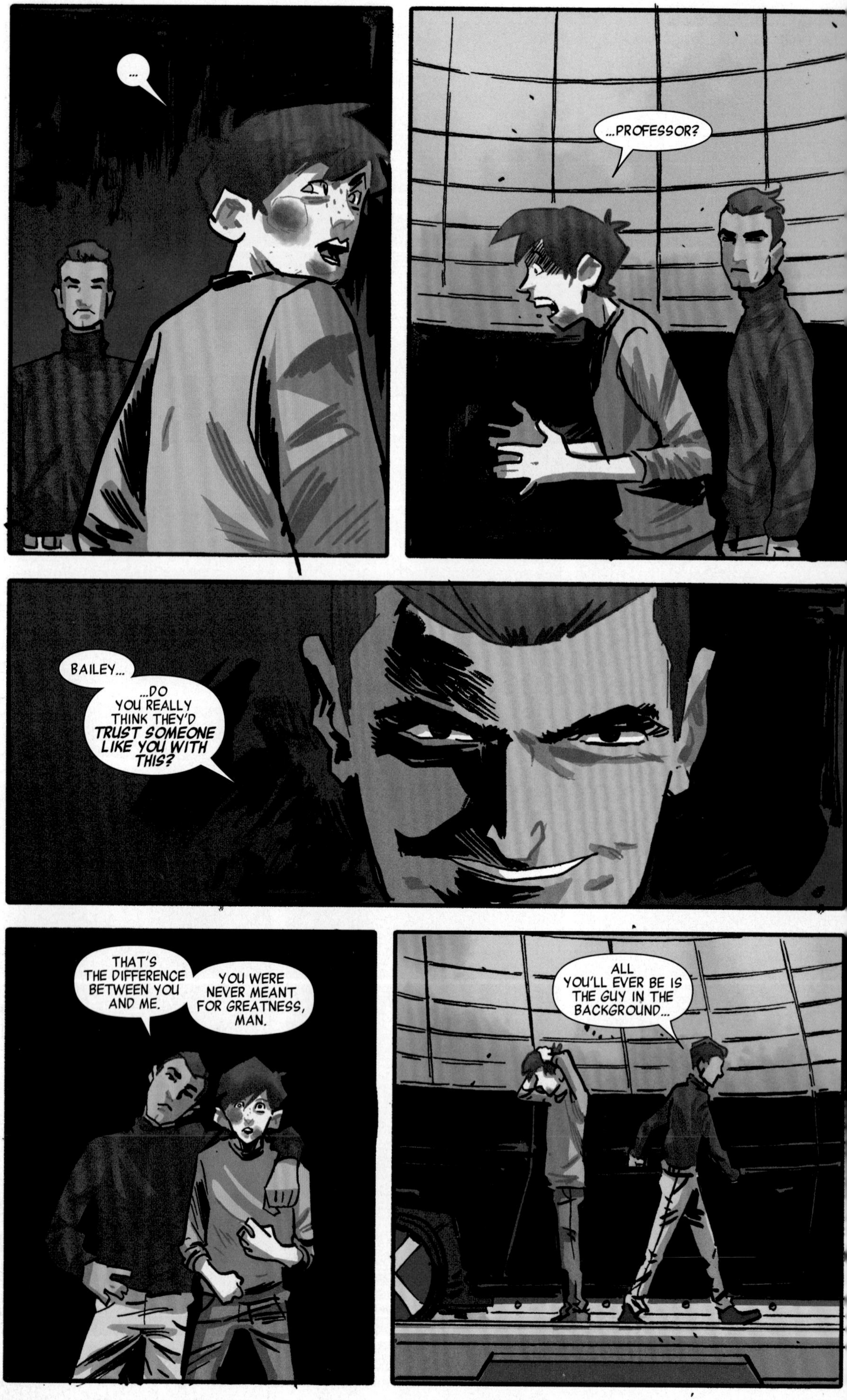
...
...PROFESSOR?
BAILEY...
...DO YOU REALLY THINK THEY'D *TRUST SOMEONE LIKE YOU WITH THIS?*
THAT'S THE DIFFERENCE BETWEEN YOU AND ME.
YOU WERE NEVER MEANT FOR GREATNESS, MAN.
ALL YOU'LL EVER BE IS THE GUY IN THE BACKGROUND...

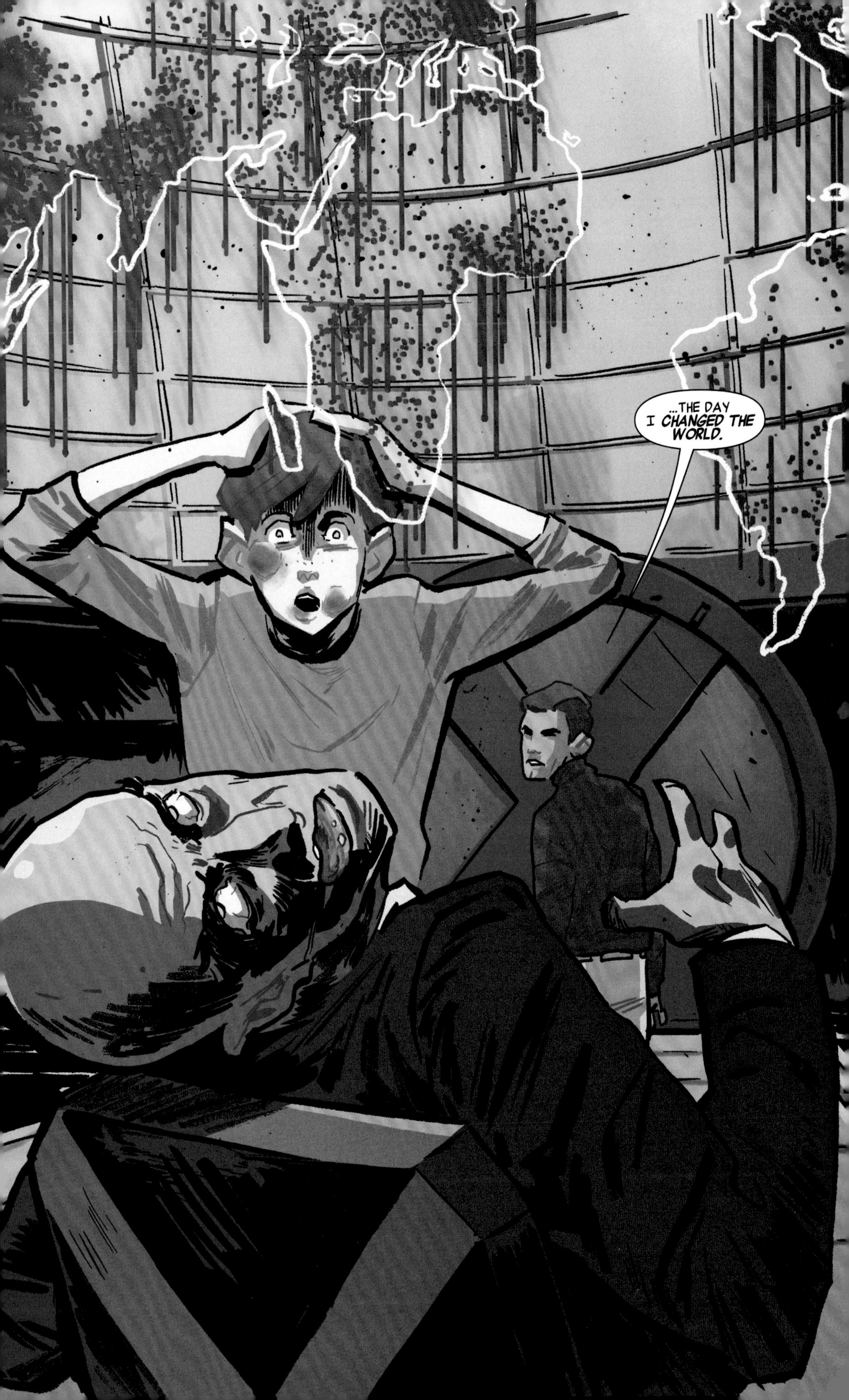
...THE DAY I CHANGED THE WORLD.

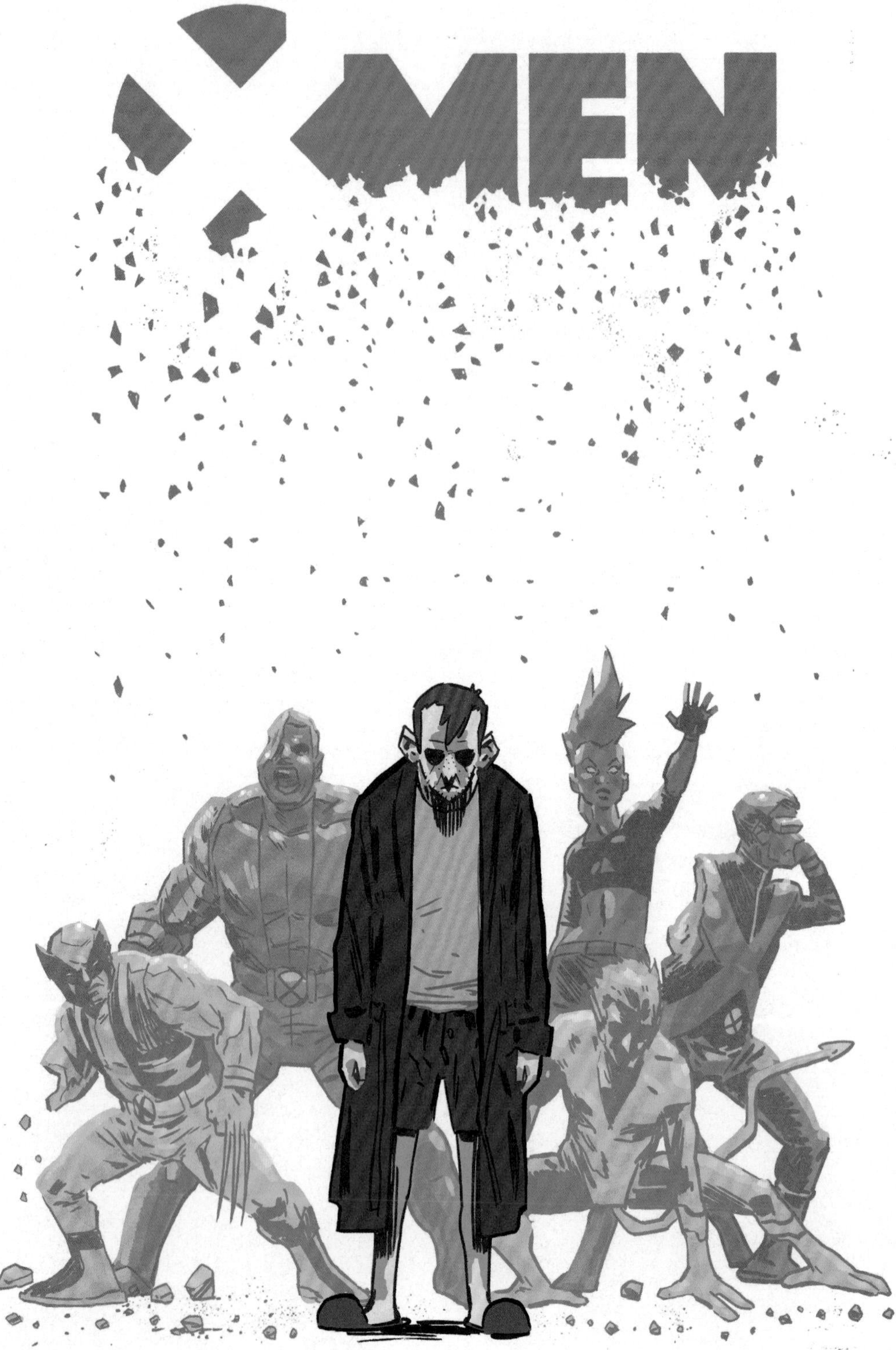
X MEN

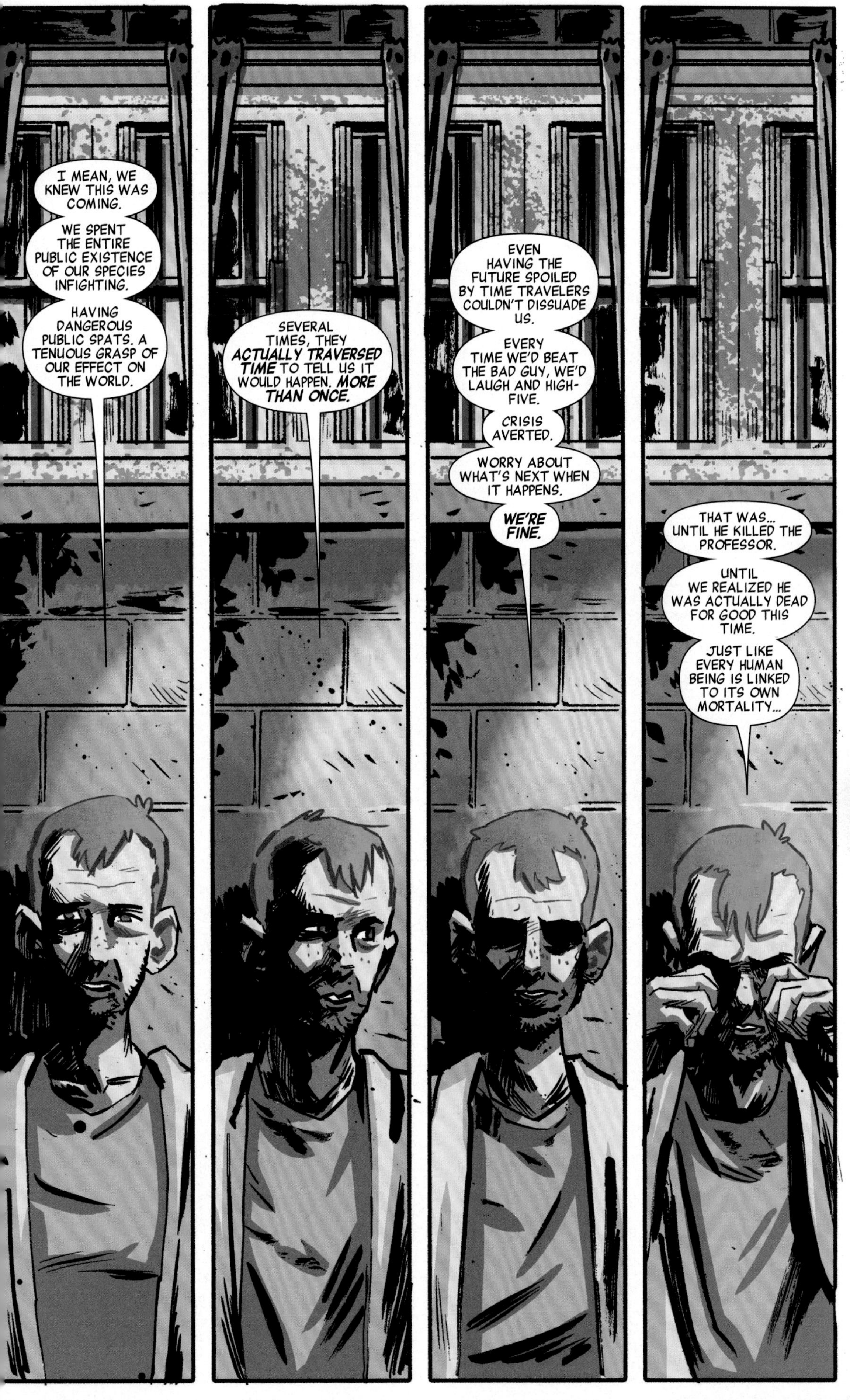
I MEAN, WE KNEW THIS WAS COMING.
WE SPENT THE ENTIRE PUBLIC EXISTENCE OF OUR SPECIES INFIGHTING.
HAVING DANGEROUS PUBLIC SPATS. A TENUOUS GRASP OF OUR EFFECT ON THE WORLD.
SEVERAL TIMES, THEY ACTUALLY TRAVERSED TIME TO TELL US IT WOULD HAPPEN. MORE THAN ONCE.
EVEN HAVING THE FUTURE SPOILED BY TIME TRAVELERS COULDN'T DISSUADE US.
EVERY TIME WE'D BEAT THE BAD GUY, WE'D LAUGH AND HIGH-FIVE.
CRISIS AVERTED.
WORRY ABOUT WHAT'S NEXT WHEN IT HAPPENS.
WE'RE FINE.
THAT WAS... UNTIL HE KILLED THE PROFESSOR.
UNTIL WE REALIZED HE WAS ACTUALLY DEAD FOR GOOD THIS TIME.
JUST LIKE EVERY HUMAN BEING IS LINKED TO ITS OWN MORTALITY...

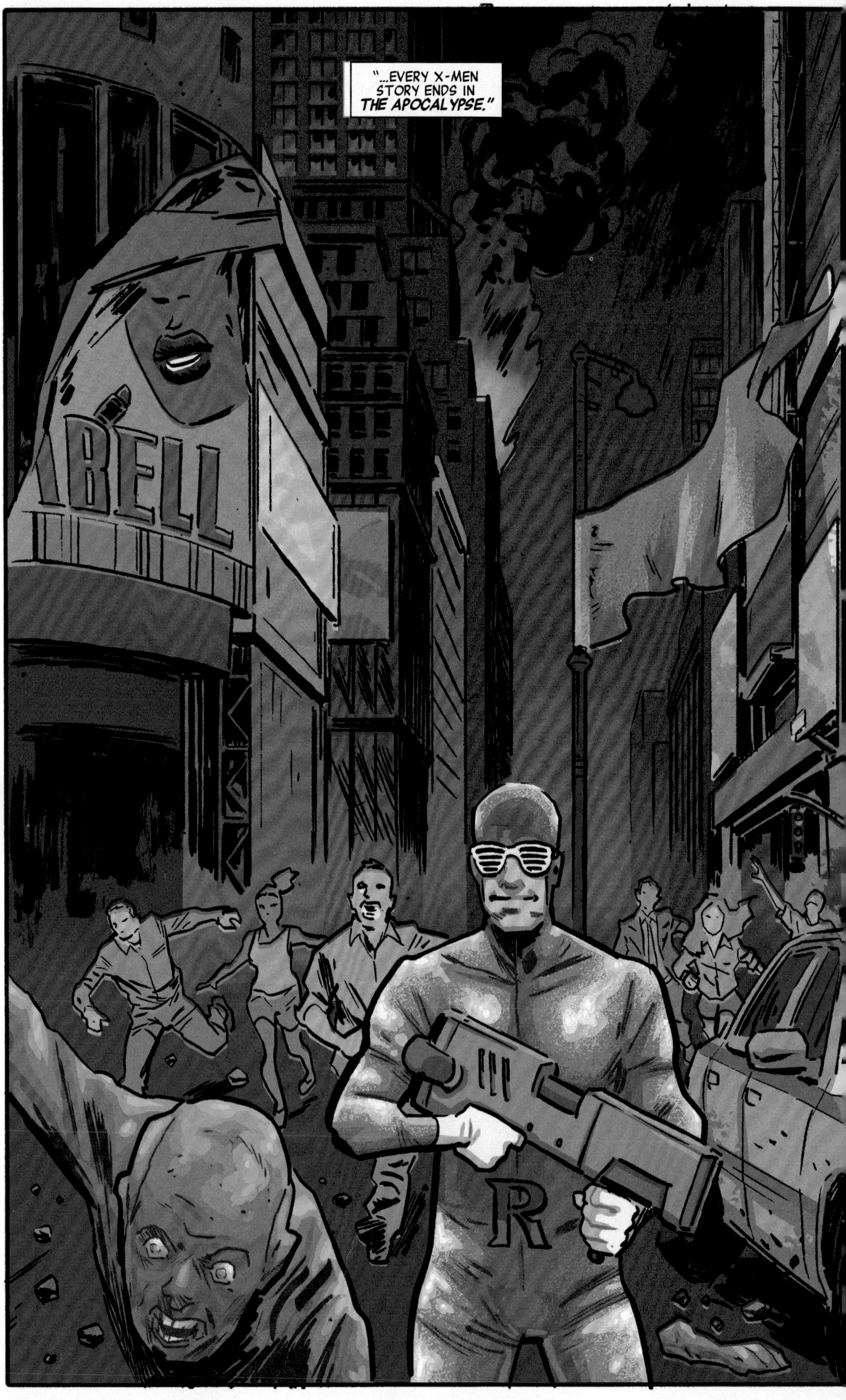
"...EVERY X-MEN STORY ENDS IN THE APOCALYPSE."
BELL
R

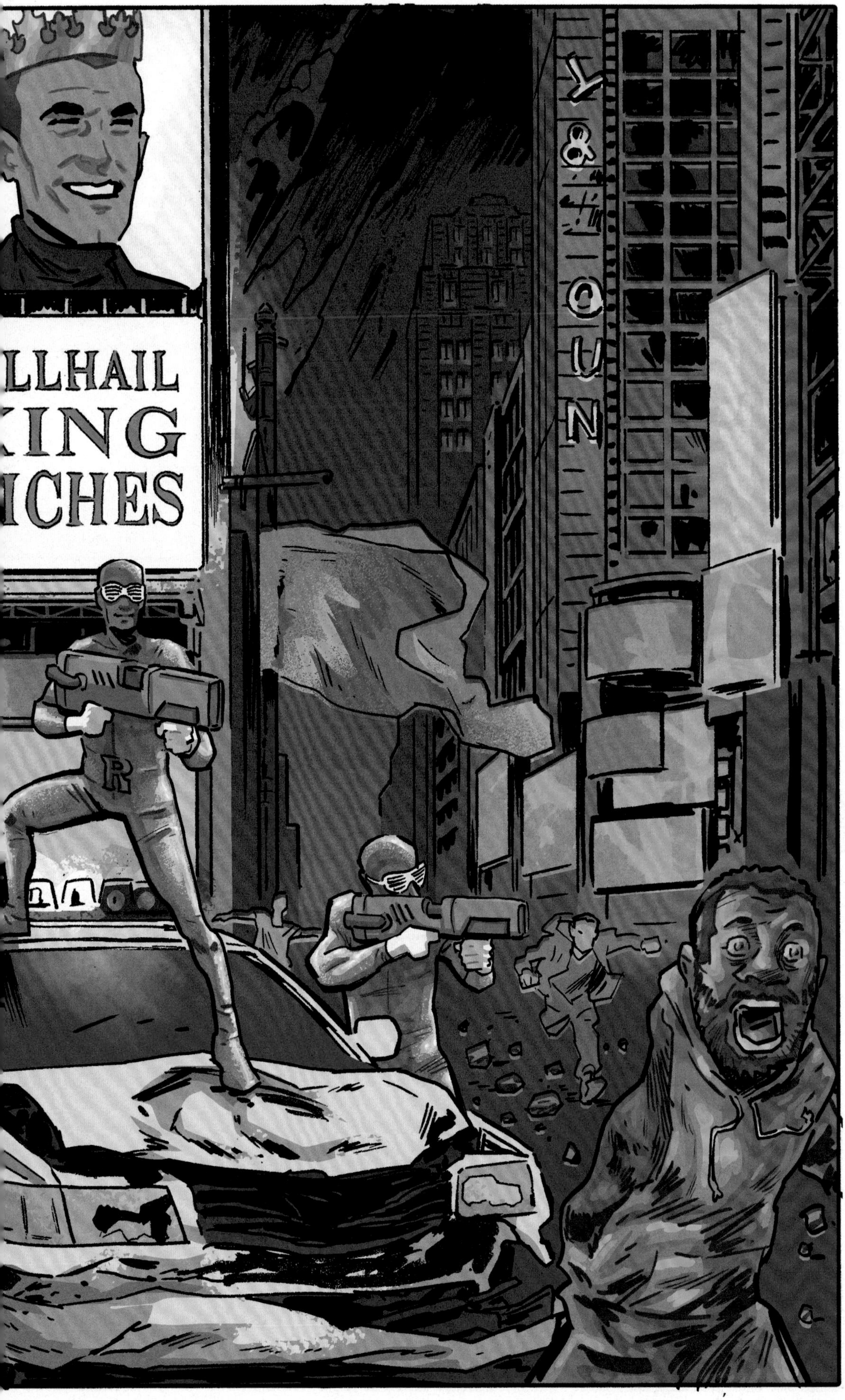
LLHAIL
KING
ICHES

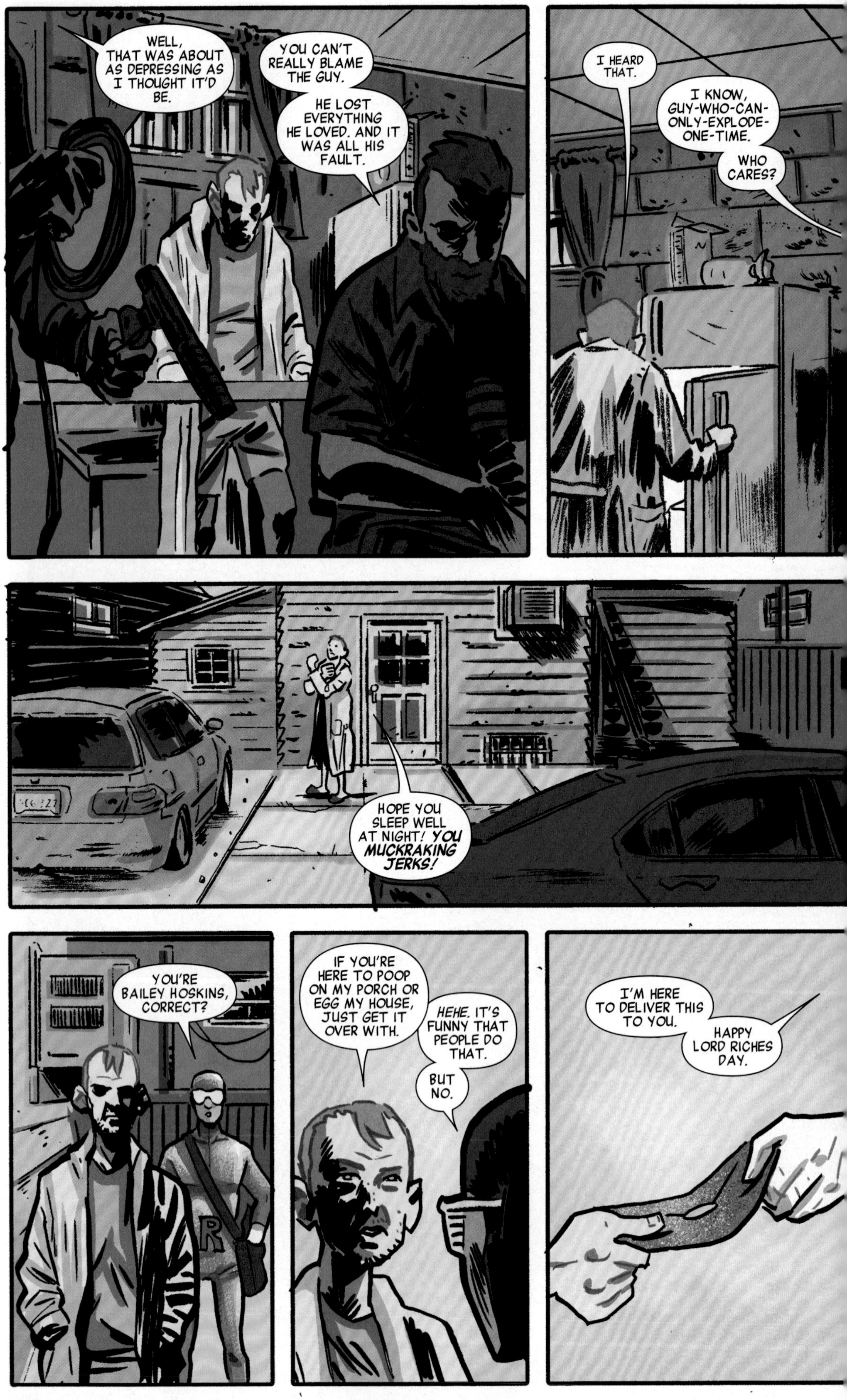
WELL, THAT WAS ABOUT AS DEPRESSING AS I THOUGHT IT'D BE.
YOU CAN'T REALLY BLAME THE GUY.
HE LOST EVERYTHING HE LOVED. AND IT WAS ALL HIS FAULT.
I HEARD THAT.
I KNOW, GUY-WHO-CAN-ONLY-EXPLODE-ONE-TIME.
WHO CARES?
HOPE YOU SLEEP WELL AT NIGHT! *YOU MUCKRAKING JERKS!*
YOU'RE BAILEY HOSKINS, CORRECT?
IF YOU'RE HERE TO POOP ON MY PORCH OR EGG MY HOUSE, JUST GET IT OVER WITH.
HEHE. IT'S FUNNY THAT PEOPLE DO THAT.
BUT NO.
I'M HERE TO DELIVER THIS TO YOU.
HAPPY LORD RICHES DAY.

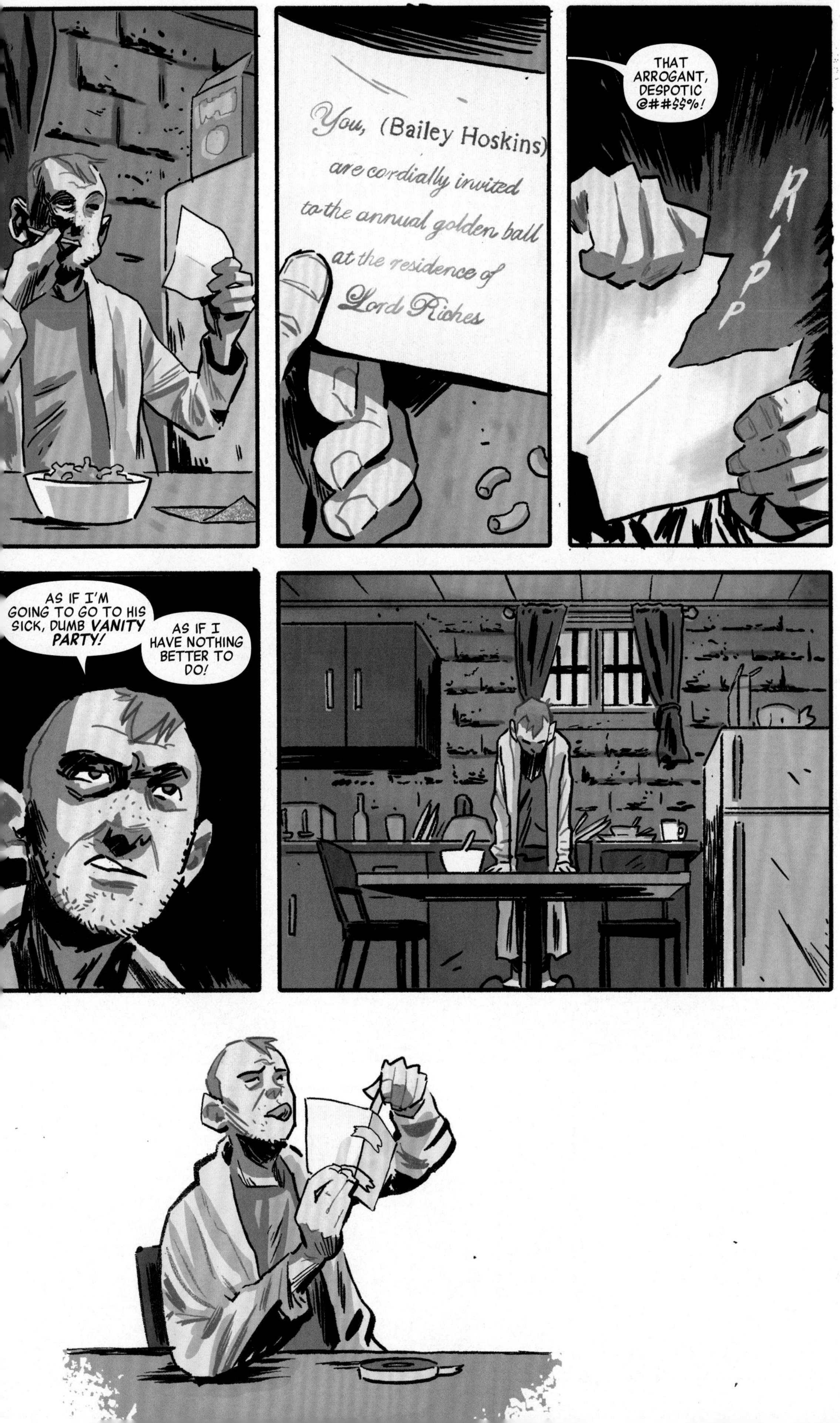

You, (Bailey Hoskins)
are cordially invited
to the annual golden ball
at the residence of
Lord Riches
THAT ARROGANT, DESPOTIC @##$$%!
RIPP
AS IF I'M GOING TO GO TO HIS SICK, DUMB VANITY PARTY!
AS IF I HAVE NOTHING BETTER TO DO!

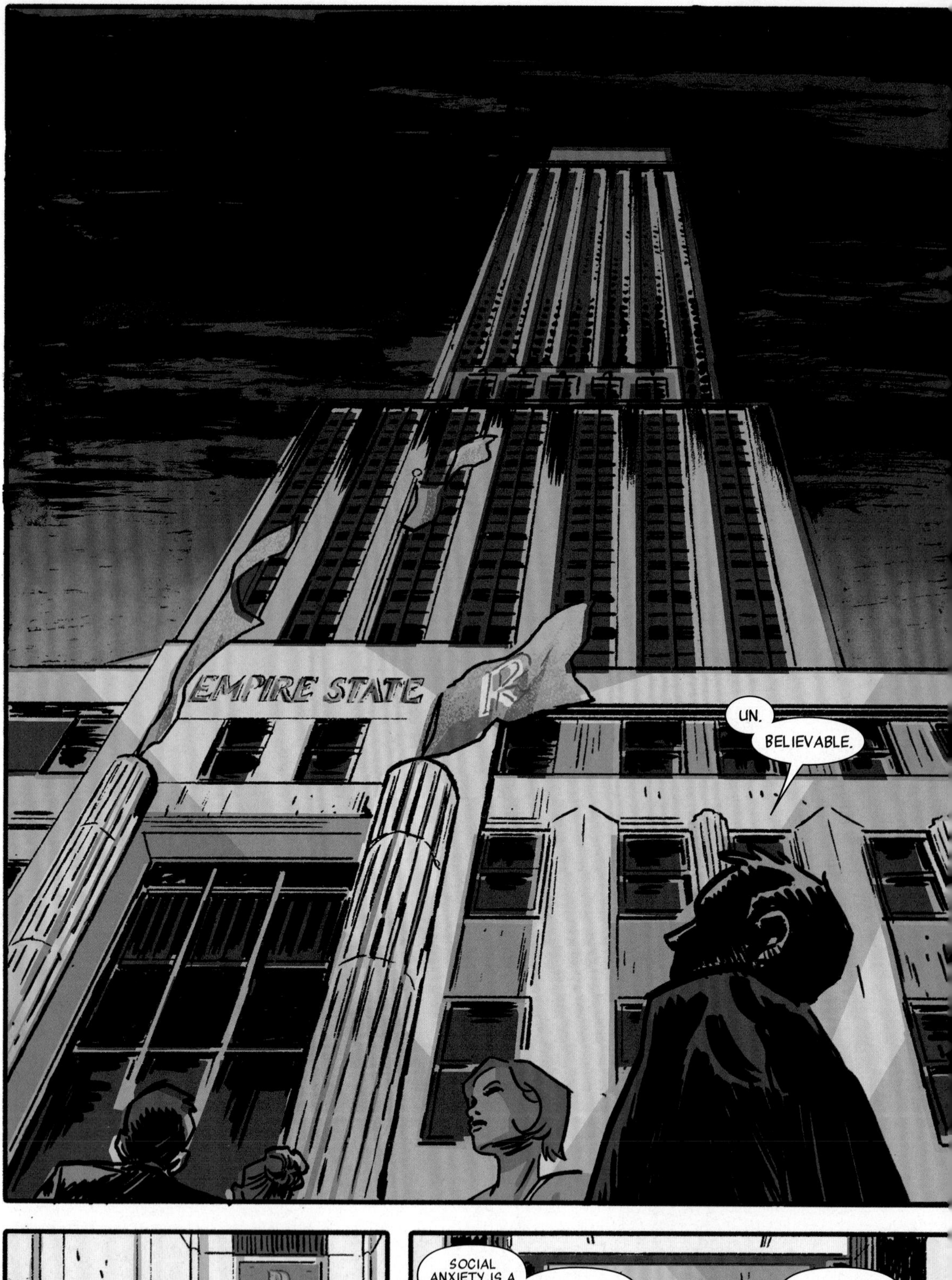
EMPIRE STATE
UN.
BELIEVABLE.

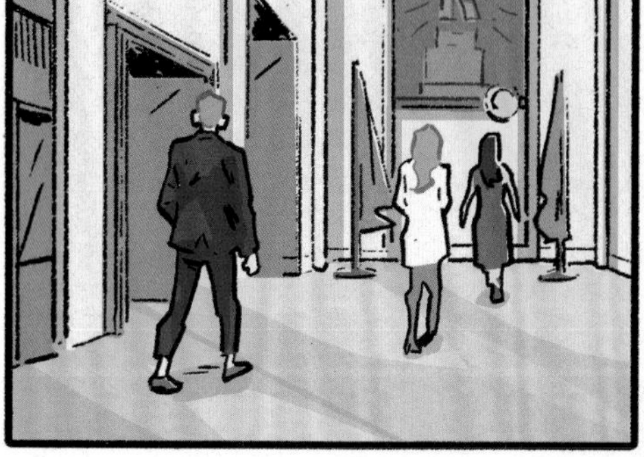

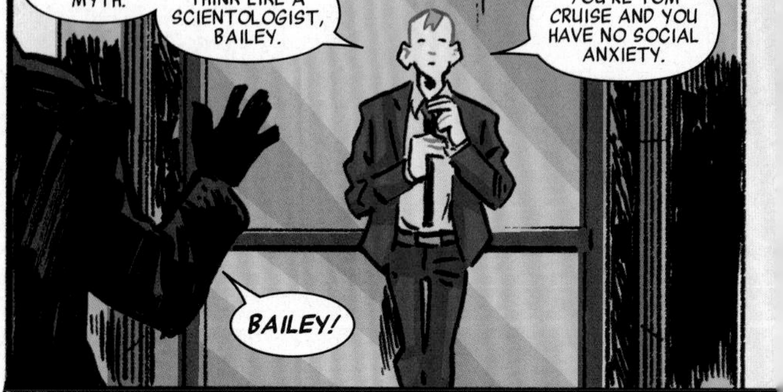
SOCIAL ANXIETY IS A MYTH.
THINK LIKE A SCIENTOLOGIST, BAILEY.
YOU'RE TOM CRUISE AND YOU HAVE NO SOCIAL ANXIETY.
BAILEY!

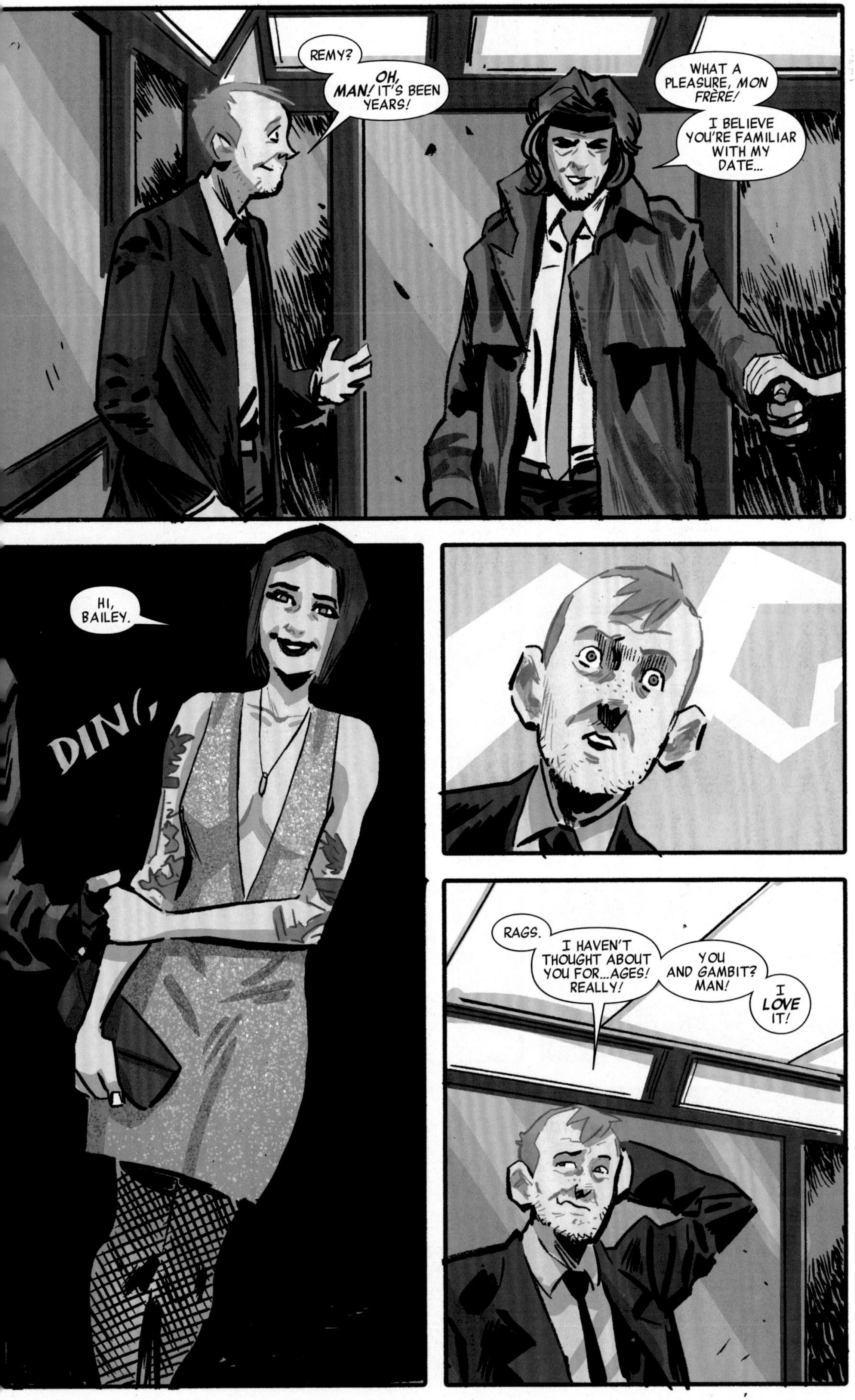
REMY?
OH, MAN! IT'S BEEN YEARS!
WHAT A PLEASURE, MON FRÈRE!
I BELIEVE YOU'RE FAMILIAR WITH MY DATE...
HI, BAILEY.
DIN(
RAGS.
I HAVEN'T THOUGHT ABOUT YOU FOR...AGES! REALLY!
YOU AND GAMBIT? MAN!
I LOVE IT!

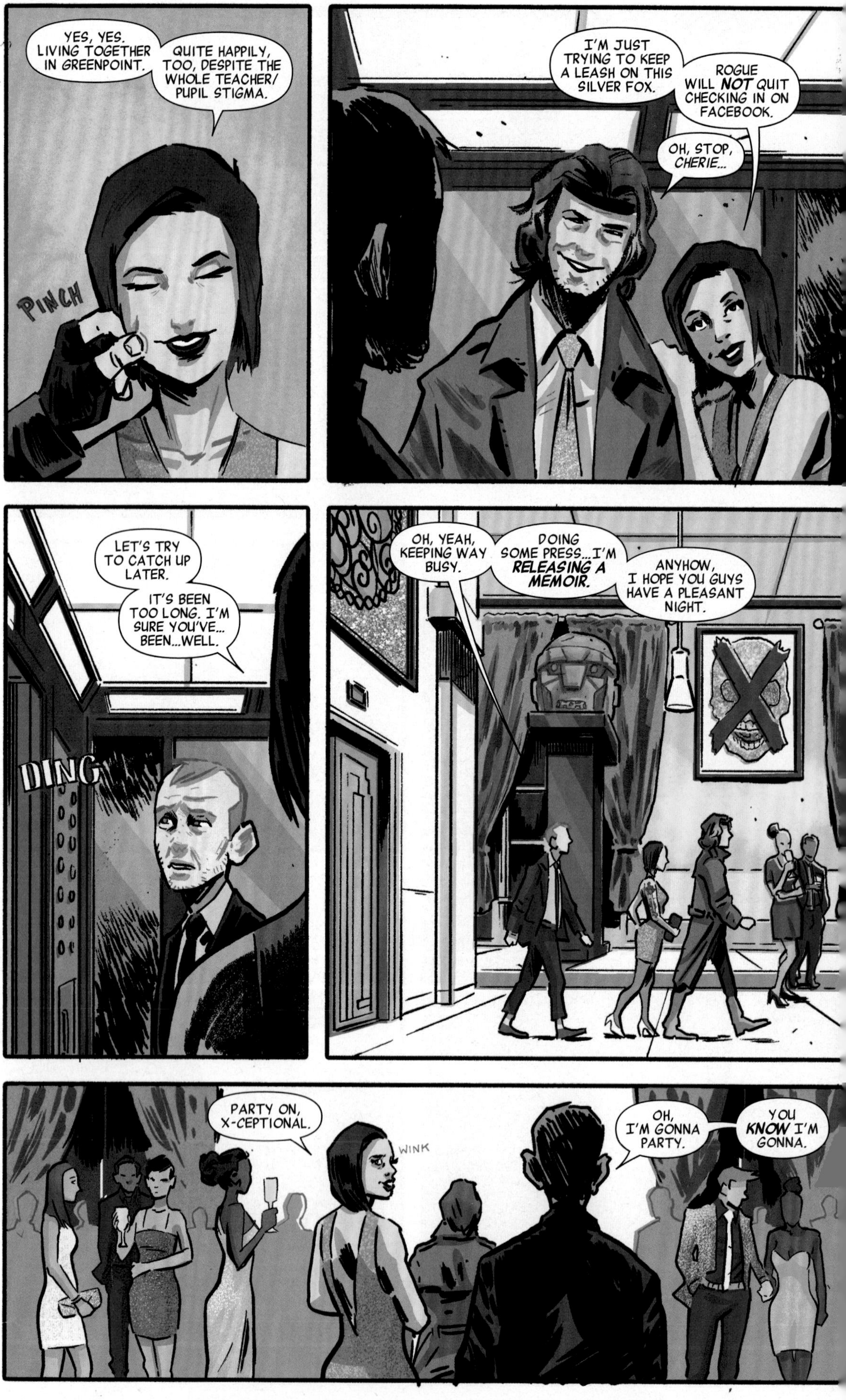
YES, YES. LIVING TOGETHER IN GREENPOINT.
QUITE HAPPILY, TOO, DESPITE THE WHOLE TEACHER/ PUPIL STIGMA.
PINCH
I'M JUST TRYING TO KEEP A LEASH ON THIS SILVER FOX.
ROGUE WILL NOT QUIT CHECKING IN ON FACEBOOK.
OH, STOP, CHERIE...
LET'S TRY TO CATCH UP LATER.
IT'S BEEN TOO LONG. I'M SURE YOU'VE... BEEN...WELL.
DING
OH, YEAH, KEEPING WAY BUSY.
DOING SOME PRESS...I'M RELEASING A MEMOIR.
ANYHOW, I HOPE YOU GUYS HAVE A PLEASANT NIGHT.
PARTY ON, X-CEPTIONAL.
WINK
OH, I'M GONNA PARTY.
YOU KNOW I'M GONNA.

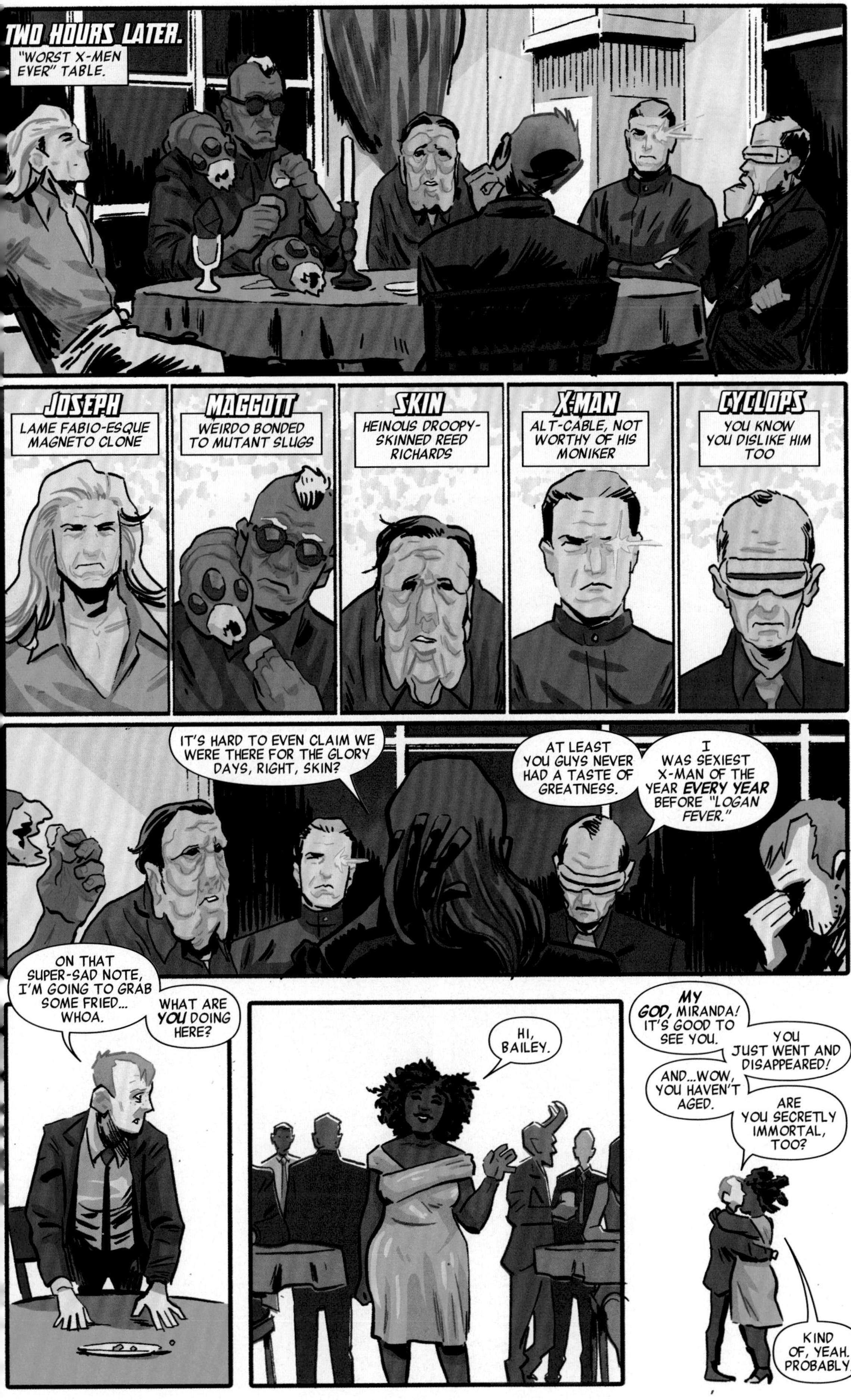
TWO HOURS LATER.
"WORST X-MEN EVER" TABLE.
JOSEPH
LAME FABIO-ESQUE MAGNETO CLONE
MAGGOTT
WEIRDO BONDED TO MUTANT SLUGS
SKIN
HEINOUS DROOPY-SKINNED REED RICHARDS
X-MAN
ALT-CABLE, NOT WORTHY OF HIS MONIKER
CYCLOPS
YOU KNOW YOU DISLIKE HIM TOO
IT'S HARD TO EVEN CLAIM WE WERE THERE FOR THE GLORY DAYS, RIGHT, SKIN?
AT LEAST YOU GUYS NEVER HAD A TASTE OF GREATNESS.
I WAS SEXIEST X-MAN OF THE YEAR EVERY YEAR BEFORE "LOGAN FEVER."
ON THAT SUPER-SAD NOTE, I'M GOING TO GRAB SOME FRIED... WHOA.
WHAT ARE YOU DOING HERE?
HI, BAILEY.
MY GOD, MIRANDA! IT'S GOOD TO SEE YOU.
YOU JUST WENT AND DISAPPEARED!
AND...WOW, YOU HAVEN'T AGED.
ARE YOU SECRETLY IMMORTAL, TOO?
KIND OF, YEAH. PROBABLY.

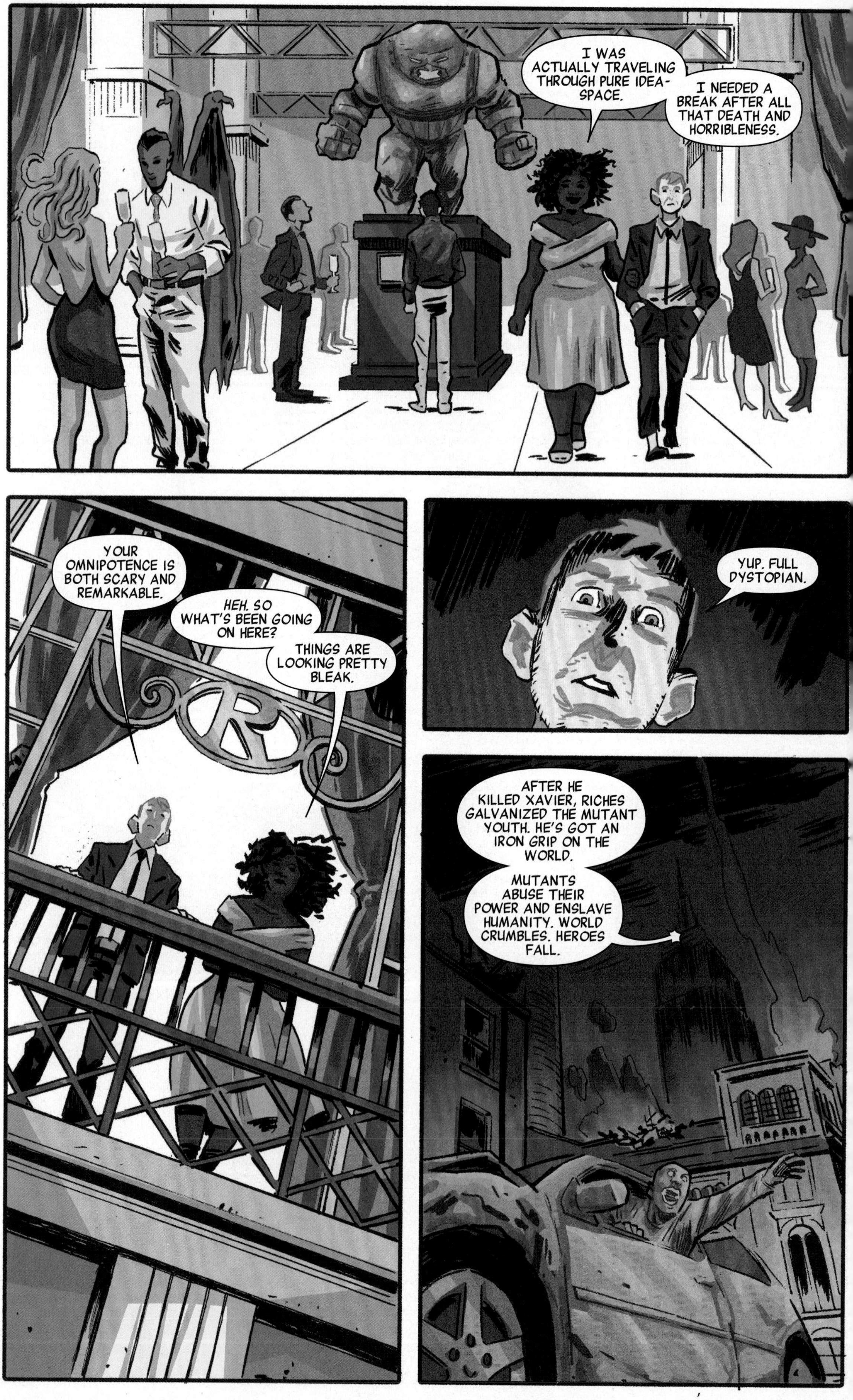
I WAS ACTUALLY TRAVELING THROUGH PURE IDEA-SPACE.
I NEEDED A BREAK AFTER ALL THAT DEATH AND HORRIBLENESS.
YOUR OMNIPOTENCE IS BOTH SCARY AND REMARKABLE.
HEH. SO WHAT'S BEEN GOING ON HERE?
THINGS ARE LOOKING PRETTY BLEAK.
YUP. FULL DYSTOPIAN.
AFTER HE KILLED XAVIER, RICHES GALVANIZED THE MUTANT YOUTH. HE'S GOT AN IRON GRIP ON THE WORLD.
MUTANTS ABUSE THEIR POWER AND ENSLAVE HUMANITY. WORLD CRUMBLES. HEROES FALL.

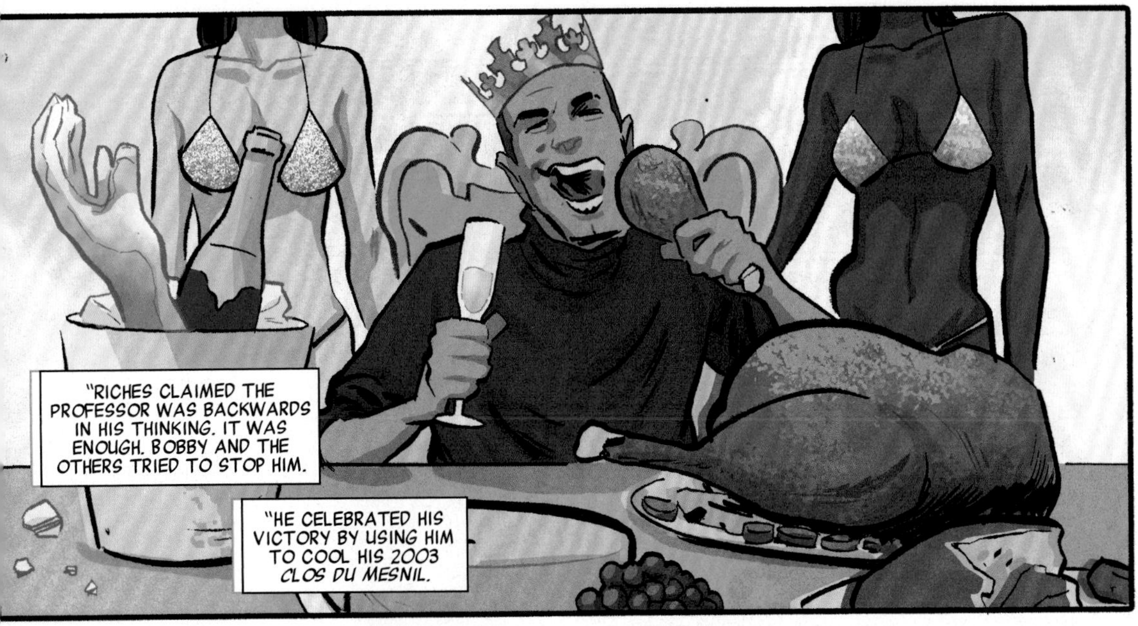
"RICHES CLAIMED THE PROFESSOR WAS BACKWARDS IN HIS THINKING. IT WAS ENOUGH. BOBBY AND THE OTHERS TRIED TO STOP HIM.
"HE CELEBRATED HIS VICTORY BY USING HIM TO COOL HIS 2003 *CLOS DU MESNIL*.

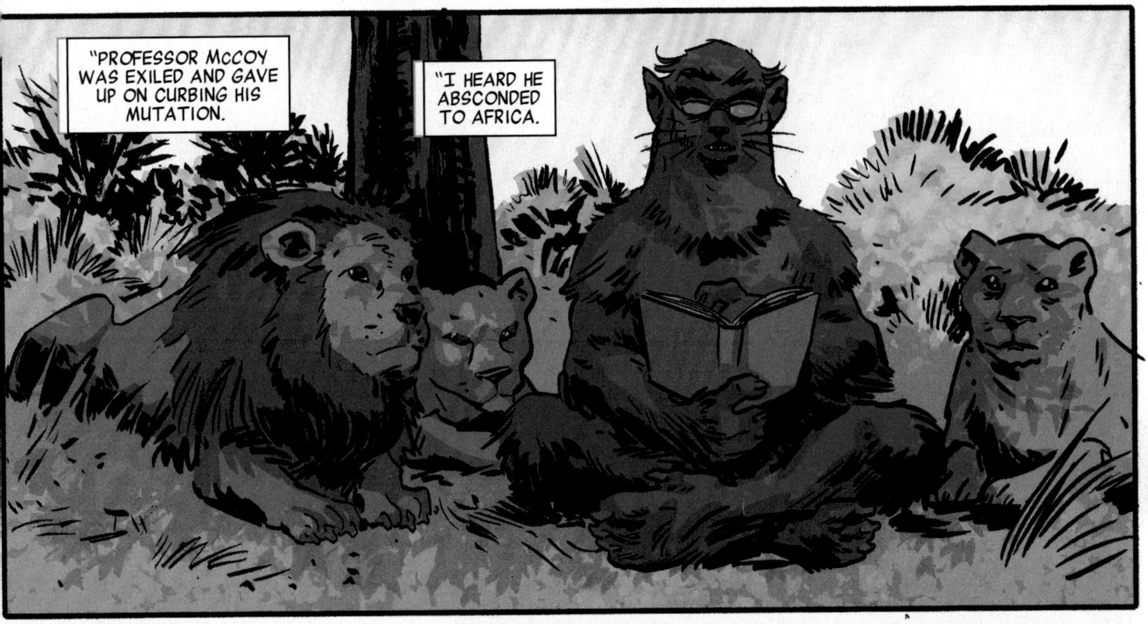
"PROFESSOR McCOY WAS EXILED AND GAVE UP ON CURBING HIS MUTATION.
"I HEARD HE ABSCONDED TO AFRICA.

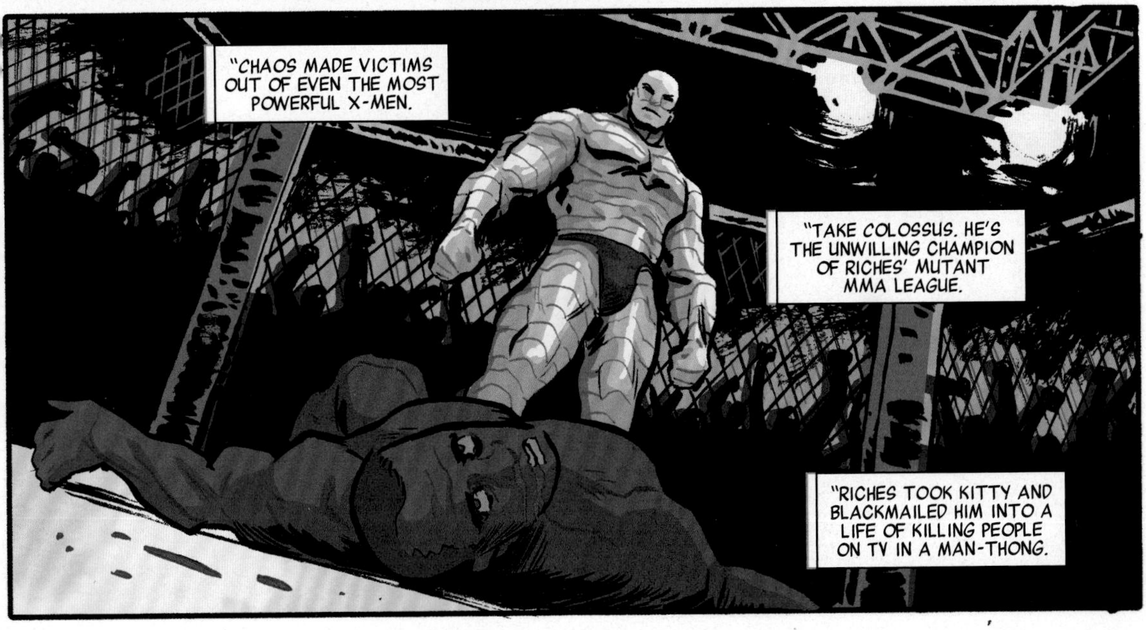
"CHAOS MADE VICTIMS OUT OF EVEN THE MOST POWERFUL X-MEN.
"TAKE COLOSSUS. HE'S THE UNWILLING CHAMPION OF RICHES' MUTANT MMA LEAGUE.
"RICHES TOOK KITTY AND BLACKMAILED HIM INTO A LIFE OF KILLING PEOPLE ON TV IN A MAN-THONG.

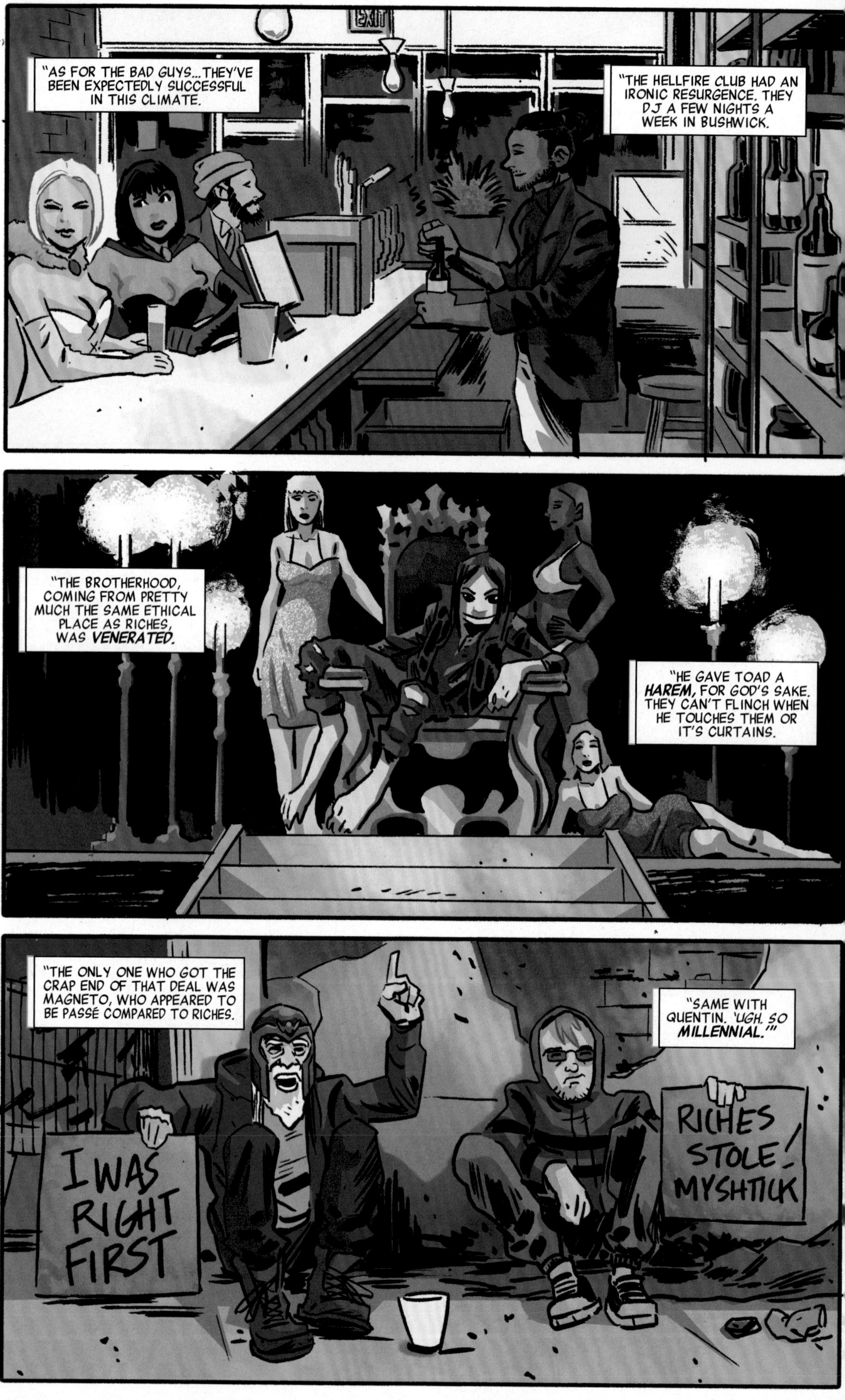
"AS FOR THE BAD GUYS... THEY'VE BEEN EXPECTEDLY SUCCESSFUL IN THIS CLIMATE.
"THE HELLFIRE CLUB HAD AN IRONIC RESURGENCE. THEY DJ A FEW NIGHTS A WEEK IN BUSHWICK.
EXIT
TSS
"THE BROTHERHOOD, COMING FROM PRETTY MUCH THE SAME ETHICAL PLACE AS RICHES, WAS **VENERATED.**
"HE GAVE TOAD A **HAREM,** FOR GOD'S SAKE. THEY CAN'T FLINCH WHEN HE TOUCHES THEM OR IT'S CURTAINS.
"THE ONLY ONE WHO GOT THE CRAP END OF THAT DEAL WAS MAGNETO, WHO APPEARED TO BE PASSÉ COMPARED TO RICHES.
"SAME WITH QUENTIN. *'UGH. SO* ***MILLENNIAL.'"***
I WAS RIGHT FIRST
RICHES STOLE MY SHTICK!

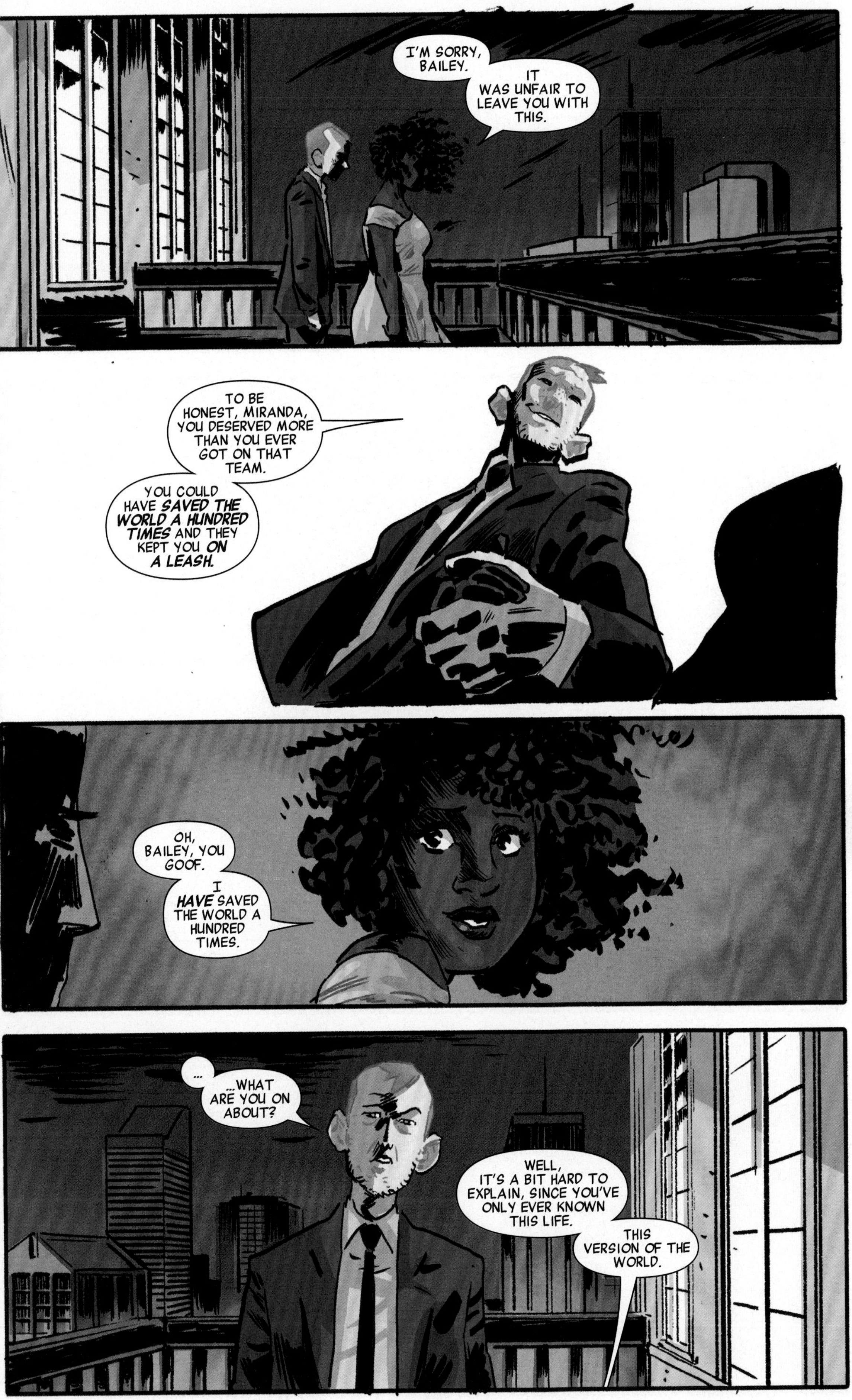
I'M SORRY, BAILEY.
IT WAS UNFAIR TO LEAVE YOU WITH THIS.
TO BE HONEST, MIRANDA, YOU DESERVED MORE THAN YOU EVER GOT ON THAT TEAM.
YOU COULD HAVE SAVED THE WORLD A HUNDRED TIMES AND THEY KEPT YOU ON A LEASH.
OH, BAILEY, YOU GOOF.
I HAVE SAVED THE WORLD A HUNDRED TIMES.
...
...WHAT ARE YOU ON ABOUT?
WELL, IT'S A BIT HARD TO EXPLAIN, SINCE YOU'VE ONLY EVER KNOWN THIS LIFE.
THIS VERSION OF THE WORLD.

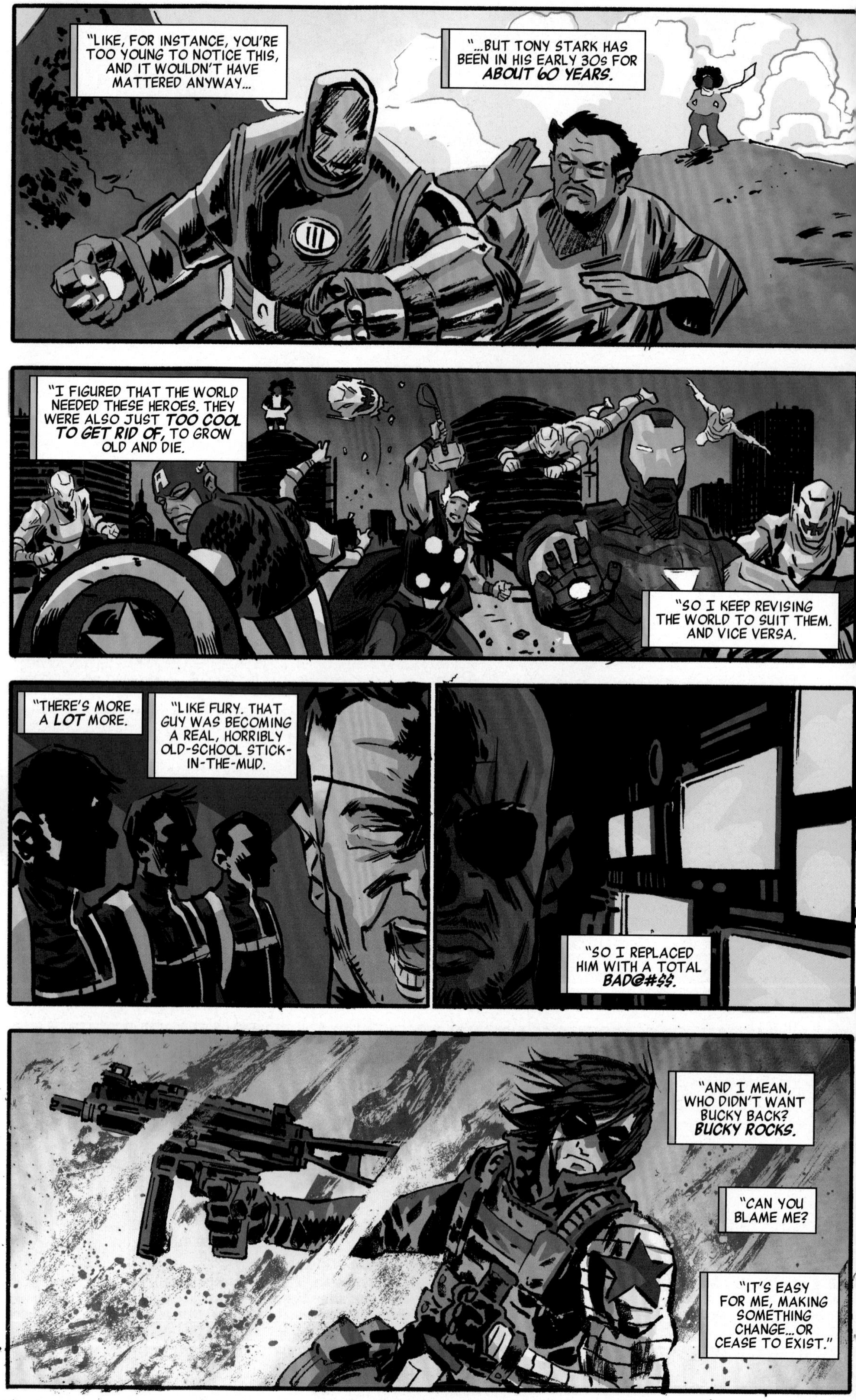
"LIKE, FOR INSTANCE, YOU'RE TOO YOUNG TO NOTICE THIS, AND IT WOULDN'T HAVE MATTERED ANYWAY...
"...BUT TONY STARK HAS BEEN IN HIS EARLY 30s FOR ABOUT 60 YEARS.
"I FIGURED THAT THE WORLD NEEDED THESE HEROES. THEY WERE ALSO JUST TOO COOL TO GET RID OF, TO GROW OLD AND DIE.
"SO I KEEP REVISING THE WORLD TO SUIT THEM. AND VICE VERSA.
"THERE'S MORE. A LOT MORE.
"LIKE FURY. THAT GUY WAS BECOMING A REAL, HORRIBLY OLD-SCHOOL STICK-IN-THE-MUD.
"SO I REPLACED HIM WITH A TOTAL BAD@#$$.
"AND I MEAN, WHO DIDN'T WANT BUCKY BACK? BUCKY ROCKS.
"CAN YOU BLAME ME?
"IT'S EASY FOR ME, MAKING SOMETHING CHANGE...OR CEASE TO EXIST."

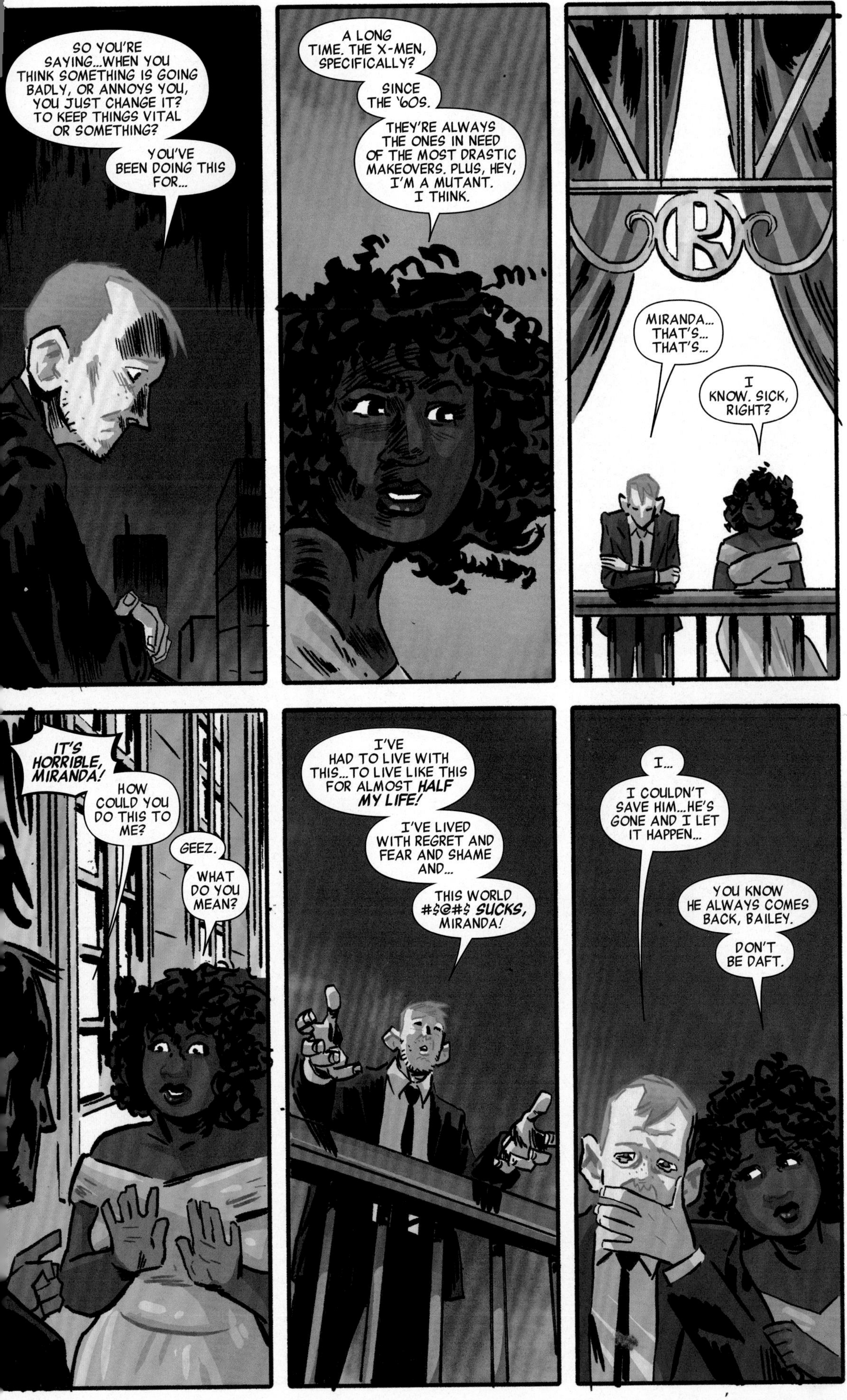
SO YOU'RE SAYING...WHEN YOU THINK SOMETHING IS GOING BADLY, OR ANNOYS YOU, YOU JUST CHANGE IT? TO KEEP THINGS VITAL OR SOMETHING?
YOU'VE BEEN DOING THIS FOR...
A LONG TIME. THE X-MEN, SPECIFICALLY?
SINCE THE '60S.
THEY'RE ALWAYS THE ONES IN NEED OF THE MOST DRASTIC MAKEOVERS. PLUS, HEY, I'M A MUTANT. I THINK.
MIRANDA... THAT'S... THAT'S...
I KNOW. SICK, RIGHT?
IT'S HORRIBLE, MIRANDA!
HOW COULD YOU DO THIS TO ME?
GEEZ.
WHAT DO YOU MEAN?
I'VE HAD TO LIVE WITH THIS...TO LIVE LIKE THIS FOR ALMOST HALF MY LIFE!
I'VE LIVED WITH REGRET AND FEAR AND SHAME AND...
THIS WORLD #$@#$ SUCKS, MIRANDA!
I...
I COULDN'T SAVE HIM...HE'S GONE AND I LET IT HAPPEN...
YOU KNOW HE ALWAYS COMES BACK, BAILEY.
DON'T BE DAFT.

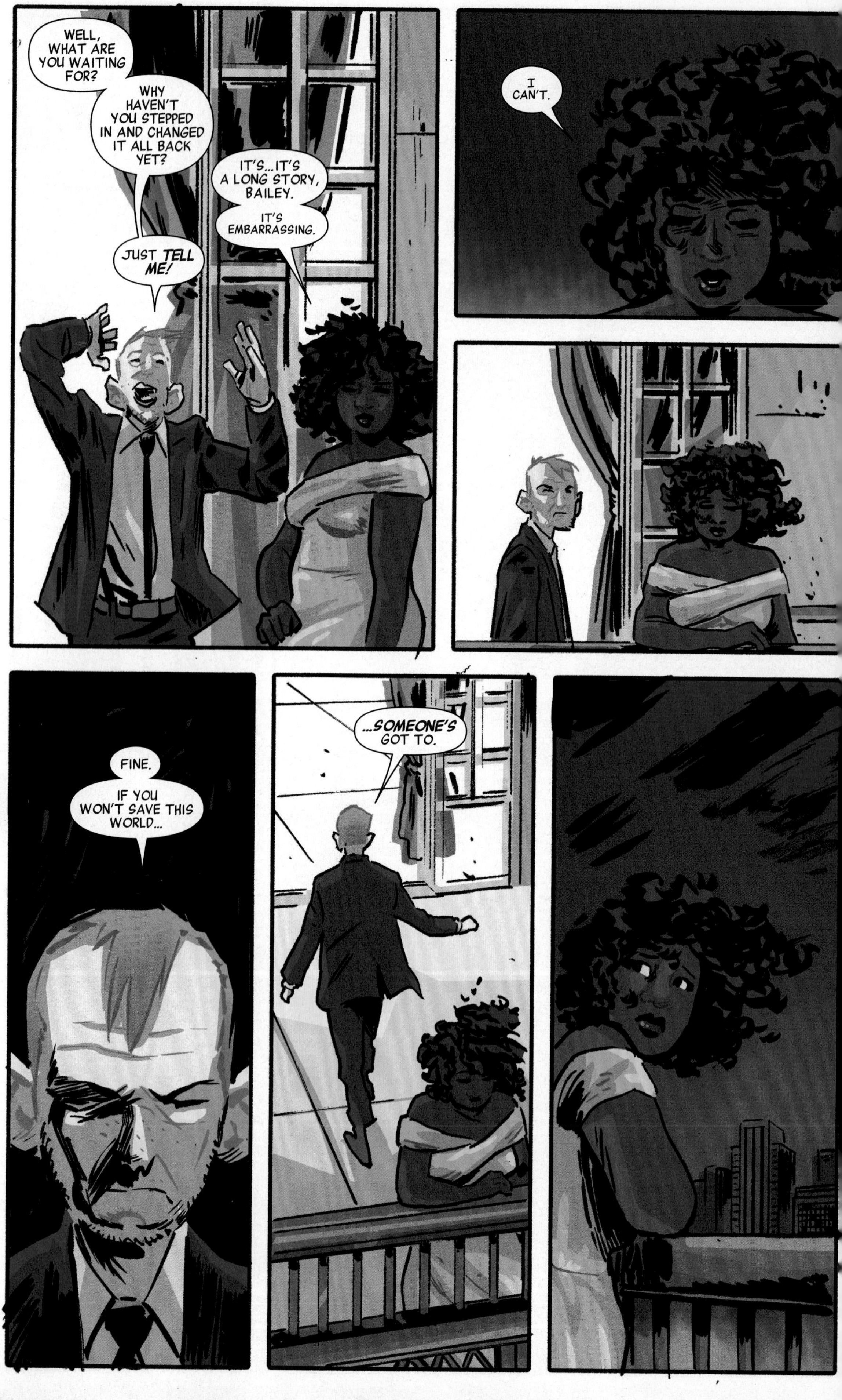
WELL, WHAT ARE YOU WAITING FOR?
WHY HAVEN'T YOU STEPPED IN AND CHANGED IT ALL BACK YET?
IT'S...IT'S A LONG STORY, BAILEY.
IT'S EMBARRASSING.
JUST TELL ME!
I CAN'T.
FINE.
IF YOU WON'T SAVE THIS WORLD...
...SOMEONE'S GOT TO.

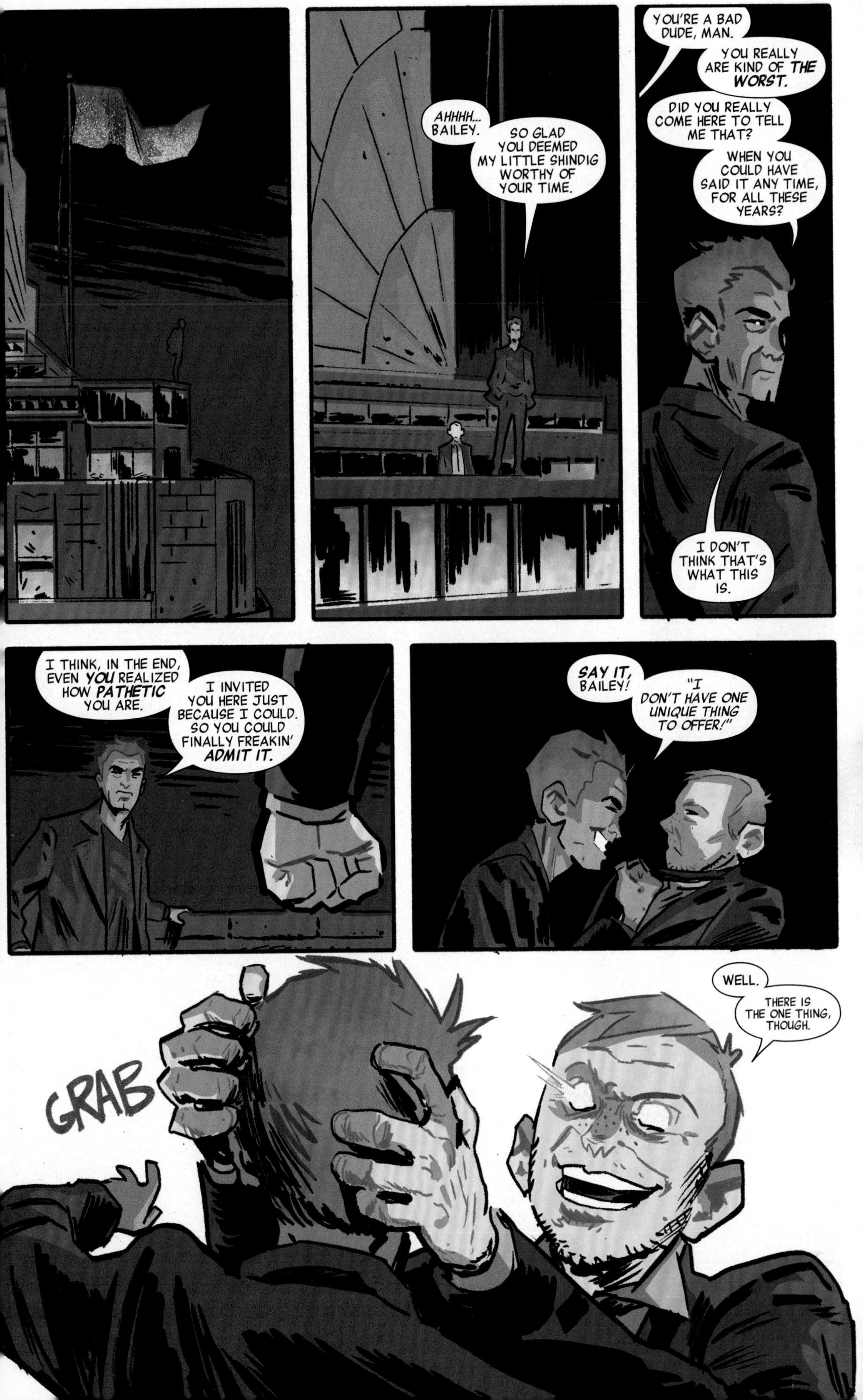
AHHHH... BAILEY.
SO GLAD YOU DEEMED MY LITTLE SHINDIG WORTHY OF YOUR TIME.
YOU'RE A BAD DUDE, MAN.
YOU REALLY ARE KIND OF THE WORST.
DID YOU REALLY COME HERE TO TELL ME THAT?
WHEN YOU COULD HAVE SAID IT ANY TIME, FOR ALL THESE YEARS?
I DON'T THINK THAT'S WHAT THIS IS.
I THINK, IN THE END, EVEN YOU REALIZED HOW PATHETIC YOU ARE.
I INVITED YOU HERE JUST BECAUSE I COULD. SO YOU COULD FINALLY FREAKIN' ADMIT IT.
SAY IT, BAILEY!
"I DON'T HAVE ONE UNIQUE THING TO OFFER!"
GRAB
WELL.
THERE IS THE ONE THING, THOUGH.

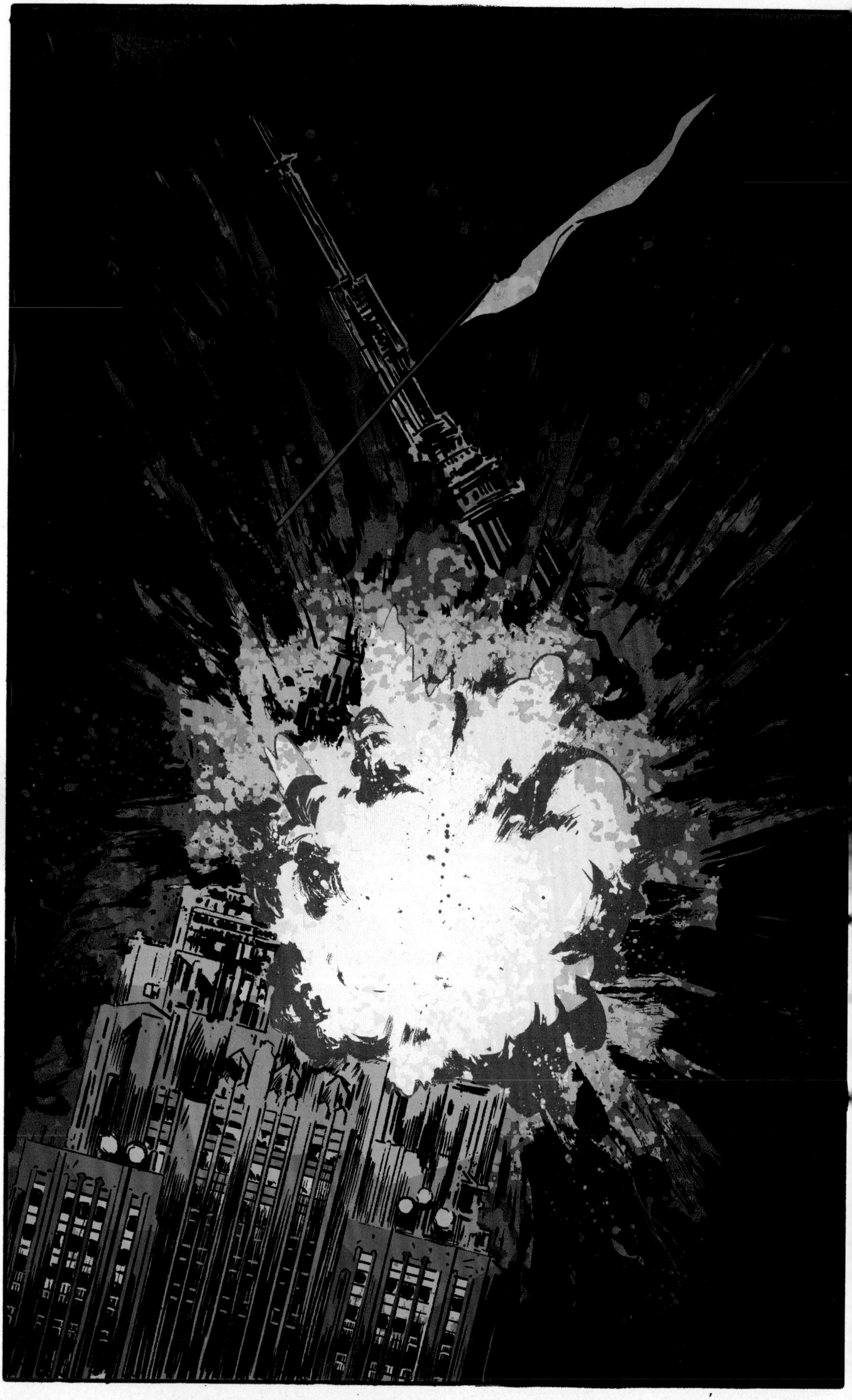

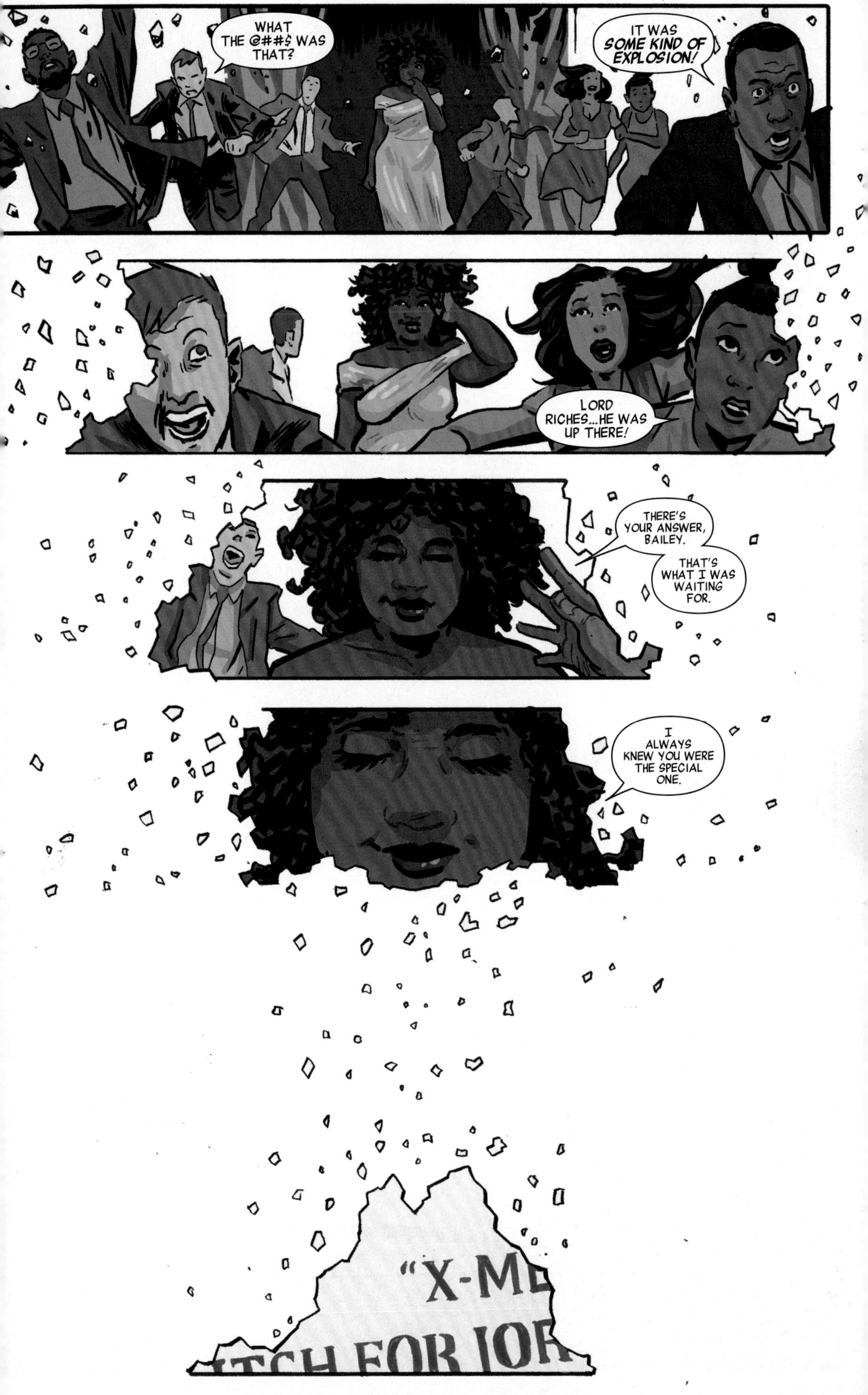
WHAT THE @#%$ WAS THAT?
IT WAS SOME KIND OF EXPLOSION!
LORD RICHES...HE WAS UP THERE!
THERE'S YOUR ANSWER, BAILEY.
THAT'S WHAT I WAS WAITING FOR.
I ALWAYS KNEW YOU WERE THE SPECIAL ONE.

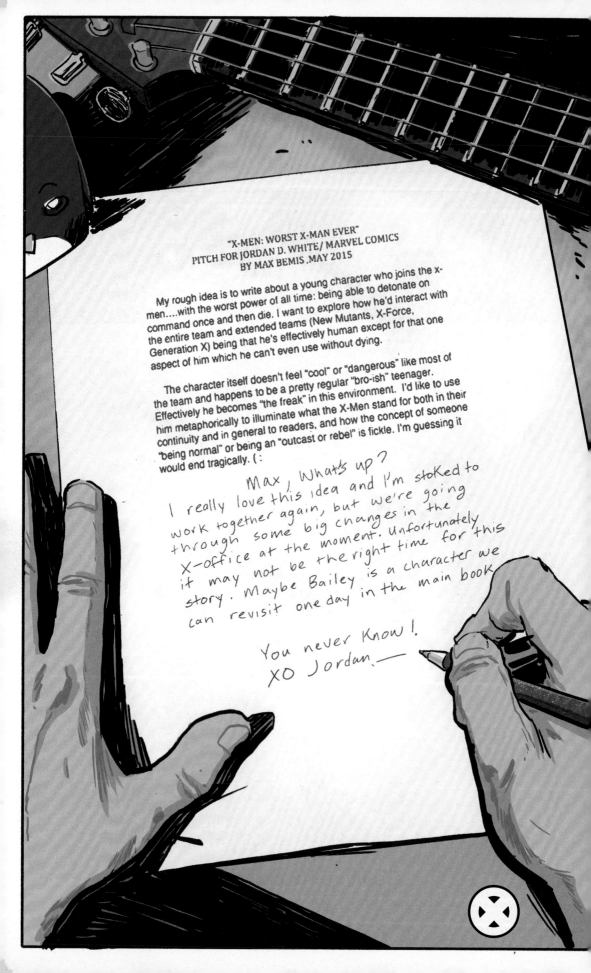

"X-MEN: WORST X-MAN EVER"
PITCH FOR JORDAN D. WHITE/ MARVEL COMICS
BY MAX BEMIS, MAY 2015

My rough idea is to write about a young character who joins the x-men....with the worst power of all time: being able to detonate on command once and then die. I want to explore how he'd interact with the entire team and extended teams (New Mutants, X-Force, Generation X) being that he's effectively human except for that one aspect of him which he can't even use without dying.

The character itself doesn't feel "cool" or "dangerous" like most of the team and happens to be a pretty regular "bro-ish" teenager. Effectively he becomes "the freak" in this environment. I'd like to use him metaphorically to illuminate what the X-Men stand for both in their continuity and in general to readers, and how the concept of someone "being normal" or being an "outcast or rebel" is fickle. I'm guessing it would end tragically. (:

Max, What's up?
I really love this idea and I'm stoked to
work together again, but we're going
through some big changes in the
X-office at the moment. Unfortunately
it may not be the right time for this
story. Maybe Bailey is a character we
can revisit one day in the main book.

You never know!.
XO Jordan.—

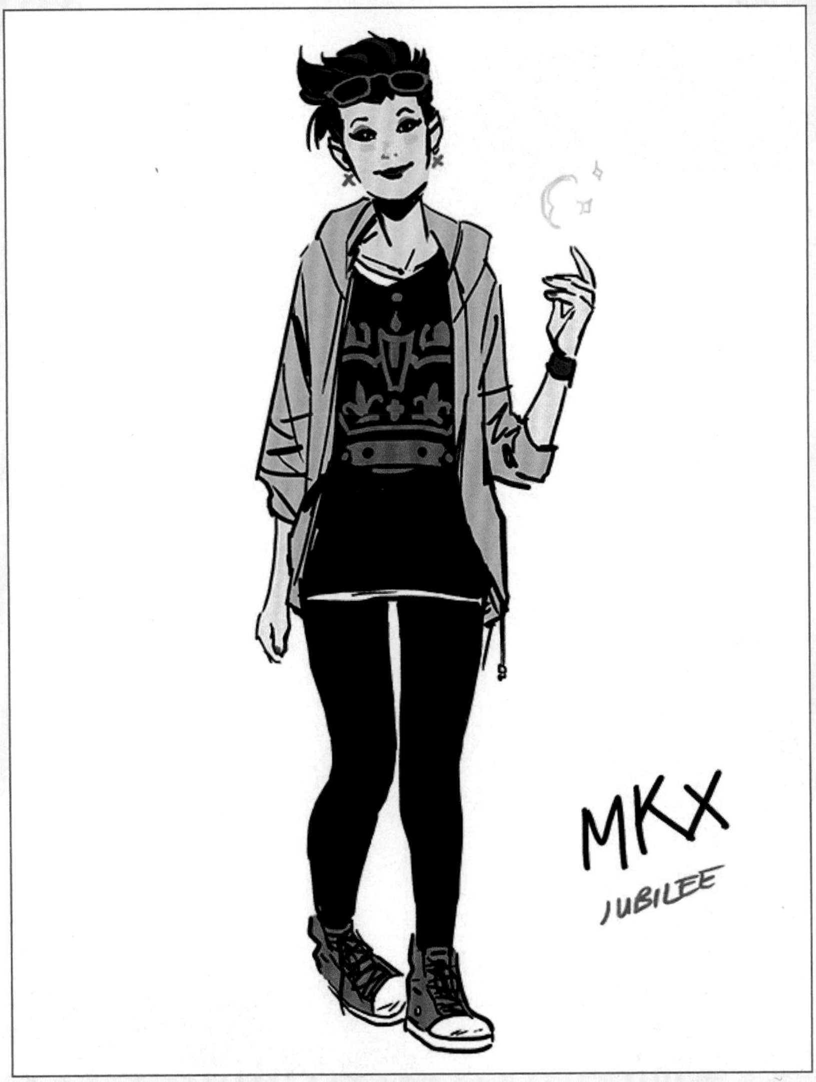
MKX
JUBILEE

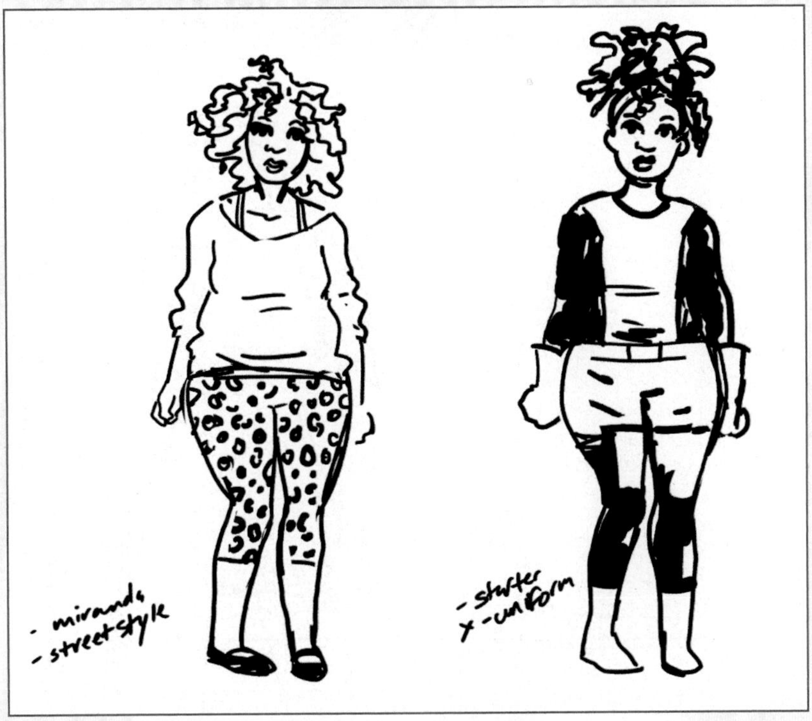
- miranda
- streetstyle
- starter
x-uniform

MICHAEL **WALSH**
CHARACTER SKETCHES

X-MEN
WORST X-MAN EVER #1 of 5
MAX BEMIS • MICHAEL WALSH • COLOR PERSON
MARVEL

X-MEN
WORST X-MAN EVER #1 of 5
MAX BEMIS • MICHAEL WALSH • COLOR PERSON

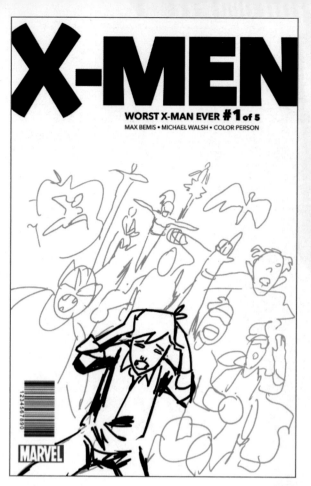

MICHAEL **WALSH**
#1-2 COVER SKETCHES

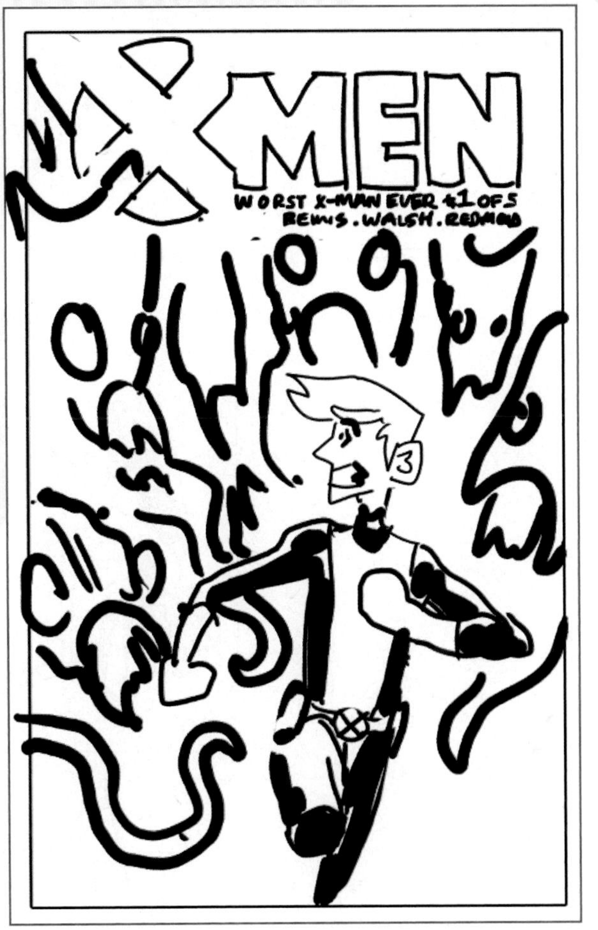
X-MEN
WORST X-MAN EVER #1 OF 5
BEWIS . WALSH . REDMOND

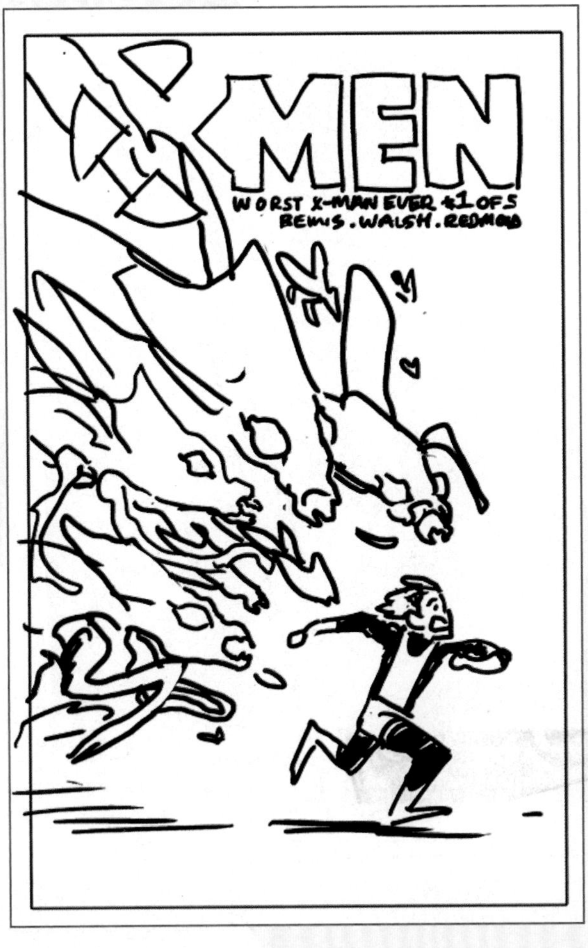
X-MEN
WORST X-MAN EVER #1 OF 5
BEWIS . WALSH . REDMOND

MICHAEL **WALSH**
#3 COVER SKETCHES

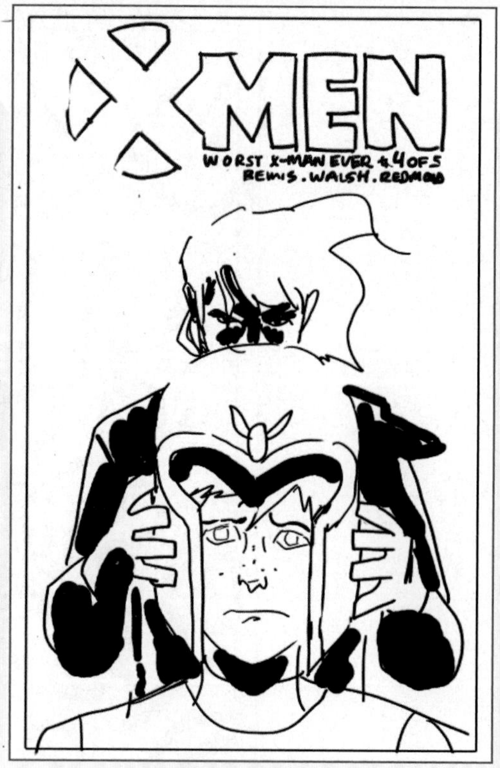
X MEN
WORST X-MAN EVER #4 OF 5
BEMIS . WALSH . REDMOND

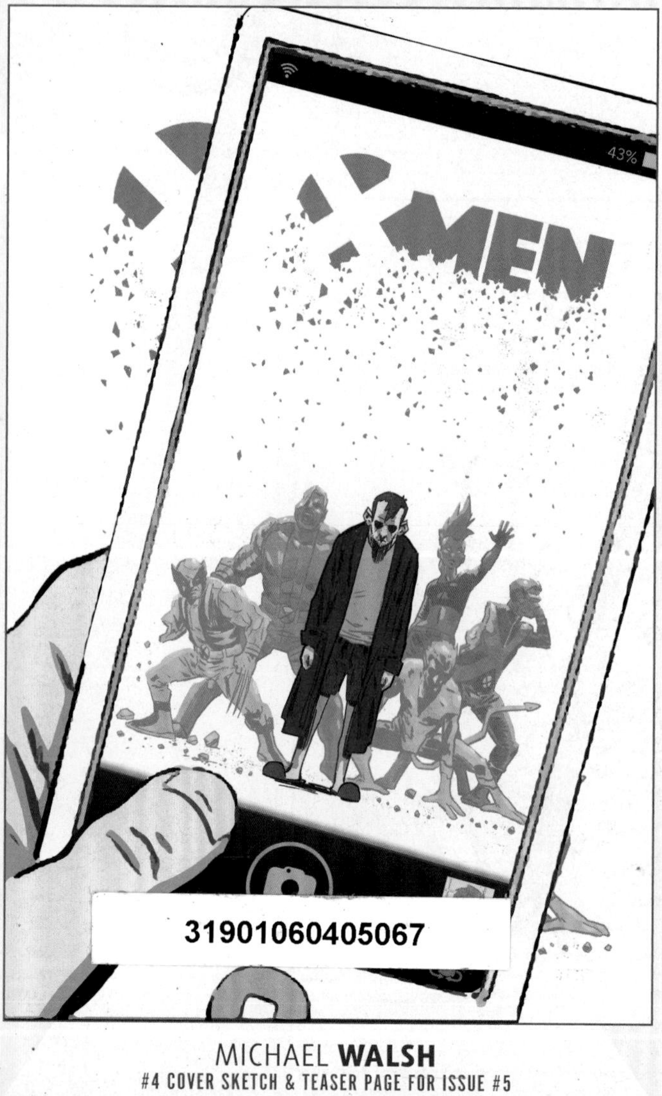
43%
X MEN

MICHAEL **WALSH**
#4 COVER SKETCH & TEASER PAGE FOR ISSUE #5